ADULT EDUCATION @ 21ST CENTURY

Studies in the Postmodern Theory of Education

Joe L. Kincheloe and Shirley R. Steinberg
General Editors

Vol. 219

PETER LANG
New York • Washington, D.C./Baltimore • Bern
Frankfurt am Main • Berlin • Brussels • Vienna • Oxford

ADULT EDUCATION @ 21ST CENTURY

EDITED BY
PETER KELL, SUE SHORE,
& MICHAEL SINGH

PETER LANG
New York • Washington, D.C./Baltimore • Bern
Frankfurt am Main • Berlin • Brussels • Vienna • Oxford

Library of Congress Cataloging-in-Publication Data

Adult education @ 21st century /
edited by Peter Kell, Sue Shore, Michael Singh.
p. cm. — (Counterpoints; v. 219)
Includes bibliographical references and index.
1. Adult education. 2. International education. 3. Globalization.
I. Title: Adult education at twenty-first century.
II. Kell, Peter. III. Shore, Sue. IV. Singh, Michael.
V. Counterpoints (New York, N.Y.); v. 219.
C5215.A3443   374—dc22   2003016259
ISBN 0-8204-6110-5
ISSN 1058-1634

Bibliographic information published by **Die Deutsche Bibliothek**.
Die Deutsche Bibliothek lists this publication in the "Deutsche
Nationalbibliografie"; detailed bibliographic data is available
on the Internet at http://dnb.ddb.de/.

Cover design by Joni Holst

© 2004 Peter Lang Publishing, Inc., New York
275 Seventh Avenue, 28th Floor, New York, NY 10001
www.peterlangusa.com

All rights reserved.
Reprint or reproduction, even partially, in all forms such as microfilm,
xerography, microfiche, microcard, and offset strictly prohibited.

Table of Contents

List of Figures and Tables — ix
Acknowledgments — xi
Preface — xv

Part One
Engaging the Dangerous Opportunities Created by Neo-conservative Globalism

Chapter 1
From the "Wall of Shame" to September 11:
Whither Adult Education? — 3
Shahrzad Mojab

Chapter 2
Global/Local Education for Adults:
Why is it a Must for the 21st Century? — 21
Barbara Toepfer

Chapter 3
Global Restructuring: New Challenges to the
Political Economy of Knowledge — 37
Liv Mjelde

Chapter 4
Questioning Developmental Globalism:
Threats to Language and Ecological Sustainability — 55
Peter Kell

Part Two
Literacy, Languages, Meaning Making, and Practices of Reflexivity

Chapter 5
Multicultural Meaning Makers: Malaysian
Ways with Words and the World   71
Koo Yew Lie

Chapter 6
Adult Educators' Talk: Responding to the Challenges
of Linguistic Normativity   89
Shanta Nair-Venugopal

Chapter 7
Reflexive Theory Building "After" Colonialism:
Challenges for Adult Education   107
Sue Shore

Chapter 8
Performing Identities:
A New Focus on Embodied Adult Learning   121
Gayle Morris and David Beckett

Part Three
Practitioner Development

Chapter 9
Adult and Vocational Educators:
Their Changing Work and Professional Development   137
Roger Harris and Michelle Simons

Chapter 10
The Work of Adult Literacy Teachers   153
Bobby Harreveld

Chapter 11
Educating Adult Researchers: Mitigating Neo-conservative
Globalism and Mediating Eco-cultural Sustainability   165
Michael Singh and Lynne Nengying Li

Table of Contents vii

Part Four
Adult Learning, Technology, and Work

Chapter 12
    Technological Literacy for Adults: Insights from Malaysia   191
    Ambigapathy Pandian and Shanthi Balraj Baboo

Chapter 13
    On-line Supplementation of Adult Education:
    A Change in Pedagogy and a Pedagogy of Change   203
    Andrew Scown

Chapter 14
    Learning Reflexively: Technological Mediation
    and Indigenous Cultures   221
    Leanne Reinke and Paul James

Chapter 15
    People's Power against the Empire:
    Re-framing Work-related Teaching/Learning   237
    Mike Brown

Chapter 16
    Learning in Complexity: Work and Knowledge
    in Enterprise Cultures   253
    Tara Fenwick

Conclusion
    Pedagogies of Global/Local Hope:
    Disobedience in the Face of Globalism   269
    Michael Singh and Sue Shore

List of Contributors   287
Index   293

Figures and Tables

Figure 9.1	Conceptualizing the adult education workforce	140
Figure 15.1	Complementary holism: The overlapping spheres of economics, politics, community, and kinship	241
Figure 15.2	Work-related teaching/learning: The interdisciplinary intersection of work and adult learning	244
Figure 15.3	A curriculum framework for complementary holism and work-related learning	246
Table 13.1	The ECI Matrix for Leading and Managing Change	216

Acknowledgments

Adult Education @ 21st Century is as much a creative product as it is a critical exploration of the historical, ideological, and localizing practices of contemporary globalization. As an expression of and response to global/local optimism, this book represents the "virtual" bringing together of researchers from across the globe around a series of interrelated problems confronting adult vocational education at the dawn of the twenty-first century. The labors of this transnational team were mediated by the new technologies of human interaction, community formation and knowledge production. However, it was their passion that overcame the distances created by national boundaries, time zones, marked seasonal differences, and disjoint holiday periods, as well as times of crisis in political and university governance that frustrated their intellectual productivity. This book, the work of a multi-lingual, multi-ethnic, multi-religious, and multi-racial team, seeks to make sense of the challenges confronting adult education in order to contribute to interventions intent on making a future that reinvents projects for forming global/local publics.

This book is the product of the Adult Education @ 21st Century International Research Network. Starting with a series of collaborative workshops, the participants in the Research Network formulated the rationale and structured the design for this collaborative venture. From these initial meetings, key researchers from around the world were identified and approached by the project team's principal investigators. It was their willingness and enthusiasm to be a part of a global/local journey and to develop a transnational network that gave this research project its shape and substance.

The editorial team thanks all project participants for their professionalism and the respect they demonstrated for each other, from conceptualizing this research project through to producing this book.

Tara Fenwick from, University of Alberta and Shahrzad Mojab from the University of Toronto in Canada are thanked for their commitment and significant contribution to this project, on- and off-line. Similarly, the considerable investment by Liv Mjelde from Akershus University College, Norway, in support of this project is most appreciated, especially her efforts in mediating cyberspace. The 2001 Literacy Education Research Network (LERN) Conference in Spetses (Greece) enabled the active and informed participation of Barbara Toepfer, the editor of *ZEP* magazine in Germany.

The involvement of Malaysian researchers was one of the major achievements arising from the 1999 LERN Conference in Penang, which gave rise to the joint Universiti of Sains Malaysia (USM) and Wollongong University International Literacy Research Program. Ambigapathy Pandian and Shanthi Balraj Bahboo from USM found in this project another vehicle for their advocacy of, and unconditional commitment to, the development of a transnational research culture that links the world's majority with its minority (South/North) and builds solidarity throughout the world's majority (South/South). Similarly Shanta Nair-Venugopal and Koo Yew Lie from the Universiti Kebangsaan Negara in Kuala Lumpur, participants in the 2002 LERN Conference in Beijing, found in this project the opportunity to give expression to their professional commitment to the sustainability of global/local public goods.

The editorial team is especially appreciative for the contributions, dedication, and support made by our research colleagues Michael Brown, Paul James, Lynne Nengying Li, Leanne Reinke, and Andrew Scown. We are especially appreciative of the work undertaken by Roger Harris and Michelle Simons from the University of South Australia Center Research in Education and Work. A special thanks to our remote area friend and scholar Bobby Harreveld from Central Queensland University for the sense of purpose she brought to using this project to reanimate our educational commitment to the public realm. David Beckett and Gayle Morris from the University of Melbourne for rounding out this transnational coalition of those willing to advocate for adult education in the face of neo-conservative, economic reductionism.

We are especially grateful to Annie Goldsmith from the University of South Australia, as well as Vasilia Tsiambazis and Veronica Luk from RMIT University, for organizing the workshops in Adelaide and Melbourne that launched the research project that led to *Adult Education @ 21st Century*. We are especially pleased that this transnational research

Acknowledgments xiii

project had the academic sponsorship of Professor Mary Kalantzis and Associate Professor Alan Reid. Their support and foresight in facilitating research initiatives such as this now requires considerable courage in the face of corporate managerialist commitments to market-driven, privatized knowledge production chained exclusively to the interests and sponsorship of speculative market capital.

Producing *Adult Education @ 21st Century* required significant co-ordination and production skills to bring it to timely fruition. The editors were fortunate to have Dr Lynne Nengying Li to co-ordinate contributions, as well as liaise and negotiate with the research team. Linda Singh is thanked for her patience, perseverance, and attention to detail in finalizing the production of the manuscript—formatting, camera-ready layout, bibliographic styling, indexing and proof-reading.

We are indebted to Professors Joe Kincheloe and Shirley Steinberg, the series editors, for their advice and support. Likewise the valuable assistance and patience of all, the production and marketing team at Peter Lang Publishing, especially Chris Myers and Phyllis Korper, is gratefully acknowledged. As "virtual" supporters of this project, their encouragement via e-mail and their patience throughout the research process sustained us.

We also thank our partners and families for their unending patience that enabled us to complete *Adult Education @ 21st Century*: Marilyn and Toby; Linda, Benjamin, and Sally. It is the sense of humanity and regard that we hold for each of our colleagues and friends that we wish to acknowledge.

Peter Kell, Sue Shore and Michael Singh

Preface

Peter Kell, Sue Shore, and Michael Singh

Adult Education @ 21st Century explores contemporary dilemmas created for adult educators by the ideological, historical, and localizing practices of globalization. This volume contributes to the critical dialogue that informs current debates about what these quandaries mean for adult educators. What will constitute our work? What will motivate our work? For whom will we be working? What will be the terms and conditions under which we will be working? The questioning of these uncertainties is grounded in empirical research and theorizing about the continuing reconfiguration of adult education.

This international team of adult educators articulates diverse standpoints about what challenging opportunities knowledge workers in adult vocational education increasingly encounter. They also provide a range of perspectives on possible responses. *Adult Education @ 21st Century* neither adopts a passive, submissive stance or a reactionary response to the dominating forces of globalization. To do so would leave unchallenged the unjust social and economic conditions that are affecting the destructuring of adult education. On the contrary, these authors dispute the taken-for-granted presumptions of neo-conservative globalism because of the limited perspectives it offers on the ideas, contexts, systems, and practices of adult education. Collectively they challenge this ideological and hegemonic project, proposing an agenda that affirms the work of adult educators as activist innovators.

Neo-conservative globalism is at the fulcrum of changes in adult education, being a flash point and catalyst for innovation as much as resistance and resentment. Diverse arguments and evidence are used by these adult educators to explore the unsettling changes wrought by economic reductionism, the dilemmas created by corporate managerialism and the opportunities these provide for renewing inclusive, democratic projects in, through, and for adult education. At the start of the twenty-first century violence, exploitation, marginalization, cultural imperialism, material deprivation, and powerlessness characterize the lives of many adults throughout the world. Desperation, bereavement, and anger drive many to suicidal self-destruction or the murder of others. These injustices have historic continuities with and stark departures from the challenges that inspired adult educators last century.

Adult Education @ 21st Century explores the problematic positioning of this field as a vehicle by which socio-economic injustices are sustained as often as adult education is used to contest them. Can adult education help surmount the inequitable power relations structured by race, patriarchy, class, sexuality, and ethnicity? To what extent can the remaking of adult education build a more socially just world?

Exploring these dilemmas requires critical engagement with the possibilities and limitations of developing new agendas for adult educators, researchers, policy-makers, and learners. Critiques are needed to challenge the chaining of adult vocational education to the regulatory forces of the transnational corporate economy and the costly and hyper-inflated promises of the new technologies of human interaction, community formation, and knowledge production. The following sections provide an overview of the constructive criticisms advanced in *Adult Education @ 21st Century* which is organized into five parts that explore the dangerous opportunities presented by neo-conservative globalism; making of meaning of the practices of globalization through literacy and language education; professional development of adult educators in the context of change and as agents of innovation; use of technology and work-sites for adult teaching/learning and formation of global/local consciousness.

Engaging the Dangerous Opportunities Created by Neo-conservative Globalization

The chapters in the first section of *Adult Education @ 21st Century* analyze neo-conservative globalism from various standpoints, exploring their implications for adult educators and their students. Neo-conservative globalism constructs the world as a seamless market for the movement of the goods, services, finances, and labor needed for maximizing profits. Governments around the world are responding to the demands of transnational capital for market-regulated economies through the radical de-structuring of public assets. This includes the deregulation of financial speculation; the downgrading of workers' terms and conditions of employment; the massive reduction in the state's underwriting of public social and economic risks; and increasing welfare subsidies for business investment and export.

This "top down" globalization has impacted on adult education in at least two ways. First, global economic de-structuring has resulted in dispossession and unemployment that has undermined the capacity of adult education to alleviate poverty by re-skilling communities. Second, neo-conservative globalism has spawned the transnational production, marketing, and delivery of adult education. Private adult education providers now compete across national boundaries with corporatized public education institutions that have formed alliances with transnational media corporations.

The transnational marketization of adult education has been accompanied by the emergence of supra-state trading blocs. Included among these are the European Union, North America's "not-so-free" trading alliance, and the Asia Pacific Economic forum. These in turn work in close collaboration with global economic organizations such as the Group of Eight, the International Monetary Fund, and the World Trade Organization. Increasingly adult education has to respond to and give expression to underpin the labor requirements of these regional trading blocs and the imperatives of these supra-national agents of global economic policies.

Neo-conservative globalism has impacted on the lives of people around the world. A global/local coalition of unions and non-government agencies have protested for labor, human, environmental, and women's rights at World Trade Organization meetings in one global city after another. Shahrzad Mojab argues for adult educators to form alliances with these organizations of global civil society to overcome the injustices that are the outcomes of rampant marketization globally. Mojab highlights the paucity of approaches to adult education that are geared solely to enhancing corporate managerialist agenda, particularly the passivity of "reflective practice" in this context. She calls for new visions, principles, and policies as a foundation for change-oriented critical pedagogies that are closely linked to the history and civic activism of progressive social movements. Redressing the oppression that led to the terrorist crimes of September 11 2001, has made the reinvention of critical adult pedagogies urgent.

Barbara Toepfer analyzes the tensions emerging from a global/local adult education program in Germany where students study the Palestine-Israel conflict. Given that globalization from above" can neither be ignored nor passively accepted, Toepfer points to opportunities for activist innovations in adult education that challenge "Othering" in concrete, local ways. As an expression of academic freedom, "global/local education" encourages adult educators to fulfil our obligation to be honest in the face of enormous political pressures to agree with and legitimize the consumerist or bellicose agendas of dominating interests.

Neo-conservative globalism involves complex and contradictory relationships that are interpreted and critiqued in contested ways within and between different communities because of its uneven effects on people's lives. Understanding these changing global/local relationships provides adult educators access to powerful tools to explore the formation of more inclusive and socially aware identities among adult learners. For instance, adult educators are responding to diasporic communities and their transnational mesh-works in ways that are nurturing and reshaping our ideas on global/local citizenship. These developments situate multi-lingualism and multiculturalism education at the center rather than the periphery of adult education. Perhaps more importantly these responses are framed around a "bottom-up" approach to globalization, albeit one that recognize the necessity of engaging with "top-down" globalization.

The challenges of reinventing adult education are manifest in the power differentials structured by class, language, gender, and race present in transnational initiatives at collaboration in an era of intensified competition. Through industry and education partnerships, the European Union's Leonardo da Vinci Program offers opportunities for adult learners to study in European countries in order to build the Union's labor capacity and an enhanced sense of European identity. The repositioning of adult vocational education within transnational regional blocs informs Liv Mjelde's evaluation of this European Union adult education program. The Leonardo da Vinci program mirrors the Erasmus project provided for university staff and students. However, Mjelde argues that the divisive boundaries between "hand" and "mind" still dog adult education and are in danger of being consolidated through these two programs.

Neo-conservative globalism has led many nation-states to forgo much of the power they once claimed in governing their domestic economies, including the formation of productive labor. Likewise, global homogenization is threatening multiculturally diverse localism. One reaction to "globalization from above" sees fundamentalists attempting to defend mono-ethnic, mono-lingual, and mono-religious state structures in the face of the growing complexity of multicultural societies. This has spawned ultra-nationalistic responses that reify and valorize fabricated notions of authentic localism based on a divisive mono-cultural politics of resentment. Adult educators are problematically positioned in these struggles as our work has often been co-opted to affirm such identity-building projects by nation-states.

A reworked "global/local adult education" now aims to develop the global/local consciousness of adult learners. This involves both enhancing their capacity for analytical and strategic thinking which is historically informed, and an appreciation of the complex investments we have in our own prejudices and stereotypes. It entails helping them understand the need for multiple perspectives to make the world a safe and sustainable place, as well as considering how the actions of one's own government are experienced by people in other nations as creating exploitation, poverty, and terror. As global/local citizens, they need to recognize the necessity for democracies to act with restraint in times of crisis, resisting calls for hatred, revenge, and retaliation in order to defend the values they claim to promote.

Throughout the world there are irreconcilable tensions between economic development and the de-skilling of Indigenous communities and the dispossession of nature. How might adult education reaffirm Indigenous and community languages during this period of global destructuring? Peter Kell explores the contradictions between the materialist imperative pursued by transnational agencies and nation-states, and its threats to the sustainability of world's ecological and linguistic diversity. His exploratory analysis signals the complexities of language education in a multi-racial, multi-lingual, and multi-ethnic nation-state. These tensions arise as a result of dramatic government policy shifts with respect to language education in response to pressures from the global business of English language teaching.

Literacy, Languages, Making Meaning, and Practices of Reflexivity

The contributors to this section are working to make sensible meanings of the predicaments neo-conservative globalism creates for nation-states and communities as they struggle to rework their adult literacy and language education programs. Using case studies they analyze the agency of adult educators as they work with and respond to the confrontational agendas of globalization from above and below.

The failure to develop inclusive strategies to incorporate and capitalize on the world's diverse linguistic and multicultural resources can be situated within the changing language policies of nation-states. Koo Yew Lie analyses the experiences of adult students in Malaysia to identify the tensions around Englishes and languages constructed as Other. While postcolonial independence policies once affirmed the work of community and Indigenous languages in nation-building, they are now being supplanted, as nation-states succumb to pressure to assign English the anti-market role of securing their economic viability in the restructured global/local economies. This reinforces the situation that existed in the colonialist era, where local languages, knowledge, and cultures were denied their place as intellectual capital in the everyday work of adult education. Given that the local remains the key site—and resource—for most of the world's population to build their sense of connectedness and belonging, Koo Yew Lie argues that the denial of their intellectual capital restricts student's social development and participation in their particular local/global communities.

Despite the complex meaning-making inherent in multi-racial, multi-lingual corporations, the diverse linguistic and cultural resources in these transnational settings are typically rendered invisible in management training. The opportunities created by multicultural diversity are rarely recognized as being productive of the sustainability of people's material welfare and life. Instead, all too often ethnic diversity is constructed as a problem to be cleansed. It is in this context that Shanta Nair-Venugopal analyses how adult educators reshape hybridized Englishes across different training situations. She provides a window into the negotiation of meanings that occurs as the local/global collide in training sessions.

Adult education was once a tool used by many nation-building states to enforce mono-cultural and mono-lingual assimilation. Then adult educators were employed to produce an ethnically and linguistically homogeneous nation-state by eliminating multicultural diversity. Of course, this was to be done without disrupting the inequitable intra-ethnic class and gender power relations of dominating interests. However, changing global/local relations of power have made it necessary for adult educators to develop more inclusive strategies that supersede these practices of marginalization and cultural imperialism. In renewing the challenge for adult educators to work on achieving the unrealized promises of emancipatory education Sue Shore problematizes Whiteness. Her critique makes meaningful the contestable power and questionable privilege of White bourgeois civility.

How might White adult educators respond to and engage with their Islamic students, especially in the post-September world of terrorizing, revengeful war? Morris and Beckett examine the embodiment of identity through a case study that challenges adult educators to break through spaces of enclosure to once again recognize the whole person. They argue against reinforcing dualisms between learner and educator, Muslim and Whiteness, to recognizing the embodied action of all of us as learners. Neo-conservative globalism is reshaping the identities of people everywhere, reconfiguring the relationships between adult educators and adult learners. Given how ignorance informs our claim to know both the changing Other and our new selves, the holistic study of human civilization is now more important than ever.

Practitioner Development

Our identities as adult educators are being reshaped by neo-conservative globalism. This reinvention of who we are is made manifest in transnational training markets as we struggle with/against making education entrepreneurs of ourselves. These changes are re-forming our identities, as adult education providers struggle with the contradictions of being institutions disciplined by the nation-state and hybridized, transnational corporations regulated by market forces. This enterprise market culture is supplementing, elaborating, and transcending the public service functions of the state. The imposition of market forces on the mix of public and private businesses has created a tenuous image of a "purchaser/provider" relationship between the state and the adult education sector. However, a major difference is that bureaucratic state control has been intensified through mechanisms of neo-conservative ideology, corporate managerialism by and technologies of compliance, while being supplemented by the regulatory power of transnational market forces. The competitive training market has dramatically changed the role of adult educators. Today we are much less teachers and researchers than we are entrepreneurs and on-line e-administrators governed by crisis management techniques.

The de-structuring of public education in the name of neo-conservative globalism has given rise to an increasingly differentiated workforce. Roger Harris and Michelle Simons's studies of adult educators in both the private and public sectors indicate significant changes in our work. The competitive training market and on-line delivery are being institutionalized to minimize the costs of teaching and the need for adult educators. This has resulted in the work of many full-time adult educators being redirected away from teaching to other activities for which they are often unprepared and not necessarily predisposed. There are tensions between the corporate imperatives and the professional development needs of adult educators in these crisis-ridden organizations. How can this differentiated workforce be prepared for these and further changes?

A coherent sense of self-efficacy is a hideous challenge in this era of management by sustained uncertainty. The identities of adult educators are being transformed from professional pedagogues to "brokers" in a training market shaped by corporate demands. Bobby Harreveld captures the dilemmas confronting adult educators as we grapple with brokering change, connections, and compliance. These complex innovative workpractices create a means by which adult educators can claim agency and renew our professional identities within global/local communities of practice.

The emergence of commodifed, instrumental research in adult education is designed to, subsidize private enterprise's engagement with, and responses to the changing global/local market forces ushered in by nation-states and new technologies. Referring to the professional development of adult researchers, Singh and Li argue for a *productive pedagogy of life sustaining research*. This could include addressing the crisis of governance in adult education due to the forces of neo-conservative globalism, as much as challenging narrow corporate models of governance and knowledge production. This would be a significant response to an education system now typified by financial mismanagement, mounting borrowers, and increasing levels of corruption. A productive pedagogy of life sustaining research focuses on pushing through taken-for-granted assumptions about the economics and politics of neo-conservative globalism.

Adult Learning, Technology, and Work

The dramatic expansion in transnational education markets has been fuelled by the new technologies of human interaction, knowledge production and community formation. The World Wide Web, e-mail, interactive multimedia, electronic databases, video-streaming, and simulation gaming are now integral to the day-to-day lives of adult educators and their students. These new technologies create important opportunities for accessing, sharing, and producing educational resources among those near at hand and far afield. Working face-to-face on a student-generated word document, it is possible for teacher and students to negotiate textual revisions and proposals for future redrafts and then to email the attached file to the students' home address for further work, with the back up copy safely stored on a file server.

This, however, is not the e-teaching/learning that interests advocates of on-line delivery. Instead, they want to capture the intellectual work of adult educators and their students, mark it as the institution's intellectual property in the form of reusable learning objects, and control its distribution via simulations of reproductive, test-like instruction. Like so many before it, this project too is driven by a mythological quest: labor and cost-savings in order to make a profit. The hype surrounding this technology papers over the digital divide: the appeal to students of face-to-face interactions; the unreliability of new technologies, the ineffectiveness of reductionist, test-driven techniques, and the huge start-up and continuing operational costs.

Preparing adult educators with the technical skills, disposition, and multicultural and political understandings to use the new technologies of human interaction, knowledge production, and community formation is a key challenge. Ambigapathy Pandian and Shanthi Balraj Baboo are working to bridge the Malaysian government's ambitious plans in this regard and the dilemmas of reforming adult education to meet these demands. The Malaysian government plans to use information technology to shift that nation from a production economy to a globally competitive knowledge economy. It is imagined that the success of these reforms will be underpinned by proficiency in the combined use of English and new technologies. Policy-makers have constructed Malaysians as having serious problems in these areas in order to mobilize the considerable anxieties needed to effect the solutions their reforms claim to offer. Pandian and Baboo identify structural barriers to young adults developing computer literacy and English language competence. There is an absence of institutional arrangements for them to enhance their English language proficiency and to use the new technologies in ways that meet the challenging agenda of Malaysia's Smart Schools plan. The gap between government policy rhetoric and the financial commitment needed to realize its goals is itself a global phenomenon.

Successful pedagogical traditions with rich religious and deep philosophical roots are being reinvented using on-line delivery to supplement adult education practices. This entails reworking those worthwhile teaching methods that comprise diagnosis and assessment, description and analysis, and intervention and reassessment. Andrew Scown brings a critical perspective to the development of on-line teaching/learning activities for a transnational course in leadership and management. He debunks the boosterism around e-learning and advocates a pedagogy of non-linear, multi-modal teaching/learning. Using the well-established teaching method of naming—reflection—action or see—judge—act, Scown provides an account of the innovative structuring of on-line teaching and learning using an Evidence-Critique-Impact approach.

Indigenous students capably and willingly employ new technologies, keen to control them so as to serve the interests of their own people and lands. Leanne Reinke and Paul James address questions about the appropriation of technology as it enters postmodern Indigenous multicultural and linguistic settings. Where the preservation of Indigenous languages is held to be a matter of generating disembodied word-banks, the relevance of this technological application and the modernist ideas framing its use prove questionable. There is greater educational value in situations where socio-technological systems are used to enhance the power and autonomy of Indigenous communities.

Life-wide, lifelong teaching/learning that re-skills workers may or may not insulate corporations and protect their workers from the competitive pressures of global/local competition. Aided by the new technologies of on-line teaching/learning, adult education is moving to dispersed and variable workplaces as determined by enterprises, workers, and communities. Changing the location of adult education so that it is not restricted exclusively to colleges valorizes the funds of knowledge and skills in a variety of working communities. Mike Brown warns that such programs are usually co-opted and distorted by corporate interests and used to reaffirm neo-conservative interpretations of global/local economic orders in uncritical ways. Brown argues for workplace teaching/learning to provide a critical, holistic approach, rather than unquestioningly accept instrumental, reductionist approaches. A pedagogy of complimentary holism invites the exploration of the overlapping spheres of economics, politics, community, and kinship through a participatory orientation to workplace teaching/learning.

Amidst the pessimism unleashed by the neo-conservative globalism that is fueling teacher-less lifelong learning to image-manage the hopes of alienated workers, there are opportunities for new and worthwhile ways of working, learning, and teaching. Tara Fenwick's exploration of enterprise education among a group of self-employed women entrepreneurs captures just such possibilities. Learning from an entrepreneurial culture that requires "knowing on the fly," adult educators might rework their traditional teaching roles of "noise makers," "interpreters," "mapmakers," and "facilitators." Arguing for an ecological approach to workplace teaching/learning, Fenwick constructs an orientation to adult education that incorporates a commitment to interaction between knowledge production, community formation, and combating social injustice.

Conclusion

The formation of a global/local consciousness that provides adult educators and learners with a sense of agency and hope about future possibilities is a key theme in *Adult Education @ 21st Century*. Michael Singh and Sue Shore see pedagogies of global/local hope as opening up new possibilities in the practices and theories of adult education. Within the global/local difficulties we face it is possible to identify spaces that become available for activist innovation in adult education. In this way the role and purpose of adult education as contributing to the pursuit of knowledge and to encouraging adult learners to think critically can be sustained across the generations. This idea and ideal may even be practiced in the face of those who insist that adult educators are merely adjuncts of government and agents of corporate enterprise.

Part One

Engaging the Dangerous Opportunities Created by Neo-conservative Globalism

Chapter 1

From the "Wall of Shame" to September 11: Whither Adult Education?

Shahrzad Mojab

The first draft of this chapter was written in the wake of anti-globalization protests in Québec City, Canada. The capital of Québec Province hosted the gathering of the Western Hemisphere's heads of state (except for Cuba's Fidel Castro) from April 20–22, 2001. This event was followed by similar protests in Italy and Sweden. These were more extensive and involved more police action than the previous ones, which had begun with the "Battle in Seattle" in 1999. They confirmed the main argument of this chapter that these struggles were not only against neo-conservative globalism or "globalization from above," but were taking an increasingly anti-capitalist turn, and have to be taken seriously by all, including adult educators.

By the end of the northern summer in 2001, it was evident that there was no end in sight to these protests, which, although lacking any central organization, were as frequent as the international gatherings of government and business elites. Governments feigned helplessness, while the determination of protestors increased markedly. Protestors, like the elites, were international in composition and global in their reach. Wherever these elites showed up, the masses were present. It is apparent that the new century is moving in a direction that is far from the wonderland promised by Thatcher, Reagan, Mulroney, and the neo-conservative "revolutionaries" of the 1980s, as well as the post–Cold War warriors who wanted to see the "end of history." However, the terrorist attacks on the United States on September 11, 2001, disrupted the pattern that the elites had woven since Seattle. In terms of its method, target, and impact this terrorist crime was unprecedented, but perhaps not so surprising given the role of the USA in contemporary practices of neo-conservative globalism.

We cannot say much about adult education without looking carefully at what is happening globally. The events of September 11, 2001, were not exceptional; many other countries have experienced terrorism and its disastrous consequences. However, the US Government has mobilized the propaganda to ensure September 11 continues to have a dramatic military, political, and economic impact on stability throughout the world. Had the attacks targeted any other country, from Indonesia (Bali) to Japan to Britain, the consequences would have been different. The difference tells us much about the unequal division of global power and the growing polarizations in a world ridden with serious crises.

The Struggle in Québec City

The heads of state of thirty-four countries in the Americas (excluding Cuba's Fidel Castro, who was not invited) came to Québec City to discuss expanding the North American Free Trade Agreement (NAFTA), the Free Trade of the Americas (FTAA), and related global and regional trade issues (Lee, 2001). The oldest city in North America, Québec City was built as a walled fortress where, in the eighteenth century, British and French troops battled for the control of the colonies. Two centuries later, the city once more became the battleground of another struggle with far wider implications than the territorial expansion of the two colonial powers. The April fortress consisted of four kilometers of four-meter-high metal fencing, which encircled the summit sites located in the heart of this historic city. Protestors named this metal fence the "wall of shame" after a Western democratic state violated the rights of its citizens to participate in the most vital economic, social, cultural, and political discussions and decisions. Shame, too, for violating the rights of its citizens to protest. The designation "wall of shame" also referred to the hard borders, such as that separating the US and Mexico, which have led to more people being killed than at the Berlin Wall.

The police forces took severe measures. An estimated 6,000 canisters of tear gas were used. There were police forces from municipal, provincial, and federal levels with dogs and water cannons. Around 2,000 soldiers with armored vehicles and helicopters were also deployed. There were approximately 350 arrests, including "snatch" arrests of some active citizens. The Royal Canadian Mounted Police emptied the city jail in preparation for the arrest of protestors and ordered the Anti-Riot Weapon, Enfield (Arwen 37), through its North American producer and manufacturer, the Police Ordinance Company. The Arwen 37 is "the first multi-purpose, multi-shot (crowd control) weapon system to combine lightweight, high accuracy and the ability to fire up to five shots before reloading" (Patriquin, 2001). Classified as a "less lethal" weapon, the Arwen 37 uses severe pain to subdue citizens. This weapon originally was developed by "Royal Ordinance, a division of British Aerospace, in the late 1960s,... to subdue rioters in Northern Ireland without killing them" (Patriquin, 2001).

Thousands of women, men, and children poured onto the streets of Québec City on Saturday, April 22, 2001. A diverse array of Canadian and international organizations was represented in the march. From Québec the participants included Convergence des Luttes Anti-Capitalistes (CLAC); Operation Québec Printemps 2001 (OQP); Summit of the Americas Welcoming Committee (CASA); Sal Accord Mulitilateral sur les Investissement (SalAMI). There was also the Groupe Oppose á la Mondialisation des Marches (GOMM) (Group Opposed to Market Globalization); FTAA-Alert McGill & Concordia; Reseau Quebecois sur l"Integration Continentale (RQIC); Quebec Network on Hemispheric Integration; and the anarchist Black Block. Groups from across Canada included; Common Frontiers; the Centre of Concern Women's Project; Canadian Centre for Policy Alternatives; Canadian Federation of Students; and Hemispheric Social Alliance.

From Toronto came groups such as Rise Up! (University of Toronto students); York Student Union; SOS (Students on Seven—the Department of Adult Education and Counselling Psychology, OISE/UT); Radical Cheerleaders (OISE and YORK factions); Mob for Glob (Mobilization for Global Justice); Transaction!; Ontario Coalition Against Poverty; the Radical Cooks (a group of chefs with progressive politics); Inter-Church Coalition for Human Rights in Latin America (IRCCHRLA); and Lesbian Avengers.

From across the border came a range of US groups including the Alliance for Global Justice; Sierra Club; Jobs with Justice; Global Exchange; Mexico Solidarity Network; Student Alliance to Reform Corporations (STARC); AFL-CIO; American Friends Service Committee; and the Campaign for Labor Rights. Other US/American groups included the Center of Concern; Committee for New Priorities; Development GAP; Friends of the Earth, U.S.; Institute for Agriculture and Trade Policy; Institute for Policy Studies; Global Economy Project; International Labor Rights Fund; Maryknoll Office for Global Concerns; Preamble Center; and Public Services International. To these were added the Inter-American Regional Office; Resource Center of the Americas; Rural Coalition, Coalicion Rural; School of the Americas Watch/NE; Tennessee Industrial Renewal Network; and United Electrical, Radio; and Machine Workers of America. US/American women's organizations were represented by the Union of Needletrades, Industrial and Textile Employees; United Methodist Women's Office for Economic Justice; Women of Color Resource Center; and Women's EDGE.

It is difficult to make meaning of this conflict in Québec City without putting it in a wider historical context. It was one in a series of global civic protests that started in Seattle in 1999, and continued after Québec City in Genoa, Italy. Along with these there were various efforts to block the transportation of nuclear waste in Germany, and to organize a shanty town set up by 2000 laid-off employees of a bankrupt cable company in Madrid, Spain. It was part of a longer history that includes the tax revolt in Britain under Margaret Thatcher.

Let me sketch the historical context for these global civic protests. In the early 1980s, a new generation of conservatives came to power in Britain, the United States, and Canada. Thatcher, Reagan, and Mulroney are familiar names. This was not a simple transfer of power from one party to another. The media dignified it as a "revolution": the "Thatcher Revolution" or the "Reagan Revolution." This generation of neo-conservatives promised prosperity and freedom by giving increased power to the market. Although conservatives in their politics, they resurrected the spirit of Adam Smith and told the people of the world that the invisible hand of the market would solve all problems. For these neo-conservatives, the market was the regulator, agency, and engine of historical change. Their agenda was to "free" trade from democratic controls, to privatize public wealth and security, and to globalize the regulatory forces of neo-conservative markets. In other words, neo-conservative economic de-structuring meant cost-cutting measures through new management techniques of labor control to create a "leaner" and more "flexible" labor force (George 1999).

The neo-conservative agenda was enhanced by the fall of the state capitalist system of the Soviet Union and Eastern Europe between 1989 and 1991. This state capitalism was called "socialism" or "communism" in the discourses of the globally dominating Western media and academia. This state capitalism was said to be less efficient than the private capitalism of the West. While conservatives were quick to call the Reagan-Thatcher agenda a "revolution," they lost no time in declaring the fall of "state capitalism" the "end of history." For them, the fall of the Eastern bloc meant the global triumph of private capitalism. Human beings had no alternative to private capitalism. The human mind could not go beyond Adam Smith and Ricardo.

The neo-conservative agenda was promoted all over the world in a well-planned manner. The agents of planning were the governments of the major Western powers, especially the United States and Britain, and their organs, such as the World Trade Organization (WTO), the International Monetary Fund (IMF), the World Bank, the European Union (EU), and the G7 (later G8) industrial powers. Even the United Nations (UN) joined their ranks as an agent for planning and promoting a neo-conservative market-based world.

The neo-conservatives have dominated the world economy and politics for two decades. What is their record? The UN Human Development Reports for 2001 and 2002 and the negative impact of globalization on the deepening of democracy in the fragmented world reveal the growth in social inequalities. Based on evidence provided by the UN, its agencies, and various governments, the following data depicts the present "state of the world" and future trends.

Ecocide

According to a detailed study released by the UN Environment Program in May 2002, "the planet is poised on a precipice, and time is running out for making tough political and economic choices that can pull it back from disaster" (Ward, 2002). According to the study, about 1.2 billion people lack access to clean drinking water, and some 2.4 billion people have no sanitation services: "the consequences include the death of 3–5 million people annually from water-related diseases" (Ward, 2002: 298). In thirty years, more than 11,000 plant and animal species will be dead or dying, including 1,000 mammal species that make up about a quarter of the world's total mammal species. The situation for marine life is no better.

Poverty

According to *Human Development Report 2001* and *2002* commissioned by the UN Development Programme, there are "serious deprivations in many aspects of life," especially in over-exploited countries (http://hdr.Undp.org/). Worldwide, there are 1.2 billion people who live on less than

$1 a day. About one third of children under five in these countries are stunted by malnutrition.

Disease

AIDS is devastating the population of Africa. By the end of 1999, about thirty-four million people had HIV/AIDS, and by 2010, Africa will have forty million orphans. In over-exploited countries, about eleven million children under five are dying annually from preventable causes; about thirty thousand children die each day.

Education

Worldwide, there are about one billion illiterate adults. By 2000, in over-exploited countries, there were some 854 million illiterate adults, of which 543 million were women. 325 million children received little or no schooling, of these, 183 million are girls. In OECD countries, 15 percent of adults lacked functional literacy skills.

Famine

Famine has been threatening the lives of millions of people in the last twenty years. In May 2002, some 70 percent of the population of Malawi were on the verge of starvation.

Slavery

Linda Chavez's (1995) study of contemporary practices of slavery reported the rise of rape and sexual slavery in different regions of the world. For instance, the armed forces of the government of Sudan use child-slaves as their main instrument for suppressing resistance movements. Here it is important to note that Talisman Energy Inc., the third largest Canadian oil exploration and production company, has vast operations in Sudan. The Inter-Church Coalition on Africa and Christian Solidarity International are monitoring the relationship between Talisman oil production and fuel for Sudan's longest civil war.

Sexual Exploitation

The trafficking of young boys and girls, as well as women, for sexual exploitation has reached alarming proportions. An estimated thirty million children are now victimized by traffickers, who almost invariably go unpunished.

War and Displacement

Military spending worldwide was $789 billion in 2000. Conflicts killed two million children in the last decade of the twentieth century and left many millions disabled and psychologically traumatized. Over ten thousand children are killed or maimed by land mines every year. Over thirty-five million people are internally displaced, of whom 80 percent are women and children.

Looking at the state of the world as it has been evolving in the last two decades, it is not surprising that there is resistance to neo-conservative globalism by citizens ranging from French farmers to indigenous people in Chiapas, Mexico. Western states, the World Bank, and IMF as leaders of the neo-conservative market-centered world have a whole army of academic experts, think tanks, and media to sell their agenda. Two decades of neo-conservative globalism provides more than enough time to make a serious evaluation of its social, cultural, economic, and environmental impacts. What might we learn from this ideological project? Who educates adult educators? I argue that we should learn from the social movements, the organizations of global civil society. They are and they provide credible indicators of the impact of neo-conservative globalism.

The dominating media engage in simplistic propagandizing by representing Seattle–Québec City–Genoa as the conspiracy of small bands of anarchists who are allegedly interested in violence for the sake of violence. There is little discussion of the failures of the neo-conservative market and the neo-conservative agenda. The anti-globalization movement constitutes a diverse opposition ranging from churches and labor unions, through youth groups to grandparents. In this diversity, we see at least two trends. First, the movement tries to address problems within the existing neo-conservative order; second, it represents a growing movement against global capitalism and in the direction of a dramatically renewed socialism.

Educating Adult Educators: The Specter of Disaster

If indeed we are not on the verge of a global disaster but already in its midst, adult education must seriously reevaluate its agenda. Does adult education contribute to the disaster or does it work, with others, to mediate and mitigate it? In order to make sense of the disaster, consider what an archeologist, V. Gordon Childe (1953), said soon after World War II. He began his study of *History* with these words:

> Within the last hundred years the societies inhabiting western Europe and North America have achieved conspicuous success in control over external nature. The spectre of famine that constantly haunted ancient and mediaeval civilizations and still threatens with annihilation peasant masses in Asia... has been effectively banished save in so far as these societies themselves evoke it by their own bellicose behaviour. Plague and pestilence which with famine still represented an ever present menace to everyone when the Church of England Litany was compiled, have been brought under control save again when war releases them. The expectation of life has consequently risen expansively. The stupendous natural forces harnessed in the turbine, the electric motor and the internal-combustion engine work for men's [sic] social—and anti-social—ends more potently than the muscles of thousands of sweating labourers or plodding oxen....
>
> Control of the social environment—of the relations between individuals, groups, nations and classes—has, on the other hand, achieved no comparable success. Within twenty-five years two world wars, not to mention continuing but localized conflicts, have released forces of destruction that threaten to obliterate all that the productive forces have slowly built up if not to extinguish mankind [sic] itself.

Childe noted that the "painful discrepancy between humanity's control over external environment and its incapacity to control the social environment" was due to the absence of adequate knowledge of society. Using the term "control," Childe did not mean the destruction of environment or the policing or surveillance of society. He was talking about the failure of social sciences to prevent war, hunger, famine, genocide, and oppression. Putting the experience of the two world wars in the context of (pre) history, he made a point that is still most relevant: human beings are capable of eliminating hunger and war and those who unleash the forces of destruction are responsible for what they do. The organized social movements of global civil society aim at preventing these forces of destruction.

Reflecting on anti-globalization movements, Roger Burbach (2001: 168), the director, Center for the Study of the Americas, observes that:

> Not since the 1960s has there been such a sweeping rebellion against the established order. It is "back to the future", and this new future is profoundly internationalist and diverse, linking up environmentalists and trade unionists, university students in the North and sweatshop workers in the South, mainline churches and destitute Third World governments, Indigenous groups and human rights activists. It is an embryonic movement that will go through many unforseen twists and turns as we agitate, organize and construct new alternatives to globalization from the bottom up.

Despite government-incited fears of nuclear annihilation, the world in the 1960s was not in the midst of a crisis as serious as the present one. Neither did the youth, students, and workers turn the world upside down. However, they taught some lessons to everyone. The academe had to change. Gender relations had to change. Consciousness about sustainability of the global/local environment began to emerge. And the struggle for peace was revitalized. What are the lessons for adult educators to be drawn from the "globalization from the bottom" protests against top-down neo-conservative globalization?

Contested Views of Globalization

Sheila Wilmot, a Canadian labor activist, and ve developed the following framework of analysis for a course that we co-taught in 2001 at the Toronto Women's Bookstore called *Women and the Violence of Globalization*. We are in the midst of a significant polarization in the struggle for saving the planet from social, economic, and ecological disaster. One pole is the people in the streets and the other pole is the major economic and military powers of the world. Street politics can offer the non-profit, non-capitalist, non-military solutions to the problems. Closed-room politics of the big powers has advanced a profit-based, capitalist, military agenda. Such a polarization is occurring in the social sciences and the humanities generally, and in the field of adult education specifically.

Within critical, left, and radical street politics, there are diverse and conflicting views on globalization. In order to advance a critical analysis of globalization, we need to grasp the policy and educational implications of these views. This chapter focuses on two critical views of globalization, namely, the social democratic or reformist view, and the feminist anti-capitalist or revolutionary, Marxist view. Both views agree that certain global situations are contributing to the worsening conditions of life for the majority of the world's inhabitants—of all species. These include putting trade above and beyond democratic controls; the privatization of public goods; the erosion of the system of public, social, and economic security; Structural Adjustment Programs (SAPs); the increasing exploitation of labor; the degradation of the environment; and increasing militarization. They are also in agreement that there is an international constitution in the making through institutions like the WTO, World Bank, IMF, and NAFTA. They argue that in the global agenda-setting process, corporations and banks, as well as government and business elites, all play a key role to the exclusion of many others. There are, nevertheless, major differences between these two views.

The *reformist* view considers "globalization from above" as a new phenomenon of the last few decades and, despite recognizing its devastating impact, considers it an irreversible and inevitable process. Their agenda is to reconstitute neo-Keynesian national economic and social reforms. This view regards the state as neutral and argues that "good" governments can look after the interests of their citizens. It is the role of citizen-oriented governments to control the movement of the multi-national corporations (MNCs) through taxing them accordingly. In other words, having lost many of their powers to MNCs and other international institutions, governments are either forced to or willingly cut social programs, minimize business taxes, and limit national laws protecting labor, consumers, and the environment. The reformist view argues that globalization from above has affected the participants in "civil society"—people of all nations who are against the corporate "values" and "rules"—and has changed the relationship between North-South by forcing all to the lowest common denominator in living standards. Reformists criticize corporations rather than capitalism *per se*, and, therefore, suggest that the localization of trade and enhanced productive capacity is an answer. They promote an uncritical return to "community."

The *revolutionary-Marxist* view, as Rikowski (2000:19) points out, addresses "the very force which creates globalization, that is, capitalism. Capitalist globalization *is* capital writ large, capital raging across the world." Neo-conservative globalism is international capitalism with two major features: 1) overproduction followed by market collapse, and 2) constant market expansion. After World War II and, in particular, since the 1970s, there have been efforts to make international profit accumulation more bold and ruthless. The trade blocs are actually competing imperialist powers, which ensure that the North controls the South. Trade is another mechanism of colonialist control.

This feminist-revolutionary-Marxist view argues that the state is not neutral. Both "good" and "bad" governments look after the interests of the elite capitalist class. Globally, too, the state has not lost its power, but has shifted it, in part, to the world level as decisions at the national level get tied more and more to the global movement of capital. In a different way, the state is being nationally and internationally reorganized as part of the ongoing competition between states to attract and/or keep a share of the world capital. Furthermore, the state has prioritized the interests of private property and ensured MNCs' access to an ever-cheapening and "flexible" labor supply, while creating the social consent necessary for this to happen and policing the social order wherever resistance "requires" state use of force. The government of Germany purposed the creation of a unified

European Union anti-riot force to assist national police forces in controlling the anti-globalization protests. In the province of Ontario, the Progressive Conservative Party is changing laws and policies in order to accommodate the interests of big business. The social democratic New Democratic Party has failed to offer an alternative to the market-based politics of these neo-conservatives.

On a global scale, the revolutionary view argues that only elites are benefiting from "globalization from above" while the working conditions and the wage levels of people of color, Aboriginal people, and especially women are getting worse. Globalizing capitalism serves privileged class, race, and gender interests. As such low-income earners, poor women of color and Aboriginal women are the hardest hit by the Structural Adjustment Programs in the South and social program cuts in the North. While this is not new, it has intensified in the last two decades (McNally, 2002; Petras and Veltmeyer, 2001; Starr, 2000).

Anti-Capitalist Struggles and Adult Education

Polarization is also in the making in adult education. Public education at all levels has effectively served the goals of nation-state building since the nineteenth century. Today, it is being restructured and repositioned to serve market-based neo-conservative globalism. Half a century ago, Harold Innis (1951: 195), the Canadian economist and historian of media, warned us about the increasing domination of public education by the market and the military: "The universities are in danger of becoming a branch of the military arm." Innis cautioned against the monopoly of knowledge that the market had created in media and academia, and their domination by the military. Glenn Rikowski (2001: 8), in his account of the significance of the "Battle in Seattle" for adult education writes:

> Education is intimately involved in the social production of the one commodity upon which contemporary capitalist society depends; that is human *labour-power* (the capacity to labour), which takes the form of "human capital" in contemporary society. Second, and related to this first point, is that education can potentially become a site of struggle and strategic engagement for the establishment of principles for critical and socialist pedagogies.

As Rikowski suggests, adult education plays a fundamental role in sustaining the capitalist economy through producing its single most important commodity: labor-power. As adult educators, therefore, we should know whose side we are on. Do the knowledge and skill we provide serve the reproduction of the capitalist relations as a way of life? Which agenda do we promote? Do we work to ensure the dominance of the neo-conservative market, its ideology and compliance regimes? Are we serving the neo-conservative agenda? Should we only issue declarations and statements in international conferences? Who is going to put into practice the nice phrases and sentences we put into our declarations? Are we responsible for anything and to anyone? Who is responsible for this mess? What is the role of adult education in this disaster? The dominant trend in adult education is to reduce humanity to labor-power through training:

> *Awareness* of this process, whilst causing uneasiness, is a crucial first step towards successfully challenging this situation—though not sufficient in itself, for a *collective* project for rescuing education from capital is essential, as the demolition of capitalist social relations in their entirety must be pursued.... No amount of "reflectivity", posing as a "reflective practitioner", indulging in textual deconstruction or sophistry can evade this. (Ribowski 2001: 36)

The rising anti-capitalist movements throughout the world are creating new possibilities for generating another "social universe." Paula Allman (1999: 40) defines this project as one of creating "a social universe not *parallel* to the social universe of capital (whose substance is *value*), but a potential form of society *suppressed* within the social universe of capital: socialism, based on addressing human *need*." What has the "wall of shame" taught us? Perhaps adult educators must choose between these conflicting agendas? Learning from these social democratic movements is crucial if adult education is to be an emancipatory political project grounded in concrete *action* learning rather than words alone.

There is no lack of ideas about a non-market, non-capitalist, citizen-based approach to adult education. But ideas cannot change the world if they are not put into practice. We have very few means for providing the type of adult education that Innis was talking about half a century ago. The state and the market have a monopoly—they are the providers, the agencies, and the architects of adult education. The "lifelong teaching and learning" project that we are engaged in is a typical case of State and market-driven adult education. It is a project for maintaining an army of skilled, mostly unemployed labor force to be on call for a market that is uncertain, undecided, and chaotic. In the absence of state and market support for an alternative approach to adult education, we must rely on socially critical movements. Adult educators can do this by strengthening our ties with organizations of global civil society. We should listen to the great majority of the people of the world who are suffering.

Adult Education in the Aftermath of September 11, 2001

The September 11 terrorist attack brought into sharp focus the web of contradictions that constitute the shattering of democracy, the impoverishment of people's lives through unrestrained capitalism, the breakup of nation-states, and the inciting of communal tensions. The instability in world politics by the USA's raging quest for vengeance has added to the current crises in the global/local public good, including adult education (Mojab and McQueen, 2002). In Saudi Arabia, a key regional ally of the United States, there is little investment in the intellectual development of the people, because education is feared because of the political changes it would necessarily bring (Ali 2002: 295). Before that event, neo-conservatives had raised the banner "All power to the market." Today, they have raised another banner: "All power to the state and its coercive organs." The market banner is, of course, firmly in place. However, the new politics openly negates freedom, liberty, and equality, the main pillars of liberal democracy. Economically, advocates of market capitalism have monopolized power in governing the world in the years since the fall of Eastern Europe. Before September 11, the United States, Canada, and the European Union were working towards effecting new controls over anti-globalization movements. Now the coercive organs of the state have been empowered by new legislation to curb civil liberties, dissent, and resistance. Ironically, terrorism has been used by the state to incite fear, thereby intimidating citizens to give up hard-won civil liberties.

Before September 11, adult education was, like other cultural, social, and intellectual efforts, subjected to the interests of the neo-conservative market. It is not clear yet how the attack on civil liberties will affect adult education. However, pressures on civil society and constraints on public spheres, including academic freedom, are already visible. While the neo-conservative market had already pushed civil society to the corner, the state and the dominating media may further reduce it to a nonentity through surveillance and the control of movements critical of neo-conservative globalism. In the absence of such socially critical movements, the power of the state and market bloc is free to continue its devastating impact on democracy. Adult education can play a role in reversing the current trend if adult educators realize the seriousness of these developments. What is the role of adult education under conditions of incessant political and economic crises that threaten prospects for democratic life throughout the world?

The assault on civil liberties has worried people with various political tendencies, ranging from anarchists to liberals, through feminists to Marxists. The following analysis of the current crisis is framed in Marxist-feminist terms. The official Canadian interpretation of the post–September 11 world is borrowed directly from the Bush Administration, and is adopted by its media arm and much of academia, and through them, by a sizeable number of citizens. According to this interpretation, the "terrorists" have appropriated the Islamic religion to destroy Western civilization, its regime of freedom and democracy and way of life, conveniently ignoring the role of neo-conservative global de-structuring of these prized public possessions. Instead, they claim that the West must protect itself by physically eliminating or disabling all those who challenge the project of neo-conservative globalism. They deny the "root causes" of "terrorism" and state that there are no links between "terrorism" and other ills such as poverty, domination, oppression, and neo-conservative globalism. We have been warned that if we find any links between U.S. foreign policy and "terrorism," we are justifying the "terrorist" attacks. Adult educators have to declare whether we are with George W. Bush, or with the "terrorists."

The Production of Terrorism

Phenomena such as terrorism have multiple causes. The question of why educated Saudis, Egyptians, and Algerians, from countries allied to the USA, would sacrifice their own lives through terrorist violence remains unanswered. However, even if (a big if) one could establish US foreign policy as the only cause, there is no justification for the mass murder of September 11, 2001. No one, individuals, groups, or governments, should feel free to commit such crimes against human beings.

Moving away from the simplistic official truth of the United States administration, it is important to recognize that the terrorism of the Taliban, Bin Laden, and their like was directed primarily against the people of Afghanistan and other Muslim nation-states. The crimes perpetrated by pro-Western Mujahideen and the Taliban, especially against the women of Afghanistan, are unprecedented in the history of the region. Moreover, the two sides, the US and the terrorists, do not form a binarism. Historically and politically, the Taliban, Bin Laden, and Western capitalism form a symbiosis, not a contradiction. The two have coexisted, and mutually benefitted from their relationship, much as slavery and capitalism or liberal democracy and racial apartheid coexisted in the United States for three centuries. Thus, Western powers, especially the US, supported, financed, trained, and led the Taliban against democratic, nationalist, and communist movements and governments in Islamic countries and against the Soviet bloc. Since the overthrow of the Taliban, much of Afghanistan is still under the rule of pro-U.S. warlords and Islamic fundamentalists. A renewed symbiotic relationship is already being put in place.

It is difficult to see how military action can defeat the type of terrorism that was centered in Afghanistan. The experience of the first twelve months of this war indicates that there is no military solution, even in the short run. Ironically, Western governments have been more successful in using these operations to constrain the civil liberties of their own citizens rather than in curbing terrorism.

Whither Adult Education?

Terrorism, in all its fascist forms, has multiple origins. The struggle against it, too, should be multi-pronged so as to be all encompassing. In Islamic countries, terrorists thrive in an environment of abject poverty in the midst of wealth, under conditions of despotic regimes, and in the absence of justice, freedom, and citizens' rights. However, in this region, as in the West, poverty and injustice are not the only causes of terrorism. The terrorist act at Oklahoma City, the blowing up of abortion clinics, the assassination of abortion doctors, and the burning of Black churches in Texas are not motivated by poverty and injustice. However, a thriving civil society and an educated, conscientious citizenry can act as a powerful check on both non-state and state terrorisms. Limiting civil liberties by silencing helps the reproduction of terrorism and may be considered a form of political and intellectual violence.

Adult education can make an important contribution to the struggle against terrorism, racism, neo-fascism, genocide, poverty, and injustice. In the twenty-first century, adult education belongs to the era of prosperity and liberal democracy. It is geared to serve the interests of nation-building, state-building, and the construction of the global empire of capital. Many adult educators know well that this type of education is far from desirable (see the Hamburg Declaration), although we do not know-how to gear adult education to the interests of global citizens.

The military revenge being enacted against Muslim opposition to US/American imperialism has targeted those forces that can most effectively curb terrorism—socially critical movements. Much of the most valuable knowledge we have today (including adult education itself), and much of the progress made since the French and American revolutions of the late eighteenth century, is due to such civic movements. From the abolition of slavery to women's suffrage rights to the abolition of capital punishment, we owe every step forward to well-educated and socially active citizens working collectively. The institutions of the state and the market were usually the adversaries of abolition, suffrage rights, and other changes. Adult education should move against the tide, and learn from history.

References

Ali, T. *The Clash of Fundamentalisms: Crusades, Jihads and Modernity*. London: Verso, 2002.

Allman, P. *Revolutionary Social Transformation: Democratic Hopes, Political Possibilities and Critical Education*. Westport, Connecticut: Bergin & Garvey, 1999.

Burbach, R. "North America," in *Anti-Capitalism: A Guide to the Movement* edited by E. Bircham and J. Charlton London: Bookmarks Publication, 2001.

Chavez, L. "Contemporary Forms of Slavery: Preliminary Report of the Special Rapporteur on the Situation of Systematic Rape, Sexual Slavery and Slavery-like Practices During Periods of Armed Conflict." *United Nations, Economic and Social Council*, 16 July 1996.

Childe, V. G. *What Is History?* New York: Henry Schuman, 1953.

Fifth International Conference on Adult Education (CONFINTEA V). *The Hamburg Declaration on Adult Learning*, 1997. Available on http // www.unesco.org/ education/uie/ confintea/declaeng.htm.

George, S. "A Short History of Neo-Liberalism: Twenty Years of Elite Economics and Emerging Opportunities for Structural Change." Paper presented at the Conference on Economic Sovereignty in a Globalising World, Bangkok, 24–26 March 1999.

Innis, H. *The Bias of Communication: A Critical View*. Toronto: University of Toronto Press, 1951.

Lee, M. *Inside the Fortress: What's Going On At the FTAA Negotiations?* Toronto: The Canadian Centre for Policy Alternatives, 2001.

McNally, D. *Another World Is Possible: Globalization and Anti-Capitalism*. Winnipeg: Arbeiter Ring Publishing, 2002.

Mojab, S., and W. McQueen, eds. *Adult Education and the Contested Terrain of Public Policy*. Toronto: The Canadian Association for the Study of Adult Education, 2002.

Patriquin, M. "Summit Police to Get Plastic Bullets." *Toronto Star*, March 22 2001, 24.

Petras, J., and H. Veltmeyer. *Globalization Unmasked: Imperialism in the 21st Century*. London: Zed Books, 2001.

Rikowski, G. *The Battle in Seattle: Its Significance for Education*. London: The Tufnell Press, 2001.

Starr, A. *Naming the Enemy: Anti-Corporate Movements Confront Globalization.* London: Zed Books, 2000.
Ward, O. "Planet's Future at Stake: U.N. Report Says." *The Toronto Star*, May 23 2002, 2.

Chapter 2

Global/Local Education for Adults: Why is it a Must for the Twenty-First Century?

Barbara Toepfer

Introduction

What are the challenges and opportunities for young people in this new century? Youngsters in Germany may say that they want a job, enough money, their own home or family, time for fun, and maybe peace, all summarized as "a future." Across the world we have heard representatives of a Ministry of Education say: "We want well-educated and well-trained people, fit for the national and global labor market. Who will contribute to our economic wealth and our democratic system?"

Around the globe we have listened to a company director or lobbyist say: "We need flexible, mobile, well-educated and adequately specialized workers who are motivated to engage themselves fully in their jobs and our economic system." The United Nations' Deputy Secretary-General says we need: "the world's businessmen and businesswomen—as creators of jobs and wealth; as promoters of trade, investment and stable markets; as innovators in the development of new technologies; in short: as full partners in our global mission of peace and development" (Annan, 2002).

Annan's deputy made this statement in a speech before the 34th Congress of the International Chamber of Commerce in Denver on 6 May, 2002.

Making a Meaningful Agenda for Adult Vocational Training and Education

Western European countries have educational systems, from primary to adult education, that are based on constitutions with the obligation that certain fundamentals like democracy, peace, human rights, the preservation of natural resources, and economic and social justice are respected. As adult educators, we are obliged to develop and administer adequate frameworks and settings that convey these values through such programs as development education, peace education, human rights education, education for a democratic society, intercultural education, ecumenical or multi-faith religious education, and ecological education. In this chapter, these programs are drawn together under the heading of "global/local adult education." If the underlying principles and values for social interaction are not consciously taken into account, there can be no constructive communication between and among peoples with different sets of values and identities. Individuals have to assure themselves who they are, in the work of finding common ground with others. One can only act globally if somehow grounded locally. Unfortunately, contemporary adult education policies and practices tend to overlook these issues.

On the other hand, advocates of global/local adult education find it difficult to place their arguments on the adult education agenda because their opponents accuse them of "moralism" or "anti-capitalism." However, a lack of these basics—these value commitments—can give space to extremist, racist, and anti-Semitic thinking and acting. This was recently evident in central European countries where voting for parties that have racist platforms enjoyed some success. This is one of the reasons why global/local adult education, particularly peace and human rights education and education for democracy, is so important in the adult education sector now. It must not be neglected at an age when students become apprentices or trainees and learn how to perform their future profession.

Insights into Adult Education in Germany

Instead of discussing adult education in a decontextualized manner, this chapter exemplifies the possibilities and limits of global/local adult education with specific reference to a "local" adult vocational education system in Germany (see also http://www.globlern21.de-Schulberatungsstelle Globales Lernen, *Aktuelles, Learning and acting in a worldwide economic and social context—a challenge for vocational education*). Germany has a complex system of adult education. There are a variety of full-time courses for all kinds of educational levels. However, adult vocational education in its more limited sense is directed at training workers for a particular profession.

As indicated by the following decree from existing legislation, Germany has a dual system of education and training:

> Within the dual system of professional training, vocational school[s] and industry share the joint task to qualify skilled personnel in the officially acknowledged training professions. In this context, the vocational school is a training location in its own right. The syllabus of the vocational school covers topics directly referring to the trained profession as well as job-related enlargement of the general education acquired earlier, especially in the areas of German and foreign language(s), social and economic affairs, religion (ethics), and physical education. In connection with the professional diploma issued by the appropriate institution the bearer of a vocational school leaving certificate can attain the intermediate school qualification, entitling enrolment for further education. The qualification attained and the entitlements combined with it are documented in the vocational school-leaving certificate. In addition, special knowledge, e.g. in foreign languages, or other additional qualifications attained can be documented in special certificates. (Federal State of Hesse, 1.02.2003; *Verordnung über die Berufsschule*. Draft, came into effect in 2003)

This decree goes along with national curriculum guidelines for job-related education, whereas each State in Germany has its own curricula for the general subjects mentioned above. While certain standards have to be achieved, teachers are relatively free to interpret existing curricula. This gives adult educators the chance, but not necessarily the intellectual or curriculum resources, for integrating global/local adult education into their programs. There are, of course, fears and hopes that, as a result of international assessments such as the Programme for International Student Assessment (PISA), teachers' professional "liberties" will come to an end through further national standardization and European-wide comparative ranking (http://www.pisa.oecd.org).

PISA and Some Consequences for Adult Education

PISA, an OECD three-yearly survey of the knowledge and skills of fifteen-year-olds in the principal industrialized countries of Western Europe, provides some answers to questions as to whether students are well prepared to meet the challenges of an unknown and unknowable future. It assesses how far these students have acquired some of the knowledge and skills that are claimed to be essential for full participation in global/local society. The focus is on reading and mathematical and scientific literacy. However, competencies across disciplinary boundaries (commonly called "cross-curricular competencies," CCC) have a growing importance in PISA as it develops over time. These competencies include approaches to learning and beliefs in their own abilities, motivation, and engagement. All these aspects of student attitudes are defined as "self-regulated learning." PISA also assesses students' ability to solve problems.

In Germany, the assessments of PISA play a particularly important role. As agreed among the OECD countries, scientists at the Max Planck Institut in Berlin are working out how to assess these CCC. As a consequence, the Hessisches Landesinstitut für Pädagogik HeLP (Institute of Further Education for Teachers) created a CCC-working group of adult educators who are dealing with concepts of lifelong teaching/learning, or perhaps better still, *teaching and learning for life*.

As feared, the tests produced some alarming results about the abilities of German students in reading, science, and mathematics. In response to these poor results, the national consortium of the Max Planck Institut für Bildungsforschung concluded that approximately one-third of the fifteen-year-old students who were tested in Germany range below or near level 1 on the PISA reporting requirements for these three disciplines. This means that students will either be unable to cope in a vocational school or will have difficulties passing the final examinations assessed by a selective board of examiners representing companies, the chamber of trade or commerce, and the school. This assessment process represents the end point of participation in the dual vocational training system noted above. While most of these students come from low socio-economic backgrounds, a significant percentage of these youngsters with poor results come from families where neither of the parents speaks German as a mother tongue.

Young people in Germany are legally bound to attend school to the age of eighteen. When they have finished general education after nine to ten years at a "Hauptschule" or comprehensive school, they usually attend full-time courses at a vocational college or school. What are the consequences of these results for vocational and adult education in Germany? What will the "future" be for these young people? Racist thinking could persuade some into action while others may "drop out."

Globalization and Global/Local Adult Education

Processes of globalization and their consequences have produced increasingly important debates and responses all over the world. This is a consequence of the imposition of "globalization from above"—which, although not a new phenomenon, has altered its speed, range, and threat to many moral pillars. It has created a situation where political, economic, and private thinking and acting is part of a worldwide web that "seismographically" reacts in one part of the world to actions in another part. This chain reaction can be seen in stock markets where global selling goods are set at commodity exchanges beyond the reach of the small producers and consumers. Where, for example, coffee is subject to constantly falling prices, which has a negative impact on the daily life of a laborer on a South American plantation (whose child, of course, is often forgotten because for the most part both laborer and child are deemed marginal to these debates).

In response to "globalization from above," many new and sometimes stunning alliances have been formed across political boundaries and factions to create "globalization from below." This development does not come as a surprise. Opponents of "globalization from above" are warned by business and governmental representatives of the consequences of following the lines of racists all over the world. These racist movements exploit populist political resentment about the negative consequences of "globalization from above," such as increasing poverty, the further exclusion of the economically powerless, the loss of orientation ("Heimat"), even in the lives of the rich, for their undemocratic and often racist political aims. This is evident in the rise of neo-Nazis in contemporary Germany as elsewhere. This is one of the reasons why global/local adult education is a must, particularly in adult vocational education, where the less privileged with poor job chances are assigned to particular classes and courses before they finally drop out of state education, or perhaps even the labor market for life.

Global/local adult education plays an equally important part in qualifying young people, who are trained for future professional responsibilities, to become "leaders" in management and the community. Intercultural competence in dealing with clients and partners from or in other countries is basic know-how in a globalized world. So too is the raising of consciousness and knowledge about issues such as child and forced labor, and developing knowledge about the mechanisms of trade and commerce. It is consideration of ecological aspects of business activities in the context of the Rio Agenda 21 Agreements. It is respect towards the Universal Declaration of Human Rights and towards religions, including knowledge and skills that shape global/local business behavior. And it is, of course, the ability to do business without undermining social and political justice or peace, or destroying often fragile, regional equilibria.

In other words, global/local adult education deals with the phenomena of "globalization from above" in a very pointed and complex way. It can be applied to single topics or practiced across fields of competence in adult education. Global/local adult education is not a "pedagogy" rather, it is a set of broad educational approaches. To give an example, intercultural education, interpreted as practices that start from situations where at least two different cultures meet, aims at people learning from each other (Zimmer, 1986). However, this does not necessarily count as global/local adult education; it adds to this teaching/learning process through a more holistic and worldwide context. Global education analyses changes in economic, political, cultural, and historical factors that may be underlying communicational processes and sharpens adult students' perceptions by offering additional ideas about reality (Führing, 1988). In summary, a global/local orientation to adult education aims to produce graduates who can act responsibly within a complex "www-system." This is regardless of whether a person is a citizen, a member of a society, or a co-worker in a particular company, and regardless of their focus on particular local/global concerns.

Another pragmatic reason for supporting global/local adult education is its role in achieving a broader and more sustainable development of cross-curricula competencies. "Competent" use of CCCs implies the ability to change perspectives and to communicate new ideas with empathy, as well as to the transference of responsibility to a team. As a foundation for self-organized learning, CCCs can help groups to solve problems and explore issues.

There seems to be a coincidence in that the skills provided by global/local adult education fit so neatly into the OECD concept of CCCs. This can be explained by the fact that global/local adult education, like the PISA, is based on and is consistent with the principles of really useful education. However, there is at least one essential aspect that distinguishes global/local adult education from more conventional approaches to the development of "generic" attributes or cross-curricular competencies. The overall aim and purpose of global/local adult education is to look closely at the reasons and explanations for injustice such as the causes of war and lack of peace, or the causes of violence against "Others."

Global/local adult education aims to assist students to understand and resist the exploitation of human beings and nature. It facilitates a closer look at adult responsibilities as part of global/local communities that benefit from aspects of globalization and understand the connections with those who have been disadvantaged by the imposition of "globalization from above." It develops ideas and strategies to alleviate some of the catastrophic consequences of neo-conservative globalism and explores how to act ethically, as for example in the development of Fair Trade policies. This is perhaps why global/local adult education is looked upon with skepticism by the economically and politically powerful. At the same time, it creates anxieties amongst parents and students who fear such studies are superfluous in an "immoral" and highly competitive labor market. Both of these issues have to be addressed.

Intercultural education is essential for our societies and also for companies that need qualified and ethical staff. The majority of people in Western European societies support democracy, human rights, respect for religions, and ecological responsibility. Global/local adult education is an appropriate response to many of these concerns. However, there are different approaches to "global/local adult education." Development education is one approach which shows how the high standard of living enjoyed by "first world" citizens depends on cheap goods, cheap labor, and cheap raw materials which can only be obtained if corporations and governments violate the basic human rights which we claim for ourselves. However, we can no longer pretend not to know the effects of these practices in which we are implicated. In a globalized world, where conflicts and wars are televised live in our lounge rooms, our unquestioning complicity with exploitation contributes to instability. Adult educators can work with their students to find answers to real-world challenges, such as the conflict between Israel and Palestine.

What does this mean for teaching activities in adult education? What does this mean for an adult education that is focussed on immediately applicable professional skills as well as concerned about educating adult learners to be active and responsible citizen who can work to find a means of solving such problems peacefully? How can a democratic government act appropriately unless its citizens think and act likewise? How can an understanding of global events be promoted where interests that keep the conflict alive are exposed and discussed? Major German companies, like Volkswagen AG, regularly send their apprentices to Israel to learn about the life and people of that country. One of the partners is Givat Haviva, a Jewish institution that offers adult education on peaceful coexistence among Jews, Christians, and Muslim Arabs.

Global/Local Adult Education in Practice: Teaching the Concept of "Israel/Palestine"

Citizen (or political) education, that addresses social and economic affairs, is legislated as part of Germany's adult vocational education curriculum. This section explores how this is implemented through teaching about "Israel/Palestine," a topic which involves education in the English language, comparative religions, and economics. Primarily, it aims at integrating cross-curricular competencies throughout a range of subjects focusing on this topic. This educational work is legitimized by the curricular obligations of adult education. Other materials specifically address the hospitality and tourism sector. Materials include presentations on hotels in Jerusalem; a speech by the Bishop of Winchester on globalization delivered on Christmas Day, 2001, and an invitation to participate in an action learning project concerning displaced Bedouins. Teachers who adapt to adult learners' needs and interests use these curriculum materials flexibly.

The teaching is conducted bilingually (German and English) and based on student research on the Internet and materials collected during a visit to Jerusalem in summer 2001. (See also http:// www. globlern21. de/s121/ israwl/ israelpalastina / html "Israel/Palästina," "Naher Osten.") This variety of contemporary methods and media is consistent with the objectives of global/local adult education encouraged by innovation activists to elaborate the pedagogy of the lecturer to include advisor and facilitator. The themes proposed are closely related to topics identified and debated in the context of this conflict. They can be replaced by themes more relevant to particular students and current political developments. While there is no prescribed order sequencing students' learning, however, the methods and the work processes used to achieve the required competencies are not supposed to be altered.

In one sequence, students were required to analyze a specific period of time, exploring Ariel Sharon's visit to the Temple Mount and the subsequent events over the next two weeks. A variety of sources from the Internet, articles, books, newspapers, and magazines were analyzed. Students worked in groups to compare and interpret the material, using such aids as a meta-plan, flashlight, and questioning with cards. The educational aim was to reflect on and test different perspectives on the same incident.

In another sequence, students were asked to put themselves (as Christians) into the position of a Jewish person living in the area, or into the position of a Palestinian from Israel or the occupied territories. The intention was to help them imagine how they might have reacted after Sharon's visit to the Temple Mount and the incidents that followed. The aim was to raise empathy for the people involved in the conflict. The results were moderated according to "Betzavta," a method that allows communication on dilemmas in a specific setting where all the participants focus on only a few central questions and are required to listen and to react to each other with respect. (This approach to moral education, which is used world wide, was developed by the Adam Institute for Peace and Democracy in Jerusalem.) (See also http://www.us-israel.org/jsource/bridges/ four.html.) The sequence was then brought to a close by a game called *Regenwald* (rain forest), with specific sounds being produced to give the feeling of belonging together.

After these tasks were carried out, there were further activities, including the exploration of additional questions. A good idea was to have students get in touch with other young adults involved in the conflict. Through the project called *Crossing Borders,* a group of adult students in Israel, Palestine, and Jordan publishe a quarterly newspaper that welcomes people from other countries to read it and join into the debate. They communicate through the Internet with a Protestant private college (Talitha Kumi) in Beit Jala (near Bethlehem) and with a range of governmental and non-governmental organizations in Germany. They also invite experts into their adult education classes and conduct interviews with them. The overall aim is to support communication between young adults from different cultural backgrounds, which in this case requires diplomacy and knowledge of language issues.

In the context of this topic, the ability to solve problems was clearly too ambitious to achieve immediate resolutions. However, research proposals for a peace agreement from various governments and alliances were submitted, such as the present and former Israeli governments, the Palestinian National Authority (PNA), US government(s), Russia, the European Union, the Arab League or non-governmental organizations in Israel and Palestine. One activity involved the students considering where agreement might be reached (e.g., for an independent Palestinian state) and where it seems unlikely to be reached (Jerusalem as the capital for both states). Students commented on the suggestions and developed ideas on how to contribute to a peaceful solution that also supported the displaced Jahalin, a Bedouin community living near Ma'ale Adumin (Jerusalem).

Each teaching concept includes accompanying documentation. This is why, in a further sequence, students were required to create a section called "Israel/Palestine" on their homepage or for a magazine. Part of the group generated a list of criteria for the assessment and evaluation of sources and the information given, which helped them to choose from the material gathered by a second group. The students then worked together to single out the material they agreed upon according to the list, which, of course, had to be debated and accepted before and during this activity. In this sequence, the students profited from the particular competencies present within the group in English language, in using the Internet, in communicating verbally, in note-taking and in essay writing. Team building and creativity were promoted. Furthermore, they all took responsibility for a "product" and a "process" to be evaluated before consluding the unit.

Evaluation of the CCCs demonstrated through global/local adult education was another major challenge which still has to be fully realized. Approaches aimed at assessing changes of practice or the achievement of skills, let alone the ability to act according to the educational aims, proved to be difficult. Results were not reliable because there was no evidence as to what extent changes in behavior (like buying Fair Trade tea) are due to deliberate and systematic educational processes, coincidence, or non-educational influences. All we could offer at that stage was an evaluation of the learning processes themselves: Are the learners involved? Are they able to express different perspectives? Are they working cooperatively? How do they deal with different opinions? The achievements of teaching approaches such as this cannot but remain speculative. There are no guaranteed recipes for "success" in any educational process, just as there are no guaranteed ways of securing peace-making outcomes.

Another important issue is whether the qualities embedded in the concept of global/local adult education are of any value for companies. Statements made in 1998 by the Bundesverband der Deutschen Arbeitgeberverbände (BDA), the peak German Employers' Association, would suggest that there are. The BDA expects workers to have the capacities for integrated thinking and to effect knowledge transfer from one situation to another. This includes knowledge about world economics and ecology as well as the abilities to work in teams on projects, to deal with complexity, to take responsibility, to have a strong and stable set of values, to feel empathy, and to be interculturally competent.

These competencies are consistent with the objectives of global/local adult education. So the question remains: Why is global/local adult education not more widely practiced in adult vocational education? This question is particularly significant if we take into consideration the fact that global/local adult education has an influential international ally in the United Nations, with its "Global Compact."

The Global Compact and Global/Local Adult Education: A Powerful Alliance

On 31 January, 1999, at the World Economic Forum in Davos, the UN Secretary-General Kofi Annan introduced to the world's businesses the UN "Global Compact," comprising nine principles for governing corporate practices and supporting appropriate public policies. These principles cover areas of human rights, labor, and the environment. (See also http://65.214.34.30/un/gc/unweb.nsf.)

The Global Compact is a value-rational platform designed to promote institutional learning. It draws on the ILO's Declaration on the Fundamental Principles on Rights at Work and the Rio Principles on Environmental Development. The Global Compact means to challenge the world's elite business leaders to help build the social and environmental pillars required to sustain the new global economy and make globalization work for all the world's people. The principles are as follows:

Human Rights
- Principle 1: support and respect the protection of international human rights within their sphere of influence; and
- Principle 2: make sure their own corporations are not complicit in human rights abuses.

Labor
- Principle 3: freedom of association and the effective recognition of the right to collective bargaining;
- Principle 4: the elimination of all forms of forced compulsory labor;
- Principle 5: the effective abolition of child labor; and
- Principle 6: the elimination of discrimination in respect of employment and occupation.

Environment
- Principle 7: support a precautionary approach to environmental challenges;
- Principle 8: undertake initiatives to promote greater environmental responsibility; and
- Principle 9: encourage the development and diffusion of environmentally friendly technologies.

These principles have definite links to global/local adult education. They are based on the assumption that co-workers and elites in the world of business will acquaint themselves with the practices and human rights as part of the social responsibility of companies. Agenda 21 is a comprehensive plan of action to be taken globally, nationally, and locally by organizations of the United Nations System, governments, and major groups in every area of human impact on the environment. More than 178 governments at the Rio Summit in June 1992 adopted Agenda 21. These governments promised to advocate and put into practice, aims of sustainable development such as combatting poverty, changing consumption patterns, and strengthening the role of major groups like women, children, youth, and non-governmental organizations. In a way, sustainable development can be seen as a U.N. tripod, based on three main pillars: Agenda 21, action by governments, Global Compact, action by companies, and Global Education, action by educational institutions

The U.N.'s Global Compact, however, is nothing but a restricted platform for such actions. Kofi Annan pointed this out in a speech to Spanish business elites in Madrid in April 2002, noting that it was designed to complement approaches that rely on monitoring and enforcement by giving business the space to try out new ideas and to make a difference through voluntary action. According to Mary Robinson, the United Nations High Commissioner for Human Rights several hundred companies from all over the world have responded to the Global Compact. At the time, Robinson was presenting a speech before the Royal Society for the Encouragement of Arts, Manufactures and Commerce in London on 7 May 2002. These include German companies like Aventis (Germany, France), Bayer, BASF, Daimler Chrysler (Germany, USA), Deutsche Bank, Deutsche Telekom and Gerling, as well as SAP (Systeme, Anwendungen, Produkte in der Datenverarbeitung).

The Global Compact is developing a learning forum that will serve as an information bank on the disparate experiences of company efforts to implement the nine principles. As Robinson states:

> We are finding that the nature of the product or service, the type and location of the relevant consumers, the size and power of the company, the prevailing human rights situation in the countries where the company operates, in addition to the proximity to potential violations, must all be part of the responsibility equation that companies, as a part of society, are obliged to adhere to.

However, adult educators are well aware that this approach—documenting examples of good practice on the Internet and assuming others will be motivated to action—is inadequate to initiate the broad structural changes proposed by Kofi Annan. The Compact cannot possibly work without business elites and co-workers in companies who are trained in self-awareness and qualified for this kind of biocultural innovation. These leaders need all the skills that make up the key cross-curricular competencies noted in this chapter. They need knowledge about the specifics of certain states, their systems, and the networks with whom they trade. They need the know-how of technical and service skills, not only based on their immediate cultural surroundings, but also from alternative experiences and points of view.

Leaders and aspiring leaders need to be educated to develop new strategies, new products, and services that fit into national and regional environments as required by these principles. They need global/local adult education in companies, schools, colleges, and in institutions of adult education. If they do not have that, the principles and other declarations of this genre will remain limited futile symbols of goodwill that reinforce popular skepticism and popular criticism of political processes. This would be a shame, because, like the Universal Declaration of Human Rights, these principles of economic action are a valuable tool for further thought and action by government and non-government organizations. They give global/local adult education the significance and place it warrants.

Important steps towards change are required in adult education all over the world. As indicated by the PISA framework, we can agree on certain standards of knowledge and competencies in adult education. Why not settle on certain educational approaches and aims that might help adults communicate and moral standards that allow us to understand and respect each other? For those who find this too challenging, Professor Klaus Leisinger offers a way forward.

> In modern pluralistic societies, it would be completely irrelevant if only we at Novartis were convinced that our own house is in order....Business today gets its social acceptance in a globalized economy through a process of external certification. Hence, we need a societal license to be able to work sustainably—and to obtain it, we must be in permanent contact with the relevant stakeholders of society. (Klaus M. Leisinger is Director of the Novartis Foundation for Sustainable Development in Basle, and Professor of Development Sociology at the University of Basle. http://www. foundation.novartis.com/organization.htm)

There are, of course, doubts that companies seriously mean to implement ethical standards like the Global Compact. The concern is that this is just another aspect of corporate public relations. There seem to be no real obligations involved other than some company self-evaluation, which holds no legal significance. It may be that, as is the case with fair trade and ecologically sustainable products, companies will have to be supervised and controlled before receiving a "Global Compact" label. However, for companies to accept the need for external certification to meet ethical standards, they *must* have global/local adult education. Existing institutions like the Notre Dame Center for Ethics and Religious Values in Business, for example, have programs that build bridges between the private sector, business studies, and the humanities. In the Center, programs are designed to strengthen the ethical foundations in the business and public policy communities by encouraging interdisciplinary dialogue and innovative research. Educators all over the world can also do so through teaching topics like "Israel/Palestine" to offer adult learners ideas on how to deal with regional problems of global consequences.

So, if companies are on the move, adult education should not lag behind and must move to the forefront of these changes. To do otherwise would be a highly risky approach that might find Ministries of Education putting the "core business" of educating for global citizenship into the hands of private enterprises and the world of business. However, it is not likely that global/local adult education could flourish in the hands of profit- and image-oriented companies. One of the major challenges for national and international political bodies is creating a network with adult educational bodies to put their resolutions into practice. As a consequence of the Rio Summit, Agenda 21 has nurtured the practice of education for environmental sustainability. It is still very much focussed on ecological aspects. Global/local adult education offers a more holistic approach that incorporates issues of social and economic justice as of equal importance. If we want a globalized world to offer a life of dignity for all its inhabitants, then as the Deputy Secretary-General of the UN said: "Businesses must behave as good global corporate citizens." Adult education has a key role in making this dictum a practical reality.

References

Annan, K. "Speech before the 34th Congress of the International Chamber of Commerce." Denver, 6 May 2002.

BDA. *Schule in Der Modernen Leistungsgesellschaft: Das Schulpolitische Positionspapier Der Bda*. Köln: BDA, 1998.

Führing, G., and L. Globales. *Arbeitsblätter Für Die Entwicklungsbezogene Bildungsarbeit*. Berlin: Hrsg.: Deutscher Entwicklungsdienst (DED), 1998.

Scheunpflug, A., and B. Toepfer. *Entwicklungsbezogene Bildung in Beruflichen Schulen. Ein Fachdidaktisches Handbuch Zum Globalen Lernen.* Frankfurt: IKO Verlag, 1996.

Solidarisch leben lernen e.V. (Hrsg.). Praxisbuch Globales Lernen. *Handbuch für Unterricht und Bildungsarbeit.* Frankfurt: Verlag Brandes & Apsel. 2002.

Zimmer, J. "Interkulturelle Erziehung Zur Internationalen Verständigung." in M. Borelli (ed.) *Interkulturelle Pädagogik.* Baltmannsweiler: Schneider Verlag. 1986.

Chapter 3

Global Restructuring: New Challenges to the Political Economy of Knowledge

Liv Mjelde

Introduction

A basic contradiction between mental and manual labor has long been a feature of industrial society. Adam Smith, a market economist, analyzed these contradictions between the division of labor and the goals of educational development in the emerging market society. Smith (1937: 340) did not see the need for public education to teach people factory skills because he thought those to be too simple or too site specific as not to warrant formal education. But he did consider adult education important for forming the moral identity of workers, stating that:

> the more they are instructed the less liable they are to the delusions of enthusiasm and superstition, which among ignorant nations frequently occasion the most dreadful disorders. An instructed and intelligent people besides, are always more decent and orderly than an ignorant and stupid one.

This problem has been contested terrain since early industrialization and the rise of adult vocational education and apprenticeship training. The idea of lifelong teaching/learning bears the traces of these contradictions. The traditions of adult education and apprenticeship with their emphasis on workplace learning are at the core of contemporary pedagogical debates. Lifelong teaching/learning reemerged as part of this agenda in the mid-1990s, not just in adult education but also in corporate settings. The discourse on lifelong teaching/learning over the last thirty years has been characterized by policy activism during certain phases and extreme stasis during others (Schemann, 2002).

The structural changes that accompany the increasing competition created by neo-conservative globalism and the transformations in employment effected through rapidly changing information and communication technologies provide the basis for this renewed interest among economic reductionists. Today, corporate managerialists are advocates of lifelong and life-wide learning. The division between adult vocational education and liberal education, the contradictions between work of hand and work of mind, between vocational and academic learning are being questioned again in new ways.

Within the education system in Norway this contradiction manifests itself in the streaming of the sixteen to nineteen-year-olds into either vocational training or academic higher education. This separation contributes to the streaming of young adults into different class and occupational positions within society. This dualism in streaming creates both different curricula contents and ways of organizing learning. There is workshop learning in adult vocational education and classroom learning in academic education (Daly and Mjelde, 2000).

Contemporary adult vocational education and apprenticeship training originated from the guild system, where learning for work took place in the midst of the working environment. Vocational programs have their learning traditions in the apprenticeship system as it originated in the feudalistic craft guilds. In contrast, the learning of the gymnasium has its roots in the old Latin school, with its emphasis on conceptual (theoretical) development being conducted apart from the world of work—both paid and unpaid work.

In response to contemporary global restructuring and the challenges it has created through the recomposition of the labor market, new questions are being posed about the development of adult vocational education (Brown, 1997; Harney, 2002). This has resulted in changes to the structural arrangements of adult vocational education throughout Western Europe. This chapter is based upon empirical work in the field of vocational education for thirty years and my participation in the evaluation processes of the Leonardo da Vinci Program as a Norwegian expert. I assessed applications during a five-year period and was the Norwegian representative in the evaluation of the whole program. Norway voted against entering the European Union both in 1972 and 1994. It is connected to the European Union through the European Economic Area (EEA).

Reforms in Adult Vocational Education in Europe

One of the crucial issues in the present reforms being institutionalized across Europe concerns the relationship between vocational and liberal studies in adult education. Recent policy developments in the European Union have placed adult vocational education at the core of debates in a number of countries. The Organization for Economic Cooperation and Development (OECD) formed a working group to compare adult vocational education in its member countries. These proposed changes include a range of new dimensions: France is developing a "Baccalaureat Technique" that integrates academic, vocational, and community-based aspects of learning in the curriculum. It has strong industry and community components. Sweden has launched a full-scale evaluation of its upper secondary education system and adult education programs. Decisions have been made to link the upper secondary school vocational fields closer to labor market needs. Denmark is taking steps within its vocational education programs to coordinate theoretical subjects with practical training in the workshops. For instance, auto-mechanic students are expected to learn Danish, English, mathematics, and physics in ways whereby all are related to workshop practice. New questions are being posed around Germany's dual system, despite its vocational training system being highly esteemed throughout Europe. While the German vocational system, with the "beruf" (occupation) at its center, was once looked upon as the ideal system, now demands for self-organized and self-directed learning are challenging it.

Issues and developments similar to these were the focus of Norway's Reform 94 that addressed challenges in the education of young adults (Norwegian Official Report No. 4, 1991). The report responded to many of the changes associated with economic restructuring borne of "globalization from above" and its impact on young adults. A characteristic of the education systems throughout social democratic post-war Scandinavia is a commitment to developing public education to ameliorate class differences through standardized universal education. A major concern has been the capacity of education to promote upward social mobility among the lower socio-economic groups and to redress issues of educational disadvantage.

Related to this challenge has been the unification of different types of educational provision under common legislation, which in Norway is enacted by means of parliamentary statutes. According to these laws initiated by social democratic governments, private education has not been encouraged. This question has been a crucial difference between the Left and the Right during most of the last century in Norway, as elsewhere. The social democrats have been wanting to use the educational system to break down class society, while the conservatives have argued for a school system to keep their privileges: separatist private schooling. On the whole, the emphasis of these governments has been on reducing the disparity between educational opportunities rather than creating tiers of privatized opportunity for the well-off.

Another feature of these initiatives by the state was the integration in 1959 of secondary modern and grammar schools into a nine-year comprehensive school. This was followed in 1976 by bringing together the gymnasia and the vocational schools to create a unified secondary school system. One of the aims of these new laws was to give equal status to both practical and theoretical education. This meant that students in the academic and vocational fields could have the right to complete three years of upper secondary education.

Until 1994, only the students in the academic field had this right. Students in vocational fields encountered fierce competition for the few places that existed in the advanced courses in upper secondary school. As a consequence, only a small minority progressed to further education. Only 11 percent of Norwegian students in vocational courses in crafts and industries entered the second year, while possibilities for a third year existed for only 3 percent (NOU 1991:4, 14). At the age of sixteen 50 percent of the cohort entered vocational streams in Norway. Vocational education has its special organization into masculinity and femininity, males in the "hard trades" and females in "soft fields": home economics, health and social services, and the aesthetic industry.

The "soft fields" have been geared to the family spheres and lower paid jobs in the service sector. These divisions are also challenged in this time of change, but this is not the main topic in this chapter (Mjelde, 2001). Vocational students have also experienced increasing competition for scarce jobs in the manual labor market during the past twenty-five years. In the period between 1972 and 1992, the numbers employed in industry in Norway fell by almost 100,000, while the numbers employed in the social and personal services sector increased by more than 350,000. Males have lost industrial jobs and women have swelled the ranks of the service sector. Former vocational students have also been moving in and out of adult education courses during these past decades as casualties of the cyclical upturns and downturns in the economy.

The 1991 policy, "Reform 94," sought to address these complex issues, arguing that human needs can only be satisfied through industrial production. There were two main questions about how this was to happen. There was the question of which areas of production would develop in Norway and what kind of skills the labor force would need in the future (NOU,1991: 4, 26; Mjelde, 1993, 1994). This stimulated other questions. Where and how would these skills be learned? Would it be in the workshops in vocational schools, in general classrooms, or in the course of working life? What kind of pedagogy would be implemented to facilitate this learning?

The vocational fields in the upper secondary school differ from the academic fields in terms of their complexity and dynamics and their relationship to the labor market. The vocational fields are more directly related to the ebbs and flows of the manual labor market than other occupations. They are more explicitly influenced by factors of gender, race, and ethnicity. The social division of knowledge in these different fields of education is also manifest in the division between workshop learning and classroom learning. The divide between practical and theoretical subjects reinforces divisions of gender, class, and ethnicity.

The crisis in production poses new questions in relation to the skills workers require for the manual labor market. These questions have been the focus of research into women and apprenticeships in Norway. The investigation of the industrial, technological, skilling, and gendering changes in the printing industry found that of the most serious weaknesses is a failure to conceptualize the ebb and flow of the manual labor market. The production processes are overlaid by market processes, whereby the labor contract is being negotiated every second of the day (Lee, 1981). These issues are at the core of reforms in Norway.

The current production crisis brought these problems into sharp focus. One of the government's proposals was to increase the importance of vocational education in schools, in combination with a structured apprenticeship program. This program stipulated two years in school and two years apprenticeship before being awarded a craft certificate. The 1991 Norwegian Policy "guaranteed" that all young people would achieve matriculation and/or a vocational qualification through establishing more flexible education structures to provide a more efficient utilization and coordination of human resources (Mjelde 1994: 200).

The development of adult education and lifelong teaching/learning programs was closely connected with these developments in vocational education in the school system and adult education centers. Adult vocational education has also functioned to replicate the divisions that exist in the post-compulsory school sector, between workshop and classroom learning practices, between work of the hand and the work of the mind. These tensions are characteristic of developments in adult vocational education.

The trend for vocational students who entered the manual labor market as semi-skilled workers during the past twenty-five years to participate in adult education courses is an expression of and a response to the ebbs and flows in the employment market. This trend is linked to government activities during economic crises. When unemployment rose, the state had lifted the level of resourcing for adult education. The resolution of the problems is a focus of the European Union's Leonardo da Vinci Program.

The European Union's Leonardo da Vinci Program

Adult education and the complexities of vocational education in particular have assumed a new importance to the European Union (EU). In this context, the EU has been promoting interaction between university professionals and students via the European Scheme for the Mobility of University Students (Erasmus) which was launched in 1987. The Erasmus Program was the first and most ambitious initiative of its kind, entailing a tenfold increase in the EU budget for cooperation in higher education. Until then it had been limited to relatively modest inter-university staff exchanges. In 1994, the Socrates program was inaugurated to subsume Erasmus, Lingua, and other similar programs in universities.

Several initiatives have also been undertaken in adult vocational education in Europe. The Leonardo da Vinci Program has been specifically directed towards the needs of the vocational training system. Among other things, it has given vocational students and apprentices an unprecedented opportunity for learning through international exchange projects.

The target groups of the Leonardo da Vinci Program are workers in craft and industry, business and services who are either vocational students or apprentices. The basis of EU policy on vocational education is Article 128 of the Treaty of Rome (1957) that instructs the Council of Ministers to establish general principles for implementing vocational training, and policies capable of contributing to the harmonious development both of the national economies and of the common market. The subsequent Council decision of 1963 developed ten principles around which the member states agreed to harmonize their action on vocational training. The second of these principles incorporated action on combining individual social and educational aspects of learning, and linking this to the economic benefits of skills training.

Flowing from this Council decision was a raft of provisions for cooperation between member states, together with the establishment of the Advisory Committee on Vocational Training. Between 1963 and 1983, the development of a framework on vocational policy for the EU took the form of several non-binding resolutions. The result of the first of these resolutions was the establishment of the European Center for the Development of Vocational Training (CEDEFOB) in 1975. The purpose of the Center was to provide information and expertise on vocational training and to stimulate research on the transferability of training standards to support the free movement of workers within the European Community. These initiatives reinforced the links between vocational education and the economic imperatives of the European Union.

The dramatic growth of unemployment in the 1980s lifted the profile of vocational training as a strategic response to long-term joblessness in the EU and the need to support the restructuring of the labor market by equipping workers to adapt to technological change. A Council resolution of 1983 (Deloitte and Touche, 2000: 19) emphasized the strategic role of vocational training as:

> An instrument of active employment policy to promote economic and social development and adjustment to the new structure of the labor market;
>
> A means of ensuring that young people are properly prepared for working life and their responsibilities as adults;
>
> An instrument of promoting equal opportunities for all workers as regards access to the labor market.

Following some twenty years of non-binding resolutions regarding vocational training, the European Community's institutions agreed in the mid-1980s to devise a legal base, founded upon Article 128 of the Treaty of Rome, for further developments in the field.

In the 1990s, two EU White Papers helped to raise the profile of vocational training to a central position in the Union's policy debates. The 1993 White Paper, *Growth, Competitiveness, Employment—The challenges and way forward into the 21st century,* identified the importance to the EU of financial investment in education and research, proposing a strategy to achieve more employment-intensive economic growth. The

White Paper emphasized the crucial importance of vocational training as a key factor in combating unemployment and strengthening the competitiveness of European enterprises. Member States introduced a community-wide vocational training program to support and supplement existing activities in this area. The profile of vocational training in the EU policy arena was further enhanced by activities such as the *European Year of Lifelong Learning* in 1986 and broader developments in the *Employment and Information Society* policy.

The *Competitiveness Employment* White Paper's theme of lifelong learning was reiterated and reemphasized in the White Paper, *Teaching and Learning—Towards the Learning Society,* approved by the Commission in 1995. This paper identified three major developments affecting the European social economy as "the globalization of trade," "the emergence of the information society," and "the progress of science and technology." The White Paper also established five objectives towards a learning society:

- to encourage the acquisition of new knowledge through the introduction of a European system of accreditation of technical and vocational skills;
- to bring about closer cooperation between schools and business through apprenticeship and training;
- to combat social exclusion by offering second-chance education to those affected;
- to ensure proficiency in three Community languages, and
- to equalize treatment of capital and training investment.

The Leonardo da Vinci Program gave expression to these policy aspirations by linking training to the growing problem of unemployment in Europe. The goal was to develop a common European vocational training policy for continuing adult education and lifelong teaching/learning. It also made a commitment to tackle socio-economic exclusion by targeting marginalized groups, such as the Romany and immigrant communities, and to promote equality between men and women.

In 1994, the European Union adopted the Leonardo da Vinci Program as a way of implementing its adult vocational training policy. The key objective of this program, originally introduced for a period of only five years (1995–1999), was to support the development of policies and innovative action in the Member States by promoting transnational partnerships. These partnerships were to involve different organizations with an interest in adult training and vocational education so as to enhance opportunities for adult participation in a dynamic manual labor market.

The program was allocated a budget of 620 million (ECU) for the first five years and was open to the fifteen EU member states and the three EFTA states of the European Economic Area (Iceland, Liechtenstein, and Norway). Progressively, it was expanded to include non-members, such as Cyprus, the Czech Republic, Estonia, Hungary, Lithuania, Latvia, Romania, Bulgaria, Slovenia, and the Slovak Republic.

A Leonardo da Vinci office was established in Brussels and a program was developed to promote cooperation among member and EFTA states in vocational education and training. The participant states were encouraged to establish their local Leonardo da Vinci offices and to explore cooperative projects between themselves and other member states. Cofinancing was demanded from the participants. Projects were promoted in the following three areas.

Survey and Analysis Projects

The participant states were encouraged to utilize different organizations such as enterprises, vocational training centers, and research institutes, as well as employer-employee unions, to form social partnerships to develop research topics responding to questions about production, economic crisis, and the labor market. A range of questions emerged. What are the skills requirements for masons, carpenters, and auxiliary nurses in at least three member states? Where does training take place in each country? What is the duration of an apprenticeship? How are assessments carried out? What are the similarities and differences between countries?

Pilot Projects

These projects involved networking programs between different partners in the fields of research, social welfare, labor unions, and employers' enterprises. The aim was to exchange experiences and knowledge within the field of vocational education and training. Projects to emerge included new curriculum for several trades in the vocational schools and the training of trainers for adults undergoing rehabilitation in companies. Other projects included the development of courses based on the application of interactive multimedia in nursing education. There was also a survey to analyze and compare the quality of vocational training programs for distance education offered by geographically isolated adults.

Mobility, Placement, and Exchange Projects

In these projects, participants were encouraged to promote mobility among vocational students and apprentices, engineers and teachers in other non-university professions. This project replicated the Erasmus/Socrates program that had operated across the European Union for the past twenty years. From 1987 to 2000, about 750,000 university students spent an Erasmus period abroad and more than 1,800 universities or other higher education institutions are presently participating in the program. The exchange program led to Italian apprentices being able to work for a period in hotels in Norway, a Norwegian dressmaker being apprenticed in the Drak-theatre in Tsekkia, and young English adults able to work in printing apprenticeships in France.

There was a requirement that at least three countries must cooperate as a prerequisite for obtaining the financial support of the EU. There was a wide variety in the applications, ranging from those involving three partners in three countries, to thirty-one partners in ten countries. In terms of priorities, the Leonardo Program stressed the acquisition of new skills; closer links between education and training establishments and enterprises; combating exclusion; investment in human resources; and use of new information technologies. The applications were evaluated by experts on vocational education from all the participating countries, as well as by Commission officers of the European Union and officials from the participating countries. Although this provided scope for a participatory evaluation, these processes were often complex and subject to contradictory and competing interests of various stakeholders.

The program ended in 1999 and was subsequently assessed by a professional research team; one expert from each participating nation followed the evaluation process. The impact of the program was significant, with over 2,993 programs being financed in the period from 1995 to 1998. The program involved 95,334 individual participants and 2,965 contracting organizations. Overall involvement in the partnerships totaled an impressive 64,510 organizations representing the diversity and complexity of the European vocational education, with in-company training programs having the largest number of projects.

For the period 1995–1999, placement and exchange projects benefited 51,047 young adult apprentices, 21,486 young adult workers and 10,750 trainers. 35 percent of the projects were from Germany, with France and the UK having the next highest proportion, a situation that poses problems, as the dominance of these in the EU raises controversial macropolitical questions. Regardless, complete classes of Norwegian hairdressers and electrical engineering students invested one-year training in England, pedicurists invested three months in Spain, carpenters went to Austria, and cooks and waiters to France.

The project evaluation report cites the following comments from participating countries. Concerning the Irish projects, participating companies said: "The company has gained considerably from working with partner organizations. Leonardo added new dimensions to our work that otherwise would have taken years to develop" (Deloitte and Touche, 2000: 70). In relation to an Austrian project, participants stated: "The co-operation with the partners was especially important to us. It has been possible to collect new knowledge and exchange experience about professional training in Europe" (Deloitte and Touche, 2000: 70). Similar positive comment came from a Spanish project: "Leonardo has been giving us considerable help in integrating disadvantaged youth into the labor market" (Deloitte and Touche, 2000: 76).

The evaluation report pointed to a number of positive benefits, including the development of networks and learning about cooperation and future participation in European programs. There was also evidence that organizational learning was improved through these partnerships. The program allowed space for the projects to remain at the forefront of technological advances, to adapt to changing market needs, and to enable the projects to become platforms for innovation in the enterprises. The transnationality of the program also contributed to the Europeanization of civil society and the growth of a European consciousness. The development of learning networks and transnational contacts enabled the exchange of skills, cultures, and learning across Europe. The question of Eurocentrism is complex. Symptomatic of this problem is that even when these questions are discussed, there is no mention of the Leonardo da Vinci Program.

The Leonardo da Vinci Program was responsible for the initiation of a number of projects that otherwise would not have come into existence. Nevertheless, there were also some problems identified which limited the effectiveness of this ambitious program. There was a failure to capitalize on the successful results of the projects because of the absence of monitoring of the outputs and products as well as a lack of dissemination of the outcomes and strategies. This was not helped by the survey and thefact that its analysis was isolated from the rest of the program. This impeded the capacity of the Leonardo da Vinci Committee to learn and develop an understanding of the program in order to influence future policy decisions. When evaluating the degree of success for the Leonardo da Vinci Program, the views of both the target groups of the program, as well as the responsible parties at different levels, were of major significance. They characterized the program as having a highly bureaucratic administrative structure centralized in Brussels that created delays in decision-making and payment processes.

In spite of these shortcomings, the decision was made to continue the Leonardo da Vinci Program for another seven years with economic development, vocational education, and the social organization of knowledge at its core. Norway, along with other countries, is expanding its involvement in the program.

In the period from the 1970s to the 1990s, little attention was directed at vocational or working-class education in Norway. The orthodox rhetoric was that Norway had already achieved equal opportunities through its education system. Learning in schools was assumed to be meeting the needs of all students. Research on adult education produced little information about the 50 percent of the youth cohort that entered vocational education and, if they were lucky, served an apprenticeship. The reforms of the 1990s changed this situation. Vocational education came to the center of economic reforms in Norway and in the rest of Europe.

Adult vocational education is linked to changes in the manual labor market in Europe, which is typified by complexity and contradictions. The hundreds of languages and dialects in Europe is a challenging opportunity for enhancing multi-lingual communication in everyday interactions. The life of sixty million Italians in the south, the birthplace of the European Union, has similarities and differences with the life of four and a half million Norwegians in the North, who have twice voted against entering the EU. They have a common European history of wars and similar political contradictions, but they also have some differing experiences in industrial and craft development and education systems. Similar divisions between mental and manual labor have developed in response to industrialization across Europe. However, there have been diverse developments in adult vocational training throughout Europe, and even within regions like Scandinavia.

The differences within Scandinavia are sizeable. In Denmark, employers and employees started to legislate for an apprenticeship system in the 1910s; Norway established its first Law on Apprenticeships in 1950; and Sweden is yet to adopt any apprenticeship law. Nevertheless, across these three countries there is a powerful hegemonic value system that allocates high esteem for mental labor and low esteem and denigration to manual labor. In this regard, Italy is no different from Scandinavia (Mjelde 1990). The Leonardo da Vinci Program has brought these contradictions to the fore. In Norway, more attention and understanding is being given to the diversity of the 250 trades under the Apprenticeship Law and to learning in workplaces than ever before.

The pedagogical focus has switched from teaching technology to student-directed learning. In support of these changes, Dr Rolf Kristiansen, the director of the Leonardo da Vinci Program of Norway said, "A focus on vocational education in Norway had emerged in a qualitatively new way. The pride in practical work and crafts traditions has been lifted among the youth with the Program" (interview data, May 2000). The present crisis has brought new challenges to these divisions. The Leonardo da Vinci Program has created awareness of and a new esteem for adult vocational education. Of course, contradictions still surround the program.

Leonardo da Vinci: Part of Globalization or Europeanization?

Globalization, as manifested in the ideological project of neo-conservative globalism, is a widely disputed and debated practice. "Globalization" was a much-used word in the anti–World Bank demonstrations in Oslo on June 24, 2002, where the slogan was: "Our World Is Not For Sale." However, the processes of globalization are not new. The processes associated with international markets and commerce have existed at least since the beginning of industrialization. Despite increasing global economic restructuring (and de-structuring) and the interdependence across the world, the processes of neo-conservative globalism differ across political and economic environments. An unprecedented expansion of world trade is creating new interdependencies that integrate national economies into a new economic order. The main agents of this global restructuring are large multi-national corporations that use information and transportation technologies to take advantage of cheap labor around the world and to expand their market reach and profits.

Measures of neo-conservative economic developments in education, employment, wages, and standard of living typically ignore the impact of globalization on social, cultural, and ecological processes. The EU's education programs and goals can be assessed in this light, not just as an emphasis on the capacity to participate in a worldwide competitive market. Fligstein and Merand (2002) argue that Western European foreign trade constitutes the lion's share of global trade and that globalization is really the Europeanization of trade. In other words, increasing global trade actually means that European firms are increasingly trading with EU firms.

The state-based political economy of the EU contradicts claims by neoconservative globalism that reduced government interventions are a prerequisite for vigorous trade and economic prosperity in the developed world. On the contrary, the work of the EU, even in adult vocational education, suggests that global markets need active states producing policies around the rules of exchange and competition, as well as adequate infrastructure and a qualified workforce. These developments must be made under the auspices of the state. The EU White Papers of the 1990s and their policies on adult education and vocational training demonstrate the need for state intervention as a means of stimulating and preparing the foundations for global/local economic growth. The emphasis on the skills of the labor force in Europe is part of state interventionist policy that has renewed the importance of lifelong teaching/learning. Programs such as Erasmus/Socrates and Leonardo da Vinci occupy a prominent role in legitimizing the work of the interventionist state. Yet many of the contradictions still exist around adult vocational education.

The Socrates Program focuses on higher education and the Leonardo Program on vocational training. This division separates one area of knowledge and skills from the other, directly mirroring the political economy of knowledge with its parallel education systems for different class positions in society. It is noteworthy how this division is reflected in the naming of the EU education programs. Erasmus/Socrates is for the academic streams, while Leonardo da Vinci is for vocational training. Socrates of Athens/Erasmus of Amsterdam represent the world of ideas made manifest in Antiquity and the Middle Ages. Leonardo da Vinci has connotations of the Renaissance world with its experimentation and the development of empirical research and applied science.

Recognizing that these distinctions are there, the EU-education programs then raise other questions. The Leonardo evaluation report found that universities conducted 18 percent of the projects. This was despite the fact that the prime targets were institutions connected to vocational training. The contradictions between the practical world of craft and industry and the academic world were revealed in the Leonardo implementation. Applicants working on practical problems of production are interested in developing solutions through research based on comparisons, but often they have no experience with the complexity of comparative research work. On the other hand, academic applicants claimed, rather naïvely, that they would solve the problems in production systems and within vocational education through a three-year comparative research project. These contradictions signal the continuing division between the mental and manual processes of labor as it has been perpetuated in the processes of industrialization and capitalist expansion.

The question of further integration between vocational and general studies has now emerged as a key issue in education policy-making in Europe as elsewhere. It cannot be solved by corporate managerialist "solutions" that force cohabitation without the explicit recognition and engagement with the tensions inherent in this much-needed border crossing. Rather, it is an acknowledgement that developments in the sphere of technology are radically changing occupational divisions, as well as the content and organization of work. This means there is increasing pressure to integrate the different elements within educational careers.

The EU agencies view these processes as both vital for the development of a European common market and for the strengthening of Europe in the global market. The agenda of European hegemonic powers might be to develop EU as a supranational state, but the implementation of this ambitious agenda is still full of tensions that reflect the many different agendas in this time of increasing global competition. The social division of knowledge between academic and vocational learning needs to be challenged in new ways. As a result of the present crisis, the Leonardo da Vinci Program has created an awareness of a new valorization for working knowledge.

Conclusion

The relationship between the abstract, conceptual world of academic education, unaffected by immediate socio-economic needs and the concrete world of vocational education, is under pressure to change. The prevailing divisions of labor that have developed during the industrial epoch are manifested in the development of vocational education for the trades and crafts. Contradictions exist between theoretical knowledge and practical knowledge, the work of the mind and that of the hand, intellectual and manual work, between practical and academic learning, and between inductive and deductive epistemologies. In vocational courses of study there are contradictions between workshop and "desk" learning, between learning in practice and theoretical learning.

This dichotomy has led to the theoretical impoverishment of vocational pedagogy for over a century. In the words of an electrician in the Apprenticeship Project, "The school cannot give you realistic training—neither for a craftsman, nor for an academic." This statement identifies the core issues that the Leonardo evaluation report highlights. The apparent complimentarity and synergy between Leonardo da Vinci and Socrates Programs shields the contradictions between them. Neither the program nor the report challenged the existing pedagogical division between theoretical and practical knowledge.

Work on developing more coherent theories in vocational pedagogy has as its core a different way of thinking about learning. Concepts like practice-theory, tacit knowledge, the reflective practitioner, and knowledge in activity give inspiration to this work in vocational pedagogy in Scandinavia. These learning concepts attempt to break away from instrumental-rational ways of thinking with their Cartesian ideal that assumes abstract thought processes precede and direct practical action. Given the relationship between "the master" and "the apprentice," the meaning of social interaction is integral to developing situated learning.

Future research in adult education and working life needs to establish and elaborate knowledge capable of demonstrating that it is the "academic breeding ideals" of the comprehensive school which are atypical in the light of history—in spite of the hegemony this cultural heritage has today. This hegemony can be observed in the EU educational programs. The programs reflect the continuing hiatus between theoretical and practical learning. In this time of upheaval, it is important that we develop an optimism that is open to new views. The germination of alternative forms of adult education for the future can transcend the debilitating social wounds which have severed the hand from the mind and the hand and mind from the heart, whether you teach or learn in Moscow, Stockholm, Sydney, or Santiago de Chile.

References

Brown, A. *Promoting Vocational Education and Training: European Perspectives*. Tampere: University of Tampere Press, 1997.

Daly, R., and L. Mjelde. "Learning at the Point of Production: New Challenges in the Social Division of Knowledge." In *Working Knowledge. Productive Learning at Work*, edited by D. Boud, 105–12. Sydney, N.S.W.: University of Technology, 2000.

Deloitte and Touche. *Final Evaluation of the Leonardo Da Vinci Program.* Brussels: The Leonardo da Vinci Office, 2000.
Fligstein, N., and F. Merand. "Globalization or Europeanization. Evidence on the European Economy since 1980." *Acta Sociologica* 45, no. 1 (2002): 7–22.
Harney, K., ed. *Lifelong Learning. One Focus, Different Systems.* Frankfurt am Main: Peter Lang, 2002.
Lee, D. J. "Skill, Craft and Class: A Theoretical Critique and a Critical Case." *Sociology* 15 (1981).
Mjelde, L. "Women and Apprenticeship: Industrial, Technological, Skilling and Gendering Changes in the Printing Industry in Norway." In *Vocational Education in Transition*, edited by A. Lindgren et al, (in press) Bern: Peter Lang Press, 2003.
———. "From Factory and Housework to Oil and Caring: Changes in Girls" Education in the Vocational Fields During the Years of Reform 94." In *Gender Perspectives on Vocational Education: Historical, Cultural and Policy Aspects*, edited by P. Gonon, (et al) 235–52. Bern: Peter Lang Press, 2001.
———. "The Promise of Alternative Pedagogies: The Case of Workshop Learning." In *Educational Dilemmas. Debate and Diversity*, edited by K. Watson (et al), 331–48. London: Cassell, 1996.
———. "Will the Twain Meet? The World of Work and the World of Schooling (Vocational and General) in Relation to Upper Secondary Schooling in Norway." In *Vocational Education and Culture. Prospects from History and Life History*, edited by A. Heikkinen, 189–204. Tampere: University of Tampere Press, 1994.
———. ApprenticeshipL From Practice to Theory and Back Again. Joensuu: University of Joensuu Press, 1993.
———. *Education and the Labor Market in the North-South Perspective.* Santiago de Chile: Cide Press, 1986.
———. "Labor and Learning." *Interchange* 21, no. 4 (1990): 34–48.
Norwegian Ministry of Education. "The Changing Role of Vocational and Technical Education and Training." Oslo: OECD Report, 1992.
———. *Veien Videre Til Studie Og Yrkeskompetanse for Alle:The Road to Further Study and Job Competence for All: Official Report.* Vol. 4. Oslo: Norwegian Ministry of Education, 1991.
Schemmann, M. "Lifelong Learning as a Global Formula." In *Lifelong Learning: One Focus, Different Systems*, edited by K. Harney, et al, 23–32. Frankfurt: Peter Lang Press, 2002.
Smith, A. *An Inquiry into the Nature and Causes of the Wealth of Nations.* New York: The Modern Library, 1937.
Teichler, U., and F. Maiworm. *The Erasmus Experience. Major Findings of the Erasmus Evaluation Research Project.* Kassel: Wissenschaftliches Zentrum fur Berufs and Hochschulforschung der Universitat Gesamthochschule Kassel, 1996.
The Norwegian Leonardo Office. *Implementation of the Leonardo Da Vinci Program 1995–1999.* Oslo: Teknologisk Institutt, 2000.

Chapter 4

Questioning Developmental Globalism: Threats to Language and Ecological Sustainability

Peter Kell

Exploring Development Economics, Language, and Ecology

This chapter provides an introductory exploration of several key dilemmas associated with economic overdevelopment, ecological destruction, adult literacy education, and language diversity in Southeast Asia. This emergent project is an outcome of research into innovation in the global business of teaching English that involved fieldwork in Malaysia and Australia (Singh, Kell, and Pandian, 2002). Analyzing neo-conservative globalism and its impact on language policy in both countries has prompted further exploration of issues that have not been widely investigated in adult literacy and language education. In the analysis of the interdependent relationship between the local and the global, the post-independence objectives of nations like Malaysia were found to center on:

- initiatives to forge unity in the post-colonial era around a set of national symbols that included a national language;
- government intervention to sponsor rapid economic growth to minimize the risks of social and political instability;
- a commitment to fast-paced industrialization through participation in various regional trading blocs;

- the use of foreign capital and the resources of agencies such as World Bank to promote economic expansion; and
- the prioritization of economic development over considerations of the sustainability of ecological and cultural diversity.

Most nations in the East Asian region combine the creation and affirmation of symbolic aspects of national identity with a strong commitment to economic development as signifiers of their nation-building projects. With the possible exception of China and Vietnam most East Asian nations exhibit hybrid forms of market capitalism and strong state intervention to direct economic development. Paradoxically, the emergence of "state-directed capitalism" is a powerful challenger to neo-conservative market capitalism (Daly and Logan, 1998). This strong state intervention has included large-scale infrastructure developments that have led to widespread social, cultural, and ecological disruption.

This chapter provides a preliminary analysis of the relationships between economic development policy, ecology, and language diversity with a view to exploring the links between unsustainable economic development, ecological destruction, and the erosion of linguistic diversity throughout Southeast Asia. It raises questions about how adult education and training at the national and regional level might respond to the challenges to linguistic and ecological sustainability. It argues the need for an interdisciplinary approach to adult education that spans economics, environmental science, and educational studies.

Asian Tigers Roaring: Neo-conservative Market and State Sponsored Capitalism?

The rapid expansion of East Asian economies has been mythologized as the "Asian miracle." However, the "Asian Tigers" emerged less as a triumph of neo-conservative market capitalism than as a result of developmentalism sponsored by post-colonial nation-states. Their economic development was steered by strong government leadership. In some cases this was dictatorial and included relatively high levels of political party and factional cronyism (Jomo, 1999). The economic success of many of these countries involved a policy umbrella of tax incentives, deregulated labor conditions, and lax environmental controls.

Aided by "open door" trading policies in the USA and Europe with low tariffs for preferred trading partners, most Southeast Asian nations experienced rapid and sustained economic growth from the mid-1970s until the financial crisis of 1997. During the period 1970 to 1989, the growth of Asian economies was underwritten by the United States military-industrial complex, which gave the region a high priority (Clammer, 2000).

The expansion of Southeast Asia can also be attributed to the transfer of capital from dormant and eroded "brown-field" sites in Europe and the United States to newer "green-field" sites in Asia where returns on investment were projected to be higher. This move to industrialize Southeast Asia was made easier by the growing dominance of transnational corporations with the capacity to transfer operations across the globe using deregulated international banking and financial structures that facilitated the rapid movement of funds across national boundaries. The transfer of international capital to South Korea, Indonesia, Malaysia, Singapore, and Thailand, where returns on investment were superior to those in Europe and the USA, was due in part to the lower costs of production. In some cases, this involved a shift from more established Asian economies such as Japan, the first beneficiary of post-colonial investment in Asia as part of a sustained campaign against the only serious alternative to capitalism, namely, unsustainable communism.

At the end of World War II, Asia was the poorest region in the world. Its rapid development has also been attributed to "Asian values" centered on discipline, compliance, and commitment to work. These claims obscure the post-colonial economic and political conditions that provided the platform for rapid development from the 1970s onwards. However, the homogenous and stereotypical European and American views of "Asianness" have not come to terms with the diverse social, cultural, religious and ecological context that typifies each country in the region. Making rhetorical appeals to "Asian values" to explain the region's economic development masks the economic and political conditions that enabled the region's "take-off" (Gomez and Jomo, 1999).

This expansion was initially driven by the manufacturing sector, where cheap (exploited), compliant (non-unionized), and skilled (educated) labor was required. As well as creating the necessary administrative and economic conditions, Asian nations guaranteed a compliant and skilled labor force or imported one. Many Southeast Asian governments guaranteed stable political conditions for business operations through a mix of repression, tight state control, and a state ethos of development. Governments anxious to attract multi-national corporations provided tax concessions for prospective investors, and manufacturers were encouraged to establish their businesses in exclusive economic zones, such as those in Malaysia (Penang) and China (Shanghai and Shenzhen). In addition, Singapore and Hong Kong moved into a high-wage economy, providing a financial hub to arrange funds and the brokering of major projects.

Malaysia and Indonesia diversified their industries, moving from a dependence on rubber and palm oil plantations and tin mining towards manufacturing and tourism. Initially, petroleum resources were used to finance much of this development. In Taiwan and Korea, the growth in the manufacturing sector was fuelled by state-run import replacement programs. Taiwan and Malaysia also developed specializations in component manufacture for electronics and information technology, while Cambodia attracted textile and garment manufacturing.

This region's economic development created differing labor patterns. This has involved a reliance on imported unskilled labor or state-sponsored strategies for filling skilled labor vacancies through adult education and training. In turn, this has led to changes in the labor market, including the increasing participation of women in manufacturing and the professions.

Accompanying these developments in manufacturing has been a continued reliance on the resources sector. While a "new" knowledge-based economy may be emerging in Indonesia and Malaysia, there is still a dependence on petroleum, mining, and timber. Logging has been characterized by rampant exploitation despite ostensible government attempts to control these industries. The forests in Kalimantan have been decimated through burning and clearing. In 1997, fires created a smoke haze that brought the region to a standstill. The economic growth in manufacturing and resources has given rise to parallel investment in infrastructure programs, such as rail, port, and road development (Clammer, 2000).

Rallying Around National Development Projects: Unity or Fragmentation?

Among the important infrastructure developments, were improvements in electricity generation to cope with an expanding industrial capacity and the parallel increase in urbanization. The Asian Development Bank and also the World Bank financed increased electrical generating capacity (George and Sabelli, 1994). This included the construction of large-scale hydroelectricity plants as a stimulus to the investment, building, and infrastructure industries.

The insatiable expansion of the building and construction industries in these countries distorted the allocation of capital and construction activity. In many cases, the construction of major projects was undertaken to pacify the development lobby rather than to service people's social and economic needs. In Japan, this has resulted in many rivers near urban centers having their banks paved regardless of the need for such construction (McGregor, 1996). An unfettered construction industry and its pipeline effect on poorly regulated financial institutions were among the major causes of the 1997 Southeast Asian economic crisis (Daly and Logan, 1998). The negative social and environmental impacts of these projects, which have been subject to minimal controls, have provided the touchstone for anti-government, anti-globalism policy activism. The construction of dams, large-scale mining, and logging have created significant political, ecological, and cultural problems, leading to a legitimation crisis in several Southeast Asian nations. Two examples usefully illustrate these concerns:

The Bakun Dam Project in Sarawak Malaysia. This controversial project has been scaled down from the initial 13.5 billion Malaysian Ringgit undertaking with 2,400 megawatt capacity to a smaller 500 megawatt dam. The construction of the 235-foot-high dam has commenced and the diversion tunnels have been completed. The dam is scheduled for completion in 2005. The project was halted due to the economic crisis in 1997 and is alleged to be the source of the falling out between Prime Minister Mahatir and former Deputy Prime Minister Anwar Ibrahim. The project was taken over by the government after its developers were unable to finance the original, ambitious plan.

The catchment includes 1.5 million acres of rainforest; 16 percent of Sarawak's log production comes from this area. Indigenous communities legally own 51 percent of the land in the catchment area. This project requires the translocation of some 10,000 Indigenous peoples of the Kajan, Kenyah, Kajang, Ukit, and Penan ethnic communities. Concerns over the destructive environmental and cultural impact of this project led to significant protest movements against the dam. The response of the government has been to argue that the dam will bring the Indigenous people of Sarawak into the capitalist economy and its consumer culture. This claim is made despite the fact that their relocation is disrupting their culture, including their environmental knowledge and skills. There are similar issues presently emerging as as a result of the proposals for a dam in Selangor begin to take shape (see http://ecanet.nat/ articles /dam.html).

The Freeport Gold Mine in West Papua (Irian Jaya) Indonesia. This is one of the largest gold mines in the world and is owned by the US multinational corporation, Freeport McMoran Pty. Ltd. The London-based RTZ Corporation has an 11 percent share in this US firm and has underwritten recent expansion of the mine site in the highlands of the West Papua (Irian Jaya). The project has caused significant political, ecological, and social disruption in West Papua (Irian Jaya) and has been one of many catalysts in the emergence of the "Free Papua" movement. This independence movement has grown from the discontent over the maltreatment of the Indigenous owners.

There are similarities with the Panguna mine in Bougainville, in Papua New Guinea, where discontent over mining rights triggered a ten-year civil war. Another source of discontent is that the mine discharges an estimated 110,000 tonnes of tailings containing toxic waste per day into local rivers with effects devastating on the downstream ecology. While the project has generated some 47 percent of the province's gross domestic product, the mine has disrupted the Amungme land and has resulted in the dislocation of an estimated 2,000 people (see Oxfam Community Abroad, http://www.caa.org.ay /horizons /december_2001/west_ papua.html).

These examples of opposition to developmental globalism indicate some of the dilemmas governments and citizens face. The creation of economic activity in provincial areas throughout Southeast Asia via large-scale infrastructure projects is riddled with contradictions and tensions. These include the need to boost existing low levels of investment in infrastructure and to lift the relatively low socio-economic investments in public education and health. The presence of ethnically diverse communities, including Indigenous peoples, with significant economic, social, and cultural dependence on the natural resources of forests and rivers, contests this political scenario. There is pressure on national governments to create and maintain the political autonomy of their provinces. The tension for government is to expand economic opportunities in these provinces whilst managing the political disunity and fragmentation that these infrastructure projects create.

Developing a Unifying National Project of Literacy and Language: Globalism, Nationalism, and Performance Anxiety

Neo-conservative views of development hold that enhanced economic performance is linked to increased worker education and training. The view is that adult education is both a personal and collective good that enhances the competitive advantage of nations in the global economy. It is in this context that English operates as an anti-market mechanism to provide a market advantage for Anglophone nations (Singh, Kell, and Pandian, 2002). These neo-conservative claims tend to ignore the significant contribution of the state in providing adult education, as well as tax and investment subsidies that enhance capital formation. From a human capital perspective, it could be expected that the Philippines, with a well-qualified, literate English speaking population, would rate well in international indicators—yet it does not. Indeed, in the manufacturing sector, worker compliance and citizen passivity, effected by state repression, are more useful in attracting global capital than accredited skills and capabilities (Rudnick, 1996; Sui Hei, 2000).

Following their independence investment in education has been a major priority in constructing Southeast Asian nation-states. The capacity of the state to fund public education at previous levels is now limited, as governments are invited to develop the private education and training sector to expand business opportunities for transnational capital (Lee, 1999). Accompanying the resource dilemmas over government disinvestment in public education are concerns over proficiency and standards in language teaching. The popular press in Malaysia and Singapore constantly question the English language proficiency spoken by their citizens, contrasting standardized British English with local English dialects (Nagara, 2001). This campaign by the media becomes particularly virulent concerning the poor performance of Malaysian students in language examinations. This poor performance is not limited to English as it also applies to Bahasa Malaysia, which also records declines in pass rates.

The press campaign attributes the poor performance to a new curriculum, the Kurrikulum Bersepadu Sekolah Menegah, that has sought to break away from functional grammar and a literature-dominated curriculum to emphasizing critical thinking. The exam results also highlighted a discrepancy between urban and rural education, with lower pass rates recorded by students in rural schools. While English passes in the Penilaian Menengah Rendah (PMR) decreased by 3.8 percent, urban areas recorded a pass rate of 72.8 percent, in marked contrast to rural schools recording a pass rate of 49.6 percent. These debates are linked to the tensions over the role of English as Malaysia's second language and the anti-market role of English as the mediator in the global marketplace for knowledge, a status that is criticized as being unpatriotic. This debate has positioned English in competition with Bahasa Malaysia, creating a situation where Prime Minister Mahathir has had to refute claims that English is a "kaffir," or infidel language, or that its use is unpatriotic. These tensions over language education create dilemmas for multi-ethnic and multi-cultural nation, such as Malaysia and Indonesia as they strive to build nation-states and simultaneously engage neo-conservative globalism (Singh, Kell, and Pandian, 2002).

The post-colonial formation of the nation-state has involved the quest for economic growth and political stability as well as the affirmation of linguistic and cultural symbols of unity. In Malaysia, national languages have been affirmed constitutionally, ensuring the legal status of Bahasa Malaysia as well as the languages of Indigenous communities. This region is subject to considerable social and ecological change due to the forces of development economics. The Iban people of Sarawak are the inhabitants of the area where the Bakun Dam is being constructed. The Kadazandusun people of Sabah are also subject to considerable economic, ecological, and social change through a combination of urbanization, tourism, mining, logging, and land clearing associated with the expansion of the palm oil industry.

Under the British colonists, the language of the Iban was afforded significant status, the "lingua franca" for trade, the judiciary, and the junior school certificate. Now, the British period is viewed in nostalgic terms, as a "golden age" when the Iban language experienced substantial development. After Sarawak joined Malaysia in 1963, the status of Iban changed. The constitutional developments of the state of Malaysia provided national status to Bahasa Maleyu (Malay), a second-language status to English, and vernacular-language status to Chinese and Tamil. Iban was included with Kadazandusun as Indigenous languages that have been offered as examinable curriculum subjects in Sarawak and Sabah schools since 1987.

Constitutionally, the Iban and Kadazandusun, along with the Malays, (Bumiputra) are considered Indigenous communities that have cultural affinities to the region and one another. Sarawak's Bumiputras include Iban, Biayah, Melanau, Kenyah, Kedayan Kayan, and Bisayah, who are guaranteed certain rights, including preferential quotas in higher education. The preservation of Indigenous languages was ambivalently affirmed under the 1995 Education Act (Act 550), which states, "Indigenous languages shall be made available if it is reasonable and practicable to do so and if the parents of at least fifteen pupils in the school so request."

Since 1987, the Malaysian government has attempted to integrate Indigenous languages into the formal school curriculum with an ambitious program of expansion. The status of Indigenous languages is interesting because constitutionally the "original" people of Malaysia consist of Bumiputera Malays, the Aboriginal people of Peninsular Malaysia, and the Indigenous people of East Malaysia. While all these groups are accorded equal status as Bumiputera, their languages are constitutionally differentiated. The national language of Malaysia is Bahasa Maleyu. Indigenous languages do not have this status, being relegated to a status subsidiary to English, a foreign language. In the case of Iban and Kadazandusun, the teaching of these Indigenous languages is confined to East Malaysia.

The Iban make up some 576,000, or 3.5 percent of Sarawak's population. The teaching of Iban in Sarawak schools involves 34,772 pupils in 453 primary schools and 16,117 secondary school students in 51 schools. The teaching of Iban is hampered by a lack of government investment in producing reading materials for schools, providing academics to educate teachers, and developing curricula to assist the 775 teachers in Iban schools. These constraints have restricted Iban teaching, not permitting the language to be offered at senior secondary school, although ambitious plans have been proposed.

The largest language community in Sabah is Kadazandusun, which has three dialects: Dusun, Murut, and Bajau. The Kadazandusun language group represents the marriage of two main dialects of the Dusunic language family, which is widely spoken across Sabah. In terms of language teaching, this has the advantage of being used widely across the community. The Kadazandusun language has been taught in schools since 1995. An ambitious three-year plan seeks to expand language teacher numbers from 30 to 507; to increase students studying the language from 316 to 8,456 and to extend the number of schools where it is taught from 15 to 231. This expansion comes from a 1997 pilot project, which engaged 15 schools in the task of collecting the lexicon from the different dialects in the Kadazandusun language family. A society for educators of Kadazandusan has been established, and they have held a preliminary conference.

The decision to adopt the Bunduwilan dialect eventuated from a 1989 conference entitled, "Towards Standardization of Kadazandusun" which involved certification of this dialect by experts from the USA. This in itself represents an interesting expression of neo-colonial dependency. The Kadazandusun are largely confined to the highlands of the west of Sabah. Predominantly vegetable growers and agriculturalists, they do not find themselves as vulnerable to the impact of logging and construction as are the Iban of Sarawak. The Kadazandusun experience makes an interesting contrast to that of the Iban in Sarawak. These social and cultural factors give the Kadazandusun significant political status in Malaysia.

This complex of economic development, the privatization of education, and media campaigns over language proficiency are integral to debates over major infrastructure projects and population relocation. In the context of rapid economic growth and translocation, adult education and training take on considerable importance in the readjustment strategies used by governments to contain potential legitimation and political crises. This includes active strategies to provide mixed employment opportunities in the development through traineeships and apprenticeships. This strategy is most effective for large-scale, long-term projects such as mines, where employment assists in transition. Passive strategies for realizing government policies include accelerating deployment of infrastructure, such as formal adult education. The strategies applied by the Malaysian government in Sarawak and Sabah suggests that the latter have broad positive impact.

Regardless of which strategy is applied, there arise questions concerning the sustainability of ecological and linguistic diversity in the face of both the forces of nationalism and globalization. There is concern about the devaluation of Indigenous languages and the knowledge they embody that accompanies translocation, especially the threat of language death after the environment in which the language is constructed and conceptualized is destroyed. The way of life of those who have been relocated is under threat of dispossession. Similarly, there is concern about the ways in which the relocation process contributes to the marginalization of Indigenous knowledge and language skills, and the extent to which the Malaysian curriculum and schooling contribute to this process.

The destruction of Indigenous ways of life, especially their forced movement, contributes to a skills gap which adult literacy education programs are enlisted to redress. Such programs can contribute to ecological destruction and cultural genocide as a result of continual economic over-development. Key to addressing this concern is recognition of the relationship between the sustainability of biological diversity and linguistic diversity. Is there a causal relationship between reduced biodiversity, the death of languages, and the loss of related socio-cultural practices? On the relationship between the environment and adult education, Coombs (1990: 117) observes:

Apart from wealth and income there can be other keys to barriers between individuals and the environment. Important amongst these are the knowledge and skills, more or less specialized, which are required to engage with many of its more complex components. The hunter-gatherer acquired skills from the older generation naturally by progressively acquiring increased involvement in these activities. Contemporary man" s [sic] skills must be acquired vicariously—frequently through institutions, to which access is rationed either by price or performance testing.

Recognizing the breakdown of this crucial relationship that developmental economics creates, Coombs (1990: 118) offers a useful strategy for working through these dilemmas:

These considerations suggest there will be value in seeing contemporary society as a series of environment activities that offer roles and experiences for those who participate in them. They suggest also that the economic system settings, from which are derived the wealth/income keys giving access to much of the environment system, and the education system (in its broadest sense), from which the skill knowledge keys are derived, still warrant special attention. Finally they suggest that experience from voluntary associations may be important and distinctive and less subject than others to the constraints of scarcity.

This introduces an alternative reading of the linkages across scarcity, economy, and ecology which is absent in the neo-conservative adult education policies. The incorporation of an environmental consciousness in adult education provides a stimulus for taming neo-conservative exploitation throughout Asia.

Economic Development and Ecological Democratization?

The complexity and diversity of Asian economic activity does not conform to the technical, reductionist models which can not explain the diverse social, cultural, and political texture of the region. Too often this view is tainted by colonial legacies. These orientalist fantasy assumptions suggest that economic developments in Asia are exotic adaptations of capitalism to changing conditions.

Developmental globalism constructs economics as a disconnected technical, instrumental activity that denies the relationships between ecology and the economy. The tension between technical rationality and eco-social rationality is often resolved by the subordination of consensus for biocultural sustainability to maximizing profits and productivity. Gorz (1994) argues that the constant quest for innovation and differentiation provides the foundation for heightened levels of consumption that fuel the systematic degradation of the environment. To avoid a technocratic and authoritarian *dirigisme*, Gorz argues that a reconstitution of the life-world is required to facilitate a fall in the production of commodities and services. This restraint is to be underpinned by joint, collaborative "own use" production. Gorz argues for a regional and multi-state approach to "eco-space." Ecological degradation is not confined by national boundaries. Moreover, ecological problems are not scientific but are linked to social and political questions associated with human rights and land rights.

Neo-conservative globalism also operates on determinist assumptions that there is an unlimited trajectory of economic growth underpinned by greater technological and industrial capacity. Developmental globalism presents an optimistic view, where growth and wealth are linked to more deregulated finance and trade. Most recently, this view of neo-conservative globalism has been depicted as a given that omits the agency of individuals and the capacity for the community to shape the future of economic policy.

In Indonesia and Malaysia, major development projects function as a rallying point for a coalition of concerns around issues of ecological survival, social justice, and democracy. Non-government groups, such as Aliran in Malaysia, are indicators of the capacity of citizens to mobilize around environmental issues. They introduce questions about the policies of the nation-state through resistance to and criticism of major construction and development programs (http://www.aliran.com). Similarly, the emergence of socially critical movements opposed to the Suharto regime was in part generated by concern about the corruption and cronyism associated with major projects. The government initiated these projects to secure economic stability and to win the loyalty of local constituents. However, these projects were responsible for prompting significant government opposition.

The neo-conservative determinist trajectory around development issues fails to account for population growth, rapacious energy consumption, environmental destruction, and the polarization of opportunities and access to wealth and resources. This unevenness of opportunity within and between nations has created the climate where racist wedge politics can undermine and threaten national consensus and unity. The use of regressive localism and hyper-nationalism based on mono-ethnic views are manifested in extreme, ultra-nationalist movements.

These movements present a major challenge, because their rhetoric enlists concerns about the environment, linking these to concerns about population levels. Often, these "population" concerns are thinly disguised attacks on internal and external migrants that blame these groups for problems created by neo-conservative globalism. This is a particularly worrying trend in multi-religious and multi-ethnic countries like Indonesia, where communal violence has erupted in Kalimantan and in Molukas and threatens to spill into West Papua and Irian Jaya. The flood of refugees from these trouble spots puts further pressure on the resources of neighboring countries such as Malaysia.

Paternalistic, neo-colonial perspectives position Asian nations as corrupt and ecologically negligent, even though American and European nations face the same issues. However, these claims reflect European and American anxiety about the challenge to their global dominance posed by Asian economic growth. Asian nations initially encountered an isolationist Bush administration wanting to thwart China's economic power with a return to "cold war" politics. Since September 11, 2001, the emerging revenge enacted in the name of a "war on terrorism" has prompted the United States of America to look for more allies in Asia by intervening militarily in the southern Philippines. The danger is that legitimate sources of opposition are being identified as "terrorist organizations." As a consequence, the key tensions around economic development and ecological destruction remain unresolved. How these global issues translate into regional issues will be of crucial importance to the future of Southeast Asia.

Towards a Local/Global Resolution

The issues raised in this chapter signal the need for detailed research into the interaction between economy, ecology, and literacy. It is recommended that multi-disciplinary approaches to adult education incorporate analyses of political economy, nation-building projects, and biocultural sustainability. This arises from the concern of Southeast Asian authorities who are seeking education assistance and advice on language teaching and Indigenous education. This is often manifested through bilateral aid programs conducted by the European, American, and Australian governments or international non-government agencies. These programs are remedial responses that fail to examine the social, economic, and environmental contexts in which they operate. Some of these programs perpetuate the myths of developmental economics and fail to respond to local and community concern for sustaining biodiversity and linguistic diversity.

One possible response to these requests is to embed adult language education within discussions about the nation-state, economic development, and ecology, the objective being to ensure that these projects are not reactive but provide an integrated approach that is useful to a range of stakeholders, of which government will be the principal one. The mix between environment and development is a politically controversial arena that ensures any adult education program will need to address these sensitivities and conflicts. Such adult education programs have to steer a course that ensures opportunities for collaboration are maximized and the needs of powerful interests are mediated. Ultimately, the impact and durability of the strategic outcomes of adult education in this context will be determined by educators' ability to address the anxieties of stakeholders.

References

Clammer, J. *Values and Development in Southeast Asia*. Subang Jaya: Pelenduk, 2000.
Coombs, H. C. *The Return of Scarcity: Strategies for an Economic Future*. Melbourne, Victoria: Cambridge, 1990.
Daly, M., and M. Logan. *Reconstructing Asia: The Economic Miracle That Never Was, the Future That Is*. Melbourne, Victoria: RMIT Press, 1998.
George, S., and F. Sabelli. *Faith and Credit: The World Bank's Secular Empire*. Ringwood, Victoria: Penguin, 1994.
Gomez, T., and K. Jomo. *Malaysia's Political Economy: Politics, Patronage and Profit*. Cambridge: Cambridge University Press, 1999.
Gorz, A. *Capitalism, Socialism and Ecology*. New York: Verso, 1994.
Hamid, R. A. "Integrating Ethnic Minorities into Mainstream Malaysian Society: The Inclusion of Ethnic Languages in the National Curriculum: Language in the Global Context for Language Classrooms." Paper presented at the SEAMO Regional Centre Conference, April 1999.
Jomo, K. S. *Rethinking Malaysia: Malaysian Studies 1*. Kuala Lumpur: Malaysian Social Studies Association, 1999.
Lee, M. *Private Education in Malaysia*. Penang, Malaysia: Universiti Sains Malaysia, 1999.
McGregor, R. *Politics, Culture and Sex in the New Japan*. Sydney, N.S.W.: Allen and Unwin, 1996.
Nagara, B. "We'll Lose Out with English." *The Star*, May 5, 1999, 10.
Rudnick, A. *Foreign Labor in Malaysian Manufacturing: Bangladeshi Workers in the Textile Industry*. Kuala Lumpur, Malaysia: INSAN, 1996.
Singh, M., P. Kell, and A. Pandian. *Appropriating English: Innovation in the Global Business English Language Teaching*. New York: Peter Lang, 2002.
Sui, H. *Assembling Gender: The Making of the Malay Female Labor*. Kuala Lumpur, Malaysia: SIRD, 2000.

Part Two

Literacy, Languages, Meaning Making, and Practices of Reflexivity

Chapter 5

Multicultural Meaning Makers: Malaysian Ways with Words and the World

Koo Yew Lie

Introduction

Malaysian learners and employers perceive a discernible gap between the promise and enactment of multiculturalism. This gap is manifested on several levels. Employers in both the private and public sectors campaign through and with the media about the levels of confidence, independence, and critical abilities displayed by graduates. They complain that graduates lack voice, creativity, innovative capacity, analytical research skills, problem-solving abilities, critical thinking capacities, the ability to undertake teamwork, and skills to communicate interpersonally and professionally.

This chapter explores some of these concerns about adult education through reference to work on situated literacies (Barton, Hamilton, and Ivanic, 2000). Specifically, I describe the literacy practices of two adult students in relation to the trajectories of the larger social, educational, political, and economic contexts in which they are studying. Through this case study, I explore the unduly constrained and submissive voices of these linguistically proficient, well-qualified, and professionally experienced Malaysian students. I discuss the findings and insights derived from this case study in the context of changing views on adult education, and the heterogenous spaces of work where these students' multiple worlds intersect.

My commitment is to engage in exploring the possibilities of multicultural resources which are largely latent or even silenced among Malaysian adult learners. The productive possibilities of these multicultural resources arise from their membership in various cultural worlds, for example, ethnicity, gender, religion, spirituality, class, and age. This chapter engages multicultural Malaysian adult learners to consider themselves producers of meaning, able to draw upon their distinctive personal and collective identities, histories, and experiences for this creative work. It provides Malaysian learners with an indication of the resources they have to develop meaning-making capabilities with the intention of affording them fuller personal, social, and economic participation in national/global spaces.

The Perceptions of "Realities" in Malaysia and Changing Global Contexts

There appears to be a general feeling of disempowerment amongst graduates and undergraduates in tertiary institutions. They seem unable to recognize any possibilities for using the extensive multicultural resources associated with their multiple membership in various cultural communities for personal self-actualization or making meaning of changing social and economic conditions. These multicultural resources include the philosophical, linguistic, and semiotic resources which belong to them as members of distinctive social, ethnic, and religious groups.

Arguably, these offer possibilities for creating new knowledges, new ways of being, new ways of interacting, and new ways of doing. There are significant constraints experienced by some Malaysian students with regard to using their own multicultural resources, especially those which are largely undervalued and/or marginalized by education institutions. The socially and economically productive possibilities of "difference" are deployed in unproblematic conformity to official discourses which are characterized by fixed notions of information transmission as the "best" model of the teaching and learning processes.

Contrast this with present-future worlds of diversity, brought on by rapid changes in information and communications technologies as well as by internationalization through migration, global economic integration of markets, and communications industries. With these changes have come tremendous possibilities as well as conflicts for multicultural peoples in terms of their productive diversity (Cope and Kalantzis, 1997; 2000). Diversity, however, has to be strategically negotiated, represented, and contested in various spaces. The active possibilities for diversity through dynamic engagement with difference, through negotiation, production, and representation, have yet to become a systemic feature of Malaysian education. Looking at the significance of humanity's diversity and its potential for productivity is largely absent, ironically, at academic sites.

The Broader Socio-cultural Contexts

This section of the chapter describes briefly the broader socio-cultural contexts within which the multicultural Malaysian reader is located, contexts which interpenetrate the teaching/learning space of Malaysian students and which influence the ways in which the students interact with texts.

The Discourse of Examinations across Sites

The prevailing social practice of copying information has arisen, in part, from the highly regulated examination-driven education system in Malaysia. It has a long-established history of valuing the top-down transmission of knowledge and convergent thinking around standardized norms. This education system revolves around performance assessment, good grades, and awards given for success in standardized achievement tests. Since these examinations value the reproduction of facts, it is hardly surprising that the ethos pervading all levels of teaching and learning practice reflects this. The literacy practices that operate within this context of learning a fixed body of knowledge can be recited without imagination or critique. This orientation to education emerged under British colonialism, which promoted a strong positivistic tradition. Malaysia is not exceptional in this regard. The United States of America, among others, has a strong positivistic education tradition which persists to this day.

The power of examinations in Malaysia is supported by private tuition businesses whose principal objective is to make money out of training clients to pass them. The principal diet for students in tuition centers consists of examination formulas, the learning of facts, and mastering techniques on how to do well in examinations. As with schools, students in tuition centers are trained to disengage their life-worlds from their learning experience, especially if they conflict with the purposes of the school and public examinations. These trends are also affirmed by a flourishing publication industry which produces review books, study guides, and extensive notes to help students pass examinations. Media attention on "successful" candidates further reinforces the expectation of a particular kind of knowledge production in this climate.

A Position-oriented, Collectivistic Society

Arguably, the general and marked absence of authoring-type literacy in Malaysia may be the effect of a hierarchical, collectivistic society. In this society, selected group interests and values are privileged over those of others, authority figures are given respect, and change is driven from the top-down. Any challenge by those in a lower position is viewed negatively. Having caused a loss of "face," there is a price to be paid on the part of the person who makes the challenge. These characteristics may account for the reason authorial literacy practices are rare, given that they would necessarily lead to perceived challenges to official discourse on significant issues. Authoring and voicing are a privilege accorded to people in positions with access to political, economic, material, and symbolic power.

In the study reported here, for example, the two postgraduate students comment on the difficulty they face in articulating their views in academic and public spaces. Holding positions as lecturers in a public university, they are expected to speak publicly but in support of official positions. Adopting a publicly critical voice is a major challenge for most Malaysians, especially when they are dismissed for risking social harmony and public goodwill. Many reasons explain the prevalence of this predisposition among Malaysians, including the existence of the University and Colleges Act and the Internal Security Act. These acts were introduced after the inter-ethnic riots in the late 1960s, and are often provided as a reason for not discussing "sensitive issues" that might stir up inter-ethnic misunderstanding and conflict. In turn, it is argued, this could threaten nation-building and economic development agendas.

The Discourse of Nation Building

Living in a country where issues related to ethnicity are a socially significant political issue has tended to constrain and been used to constrain Malaysians. They tend to be cautious of any threat to existing inter-ethnic power relations. The focus has been on national economic development. Submission to dominant nation-building discourses is, as the safe option, mobilized for maintaining prosperity and peace. The contestation of alternative views in public spaces is avoided, as the risks can be unduly high. There is a lack of well-functioning public spheres with open communication that permit discussions that could lead towards greater self-understanding. Nevertheless, alternative media on the Internet is being accessed privately. However, the media is strongly regulated and controlled by the ruling political parties. Independent analysis and comment is generally constrained. Text production within the media is limited to officially sanctioned facts and opinions. The local media is constrained by "nationalistic" policies that feed nation-building agendas.

The political and socio-cultural contexts of Malaysian meaning-making impacts on text mediation by readers and writers. In turn, this impacts on the larger contexts. At one level, the unquestioning "respect" for officially institutionalized power has silenced Malaysians. There is a strong literacy of compliance and obedience which hinders the expression of difference and the articulation of diversity in education. There is a lack of public articulation of the everyday negotiation with the different that faces Malaysian adult worker-learners. Paradoxically, these very spaces also offer potential for learning to produce dialogic exchanges.

Social and Productive Diversity in Everyday Life

The dynamic processes of meaning-making and representations of multicultural adult learners are manifest in spontaneous translations, word play in Malaysian Englishes, and heterogeneous discourses in daily life. Creative works by Malaysian writers, artists, and designers show a complex of hybridized discourses involving multiple life trajectories (Sabapathy, 1998). However, these creative productions remain limited to well-known and "recognized" writers and artists ratified by institutional power. Their texts are constructed as unproblematic representations of "culture." The more important question concerns how access to voice, creativity, and representation can be provided to many more Malaysians.

This section has described the broad socio-cultural contexts within which multicultural Malaysian learners are located. It has focussed on the possibilities, realities, and conflicts for multicultural meaning makers. The next section focuses on the theoretical perspective informing this case study involving multicultural adult students. Concepts of identity, literacy, power, reflexivity, and globalization are especially important in this context.

The Theoretical Underpinnings and the Case Study

This chapter draws on theoretical work which considers literacy as a social discursive practice (Wallace, 1988; Street, 1988; Gee, 1996; Barton,

Hamilton, and Ivanic, 2000). Literary practices are the historically constituted aggregates of worldviews, ideologies, values, attitudes, behaviors, and thinking of particular communities in situated contexts. Literary practices are expressed through socially sanctioned performances and displays, like listening, speaking, reading, writing, and the production of texts. Through these particular practices, identities are constituted and membership of cultural communities recognized. Literacy practices can be inferred from the attitudes and feelings of literacy participants to their multiple ways of meaning-making. Literacy practices also include the participants' perceptions of what counts as knowledge, and the people and institutions that have rights to legitimize knowledge.

In this chapter, a key assumption is that literacy is a social discursive practice involving the acquisition or learning of the complex of participant roles, identities, language/s, texts, representations, and artifacts. Embedded within this configuration are privileged philosophies, ideologies, values, and attitudes that are often invisible to insider-participants. Literacy is necessarily plural. We need to talk about literacies by virtue of the fact that all human beings belong to a number of primary and secondary discourses (Gee, 1996). Literacy practices are privileged by discourses of particular communities in particular sites.

Further, literacy practices are embedded in ideological and power relationships. Underlying reading and writing practices are assumptions, ideological commitments, beliefs, and values of the particular social-cultural contexts from which they emerge. Some literacy practices are more dominant and visible when compared to others. Given the hierarchical structuring of communities, those literacy practices which protect and preserve the power of elites are valued above all others by them. The learning of literacy practices valued by these communities and their institutions may lead to the acquisition of power, money, and status. However, the acquisition of vernacular, everyday literacies are necessary for the affirmation of particular identities from one's primary life-worlds, especially the family. Here, "life-world" is understood in terms of Gee's (1996: 181) definition as "that space where people can claim to know things without basing that claim on access to specialized or professional discourses with their special methods for producing knowledge."

Multicultural adult learners need to become more aware of the reasons, processes, and effects of traversing and hybridizing life-worlds. This may help them engage strategically in contemporary local-global spaces, a requirement of new learning and work where plurality is significant. For example, multiple interaction patterns, communication styles, ways of speaking, and self-presentation are now required for teamwork involving culturally diverse members of different life-worlds and disciplines brought together by possibilities of globalization and communication. The creation of new knowledges is a requirement at post-Fordist work sites where "new" involves new ways of looking at a problem, and the need to accommodate new sociality, new commodities and new ideas.

Submissive and assertive literacies (Koo, 1998) operate at a number of interacting levels, both as generic social practices as well as singular pragmatic-interpretive acts. Submissive literacy occurs where a participant assumes the role of an animator or articulator, mouthpiece, or scriptor of texts with little responsibility for the origin of ideas in the source texts and little commitment to the ideas in the text. Such submissive literacy practices may have developed due to the influences of social, political, and economic institutions. They are marked by unequal power relationships. The globally dominating neo-conservative ideology promulgated by the mass media and throughout the capitalist marketplace also finds expression in the production and interpretation of texts, as well as the prevailing values sanctioned by societies' elites. This work occurs within the home, school, workplace, spiritual or religious sites, and bureaucracies.

"Assertive literacy" (Koo, 1998) is the practice where the participant assumes the role of author, the sayer or originator of the message of the text, or a transformer of an input or source text. He/she exercises some responsibility for the origin of ideas in the source text and comments upon it or has some reasoned commitment to or detachment from the source text. Such assertive literacy practices may emerge due to changing power relationships in dominating institutions, ideologies, beliefs, and values existing in particular domains of societies such as home and school. However, in the case of Malaysian students, assertive literacy practices in formal institutions are rare. This is due to Malaysian enculturation in both their primary (family) and secondary life-worlds (communities including religious, educational, bureaucratic, and governmental institutions).

Reasons for the dominance of submissive literacy practice include the history of the Malaysian education system, positivistic and privileging pre-established knowledge, viewed as unproblematic, universal, and true.

Ways with Words in the Worlds of San and John

The empirical work reported in this chapter is based upon a longitudinal case study that focuses on two Malaysian adult readers' literacy practices.

Evidence is being generated via interviews and observations of their interactions with texts. The readers are middle-class Malaysian students who are in their thirties. The first reader, San (a fictitious name), is a Malaysian Chinese woman from a middle-class urban family. The second reader, John (not his real name), is a Malaysian Indian male. Both readers have at least ten years of experience in teaching English as a second/foreign language and are English language lecturers at a Malaysian public university. This chapter focuses on selected findings obtained from the larger qualitative study involving reader history and profiles, and reader responses in questionnaires and informal interviews. Data were also obtained from reader think-aloud protocols in relation to discourse interactions with two texts which are representative of the type of texts used in their workplace. The first text was taken from *Aspects of Language Teaching* (Widdowson, 1992), while the second was a newspaper article, *"The Status of Bahasa Malaysia,"* written by Malaysian writer Jocelyn Tan.

Literacy Practices of Malaysian Readers in Relation to Texts and Contexts

This section provides an analysis of the literacy practices of Malaysian readers undertaken by interweaving findings from data obtained from participant profiles, questionnaires, interviews, and think-aloud protocols.

Privileging Formal Learning and Imagination

The two participants perceived a dichotomy between reading for formal learning and reading for imagination or pleasure. In part this reflects the social values within the larger society which tends to privilege utilitarian learning for content knowledge against and above reading for pleasure and the development of the imagination. San and John explained that the Malaysian education system is tightly regulated, with official sanctions controlling knowledge through the use of approved assessors and examiners.

Disempowerment and Critical Thinking in Academic Space

John enjoyed literature in Form Six (pre-university studies) until the rigid formal assessment system "killed his love" for it. Although he has a long history of academic success, he was traumatized by his "failure" in one subject at postgraduate level in university. This affected him so badly that he did not complete his graduate studies. The positioning of his inability to think critically by one of the lecturers was the reason for his inability to complete, although he was an intelligent and motivated student. Indeed, he had many years of experience in language teaching and learning to draw upon for his interactions with text. However, he found himself helpless after a literacy encounter when a lecturer described him as lacking in the ability for critical thinking. This seriously affected his confidence in his academic ability. No doubt there could be other reasons to account for his disempowered condition other than the lecturer's crippling depiction of him as being unable to think critically.

In John's case, there is a disconnection between his everyday literacies and the academic literacy he wishes to acquire. John's repertoire of vernacular literacies could be engaged critically through a reflexive pedagogy which juxtaposes the differing discourses so that he reflects on the purposes and processes of each genre underlying politics and the ideology of each. This is especially important in societies which are highly collectivistic, where approval is dependent on gatekeepers like adult educators who have a major say in their students' life opportunities.

San reported that she reads imaginative literature and is very proficient in the English language having a privileged middle-class family background where English was widely spoken and read. Those who taught her described her as academically able. However, when it came to her interactions with academic texts, she found herself silenced by the power of the writer's ideas and the erudite ways in which some of the "native speakers" write. Her definition of "native speaker" privileged the (White) people situated in Kachru's (1988) "Inner Circle" and is indicative of her unquestioning submissive positioning of herself in relation to these privileged texts.

Like John, San reported she was overpowered by the English language text she read, finding it difficult to draw upon her own experience to interrogate the text, its knowledge claims and authority. There is a crucial need here for peoples working out theories in the context of the outer regions to learn how to negotiate the meanings captured in texts located within the privileged Inner Circle. Learners need to be taught how to reflectively draw from their own memories, experiences, and views—to mediate local meanings from privileged texts. However, this dialogic engagement is often a difficult, if not alien, experience for readers who have been trained to see the truth as being "out there." It is in this sense that the two readers remain positioned, appropriating the mind of the perceived Other.

The observed silence of otherwise intelligent adult interlocutors in an academic site suggests the power of abstract claims to universal truths are understood as above and beyond challenge. As yet they are unable to find within themselves the resources to challenge master discourses to which the non-native English speaker must submit. The linguistic rhetoric and discourse of the native English-speaking writer silenced San. This was despite her rich experiences in the academic world and her wide knowledge of the world acquired from a childhood habit of reading. As San put it in relation to the Widdowson (1992), "He writes so well and elegantly that I could not find a space to squeeze for myself."

Fluidity in Everyday Life and Stratification in Academic Space

San and John reported having a rich and successful history of using multiple literacies in their everyday life-worlds. In terms of vernacular literacies in their day-to-day life, both readers traverse purposefully and fluidly from mother-tongue literacies to Bahasa Malaysia literacies and English language literacies. These adaptive and adroit literacy mediators have acquired the art of submissive convergence to gatekeepers in academic sites, having appropriated the ways of "doing texts" privileged by those sites.

At the same time, they are able to use their vernacular literacies to create hybridized texts in their other life-worlds, keeping these literacies distinct for their own purposes. For example, John has various literacies in Tamil, standardized Malaysian English intertwined with Liturgical Colonial British English in the Tamil church domain. He shifts to Malaysian Tamil for informal conversations at home. Then John switches to colloquial Bahasa Malaysia when communicating with cabdrivers and the hawkers at the night market. He is able to move fluidly between these cultural and linguistic spaces for his purposes.

However, this adaptive capacity is not used in pedagogy of adult education to help disempowered learners to build upon their representational resources to access let alone transform, dominating literacies and discourses. A multiliteracies framework could help John explore the use of this capacity in adult education classes so that a dialogic interaction between texts and contexts may be engaged in the formation of a richer authoring capability among adult learners (Cope and Kalantzis, 2001).

However, the pedagogical and gatekeeping functions of adult education undervalue the creative and innovative capacity which John has, as manifested in his ways with words in less risky, less face-threatening spaces where multi-lingualism is acknowledged and valued. The learned practice of submission has a negative impact on the creative and critical capacities of adult learners. To the extent that adult learners confine themselves to submissive academic literacy, adult education does not empower them to further their academic and work life.

Assertive literacy is crucial to creating new knowledges and new identities for the twenty-first century. There is a pedagogic and social need to articulate spaces for the contestation of varying discourses in and through adult education so as to allow for the engagement of linguistic diversity openly. This would allow for greater linguistic and semiotic productivity and representation of meanings. This would allow for the adult learner's development of voice (Bakhtin, 1986). The meaning maker's expression affirms and recognizes her/his situatedness in engagements with peoples, communities, and contexts where voices are multiply constructed by class, ethnicity, and gender. Empowerment through the recognition and affirmation of the adult learner could allow for the fuller realization of adult learner's meaning maker potential and therefore the enrichment of community, nation, and state.

The Compartmentalization of Vernacular Literacies and Academic Literacy

These two adult learners recognize the importance of the indigenized languages like Straits Chinese patois, Malaysian Cantonese, Malaysian Tamil, Malaysian Englishes, and varieties of Bahasa Malaysia for expressing multiple Malaysian subjectivities. The hybridization of identities and discursive transformation is manifested in the lighthearted entertainment programs on Radio and Television Malaysia and on the Internet, where global/local texts interact. San and John have learnt to view these languages and the cultures as insignificant for creating serious knowledge and cultural capital. Neither they nor their teachers view them as fluid, versatile ways of interacting and perceiving in a multicultural world, denying their role in contributing to a distinctive and new adult education.

San and John have not learnt to use vernacular literacies to create new designs of meaning and representation that are socially and economically productive. They are not able to see the transformative potential of these linguistic and semiotic resources that they have as multicultural meaning makers for living with difference. What is clear from these adult learners is a lack of agency in relation to their serious engagement with the multilingual knowledge society of the twenty-first century.

English Language as Liberatory and Constraining

In interviews and questionnaires, San and John report that they perceive Standardized Malaysian English much like international English. In particular, they construct it as being "neutral." Ironically, when compared to the mother tongues of the various ethnic groups, English is viewed as a "neutral" language because it is not related directly to any particular ethnic group in Malaysia. The English language is perceived as having an important "neutral" status for the development of the imaginative and the epistemic, and for transcending spaces vis-à-vis the personal, community, national, and international spaces. The two subject participants are generally accepting of the English language as being an international language useful for accessing national, international and global education, business, trade, diplomacy, and wider communication. The English language is seen as offering a modern way of being, a way of escaping patriarchal, ethnocentric, and traditional ways of being.

However, there is a stark contrast between what these adult learners have been led to believe are the possibilities represented by learning the English language and what they actually do with English in everyday dialogic interactions. My own observations of Malaysian learners tend to confirm that this is a common perception and/or confusion, perhaps indicating the conflicts felt but not always articulated. The unquestioning acceptance of the claim that English is socially, culturally, and economically neutral is again a manifestation of the participants' general unawareness of the historical, social, political, and power-centered relations of systems of language, knowledge, and social practice.

The disempowerment of adult learners rich in life-world experiences means that they are not able to engage their cultural knowledge imaginatively to represent their own meanings of the texts with which they are interacting. This is a manifestation of the structuring of power in adult education that hinders the valuing of the views of those adult learners occupying a marginalized subject position. Such deficit thinking comes from politics, the media, bureaucracy, education, and workplaces that depict knowledge and power as belonging to an unproblematized abstract, universal, truthful realm. Pedagogies of intercultural reflexivity may help challenge this perspective.

The two Malaysian adult learners represented in this case study were able to draw upon their multicultural resources to come thus far in the educational system and to negotiate this diversity of resources in their everyday lives. However, they were not fully aware that their voices could be represented within academic space. Their voices were silenced because they were viewed as unimportant or as presenting a risk to dominating interests. These adult learners had not acquired the confidence to use their memories and histories when interacting with academic knowledge and texts. There was a chasm between the potential and the actual—actual processes that they constantly draw upon. In their everyday (non-academic) life, they regularly draw upon creative practices such as translation, shifting between subject positions. However, these practices are trivialized as being appropriate only for everyday life but not for the forging of knowledge in academic sites.

Another dynamic meaning-making practice engaged everyday by these Malaysian adult learners is that of intra- and inter-language translation. This involves the multiple and fluid uses of Malaysian English in different contexts. This practice is taken for granted so much so that its normality renders it invisible. The advertising and marketing industry has now appropriated Malaysian English to mobilize the transnational culture of consumerism. The transformation of discourses in adult education may have to wait for further legitimation in those sites committed to consumerism.

As multicultural, multi-lingual peoples, Malaysians draw upon these practices to negotiate variations in ethnicity, class, age, gender, ideology, religion, and spirituality. This capability, which is reflected in their everyday experiences, is undervalued in the creation of cultural capital.

The two participants perceive English language discourses as having potential in terms of the transformation and redesigning of their present texts and contexts. Specifically, they see possibilities for using English in reframing the realities of informal contexts. However, they do not see their repertoire of other linguistic resources as having innovative potential for serious economic and social capital creation, as required by the knowledge producers of the twenty-first century. This dominating practice has emerged partly from the deep structural institutions in the society and in adult education where top-down gatekeeper text interpretation and production are unproblematic, accepted as "universal" and "true."

This general accepting attitude toward inequitable power relations has silenced the creative potential and productivity of Malaysian adult learners. This poses difficulties for "knowledge" creation in academic sites. The creativity expressed in their flexibility and resilience in crossing and hybridizing informal cultural and linguistic texts and contexts is especially evident in informal sites outside academia. The creativity present in these casual conversations has yet to be transferred into sites of knowledge production. A paradigm shift within Malaysian adult education is vital so that we remain strategically attuned to the possibilities of localizing the globalization in the economy, politics, and society.

Twenty-first Century Malaysia

Multicultural Malaysians are confronted with rapid changes in the twenty-first century brought about by national development and globalization, both of which are underpinned by dramatic changes in information and communications technologies. This makes it crucial to reconsider a systemic commitment for negotiating the cultural diversity that is a significant feature of Malaysian society. While undervalued and generally rendered invisible, the meaning-making resources for doing so are already present in multicultural students. The negotiation of diversity in multicultural societies is an important requirement for producing transnational learners, workers, and citizens in the twenty-first century. It brings with it the hope of moving Malaysians toward becoming a more democratic and participatory peoples; meaning makers coming to voice their changing spaces through their rich spiritual, philosophical, semiotic and cultural resources.

Given rapid changes and the fluidity of nation-states, multicultural Malaysians are embracing new subjectivities, new literacies of being, new knowledges, and new discourses. However, it appears that adult education in Malaysia continues to reproduce and privilege hierarchical power relations, top-down interactions, and structured monologic discourses. The adult learner-workers graduating from this system meet industry requirements for global workers who perform submissive, mindless, and repetitive work (Gee, 1996). In this sense there seems to be continuity between adult education literacy practices in Malaysia and those characterizing the spaces of transnational work. However, if the Malaysian government and industry wish to pursue original knowledge building, design, and creative work, they need to draw upon the multicultural-intercultural resources which already exist in the everyday taken-for-granted and pluralized articulations of Malaysians. They can help forge distinctive new knowledges from their diversity for the complex of multiple local-global spaces.

Malaysian literacy education continues to be narrowly utilitarian, grounded in decontextualized, skills-based functional discourses, where the specifics of reading and writing are lost in the rote learning of a body of facts. Consequently, adult learners find themselves disadvantaged in the pluralized, albeit contested, local/global spaces. A discontinuity exists between the literacy practices of adult education providers and the new work-place literacies of the twenty-first century, with contradictory demand for factory hands and knowledge producers. The capacity to negotiate the cultural diversity involved in teamwork produces new ideas, and thinking out of the box is the basis of the multi-lingual knowledge economy.

Presently, these resources are not systematically articulated nor valued in adult education, which focusses on the knowledge claim of the external, native English speaker. Until multicultural adult learners systemically and actively value their multiple ways of knowing as worthwhile resources for self-actualization, problem solving, teamwork, and research they will be powerless second-class workers. This should not be the case in a global work order where specific kinds of diversity is the norm (Cope and Kalantzis, 2000).

Malaysians are adaptive and resilient boundary-crossers, some more visibly so than others due to their control of material and political power. They have indigenized and hybridized their meaning-making discourses in their everyday educational and working lives. However, what is not explicated clearly are the particular participant identities which they adopt, and the very processes which they draw upon to cross and mix cultural lifeworlds—the very knowledges and resources which they take for granted in their hybridization of discourse. This symbiotic creative mixing of lifeworlds is generally not valued in adult education.

A Pedagogy of Intercultural Literacies: Access, Empowerment, Plurality, and Transformation

This chapter has argued that adult education can provide greater equity and access for disempowered peoples in order for them to have a voice in the educational, work, and civic spaces of the future. This poses an important challenge for adult education at the beginning of the twenty-first century. To empower adults as meaning makers for active participation in an increasingly integrated world of global production and consumption, a reflexive framework of intercultural literacies offers resources of hope. At least five attributes are integral to this pedagogy.

- First, making visible the operations of dominating literacies and modes of accessing them, are not naturally acquired;

- Second, rearticulating the interface between dominating literacies and resistance literacies to explore new ways for redressing the silencing and disempowerment both can effect on heterogeneous voices and perspectives;
- Third, rearticulating ways of problematizing dominating and resistance literacies by critiquing them and focusing on possibilities for forming projective literacies in relation to one's own representational resources;
- Fourth, rearticulating a pedagogic grammar of adult learners' primary and secondary life-world knowledges to show how the creative hybridization of everyday literacies from various domains help multicultural literacy brokers mediate the conflicting, uneven and challenging global/local spaces between the goals and purposes of particular discourses, and
- Fifth, rearticulating intercultural and multicultural literacies in terms of multiple and variable participant roles, purposes, processes, and outcomes. This includes enhancing adult learners' skills with meaning-making in print, visual, and multi-modal forms and as expressed in hybridized languages, discourses, and semiotic forms.

Adult educators now need to engage their students dialogically across ethnic, religious, and cultural structures, as well as across the state's systems of racialization in heterogeneous spaces. The challenge is to bring inter-ethnic, global citizens spatially and temporally closer together to face potential conflict, so that differences can be strategically negotiated. Inter-cultural and, specifically, inter-ethnic dialogue is fundamental to change and continuity for adult education students and the communities they inhabit.

References

Bakhtin, M. "The Problem of Speech Genres." In *Speech Genres and Other Late Essays*, edited by C. Emerson and M. Holquist. Austin, Texas: University of Texas Press, 1986.
Barton, D., M. Hamilton, and R. Ivanic. *Situated Literacies*. London: Routledge, 2000.
Cope, B., and M. Kalantzis. *Productive Diversity*. Sydney, Australia: Pluto Press, 1997.
———, eds. *Multiliteracies*. London: Routledge, 2001.
Fairclough, N. *Critical Language Awareness*. London: Longman, 1995.
Freire, P. *Pedagogy of the Oppressed*. New York: Continuum, 1970.
Gee, J. *Social Linguistics and Literacies*. London: The Falmer Press, 1996.
Heath, S. B. *Ways with Words*. Cambridge: Cambridge University Press, 1983.
Kachru, B. B. "The Sacred Cows of English." *English Today* IV, no. 4 (1988): 3–16.

Koo, Y. L. "Reading as Social Practice." In *Writings in Applied Linguistics, a Festschrift to Honour of Prof. Madya Dr Abdul Aziz Idris*, edited by M. Maros and Q. C. Kin: Faculty of Language Studies, National University of Malaysia, 2002.

———. "People, Voices and Discourses Mediating Spaces." In *Voices and Discourses Mediating Spaces: A Festschrift to Honour Prof. Madya Dr Harriet Wong*, edited by Y. L. Koo, Faculty of Language Studies, National University of Malaysia, 2002.

———. "Participant Roles of Multicultural/Lingual Malaysian Readers in a Tertiary Context." Unpublished Thesis, University of London, 1998.

Kress, G., and Van Leeuven. *Reading Images: The Grammar of Visual Design*. London: Routledge, 1996.

Lankshear, C., and P. McLaren, eds. *Critical Literacy, Praxis and the Postmodern*. Albany, New York: State University of New York Press, 1993.

Lee, K. H., and C. B. Tan. *The Chinese in Malaysia*. Malaysia: Oxford University Press, 2000.

Sabapathy, T. K. *The Art of Yeoh Jin Leng*. Singapore: University of Singapore Press, 1998.

Street, B. *Literacy in Theory and Practice*. Cambridge: Cambridge University Press, 1988.

Wallace, C. *Learning to Read in a Multicultural Society*. Cambridge: Prentice Hall International, 1988.

Widdowson, H. G. *Aspects of Language Teaching*. Oxford: Oxford University Press, 1992.

Chapter 6

Adult Educators' Talk: Responding to the Challenges of Linguistic Normativity

Shanta Nair-Venugopal

Introduction

In workplaces worldwide, the widespread use of Englishes is exerting almost irresistible pressure towards global linguistic uniformity and yet simultaneously results in the emergence of numerous local hybrid Englishes. This chapter critically examines these contradictory sociolinguistic tensions between the press for linguistic homogeneity and normativity on the one hand, and fragmentation and variability of Englishes on the other (Graddol 1997; Lietner and Sieloff, 1998; Crystal, 1997). To do so it explores the nexus of normativity and language "choice" and use in the situated discourse of adult educators in Malaysian business settings.

Nowhere is the use of (one or more) Englishes more entrenched in Malaysia than in corporate business and industry, and banking and finance, although the Chinese languages and dialects dominate local/global Chinese diasporic business interactions. Moreover, *Bank Negara,* the Malaysian Central Bank, along with government corporations and agencies, make extensive use of English. (Nair-Venugopal, 2001). The language of global/local Anglophone businesses, English has remained the normative language "choice" for corporate business communication in Malaysia. Although English is no longer an official language in Malaysia, its domination of transnational business and government activity is a large legacy of the British colonialist enterprise here and there. It now makes possible continuing links with the English-speaking world, with countries such as Singapore, the Philippines, and India.

The pervasive influence the English language achieved under British imperialism is being carried along by the juggernaut of contemporary globalization and regularized in many of its contexts by the practices best characterized as "McDonaldization" (Ritzer, 1996). Emerging from globalized workplaces in multi/transnational corporations is the hegemonic view that English is *the* international language of global/local business practices, *the* language of international capitalism (Naysmith, 1987). Of course, it has to contend with other global/local languages that include Mandarin, Spanish, Arabic, and Portuguese.

But the ideological project of producing a single standardized or normalized international English is confronted by the ascendancy of linguistic variation in Englishes across the world's workplaces. Paradoxically, at the same time as English is becoming a *lingua mundi,* that is one world language among others, as well as a *lingua franca,* one of several key languages for conducting commerce, media, and politics globally, the globalization of English is also giving rise to its localization. There are emerging "multiple and increasingly differentiated Englishes, marked by accent, national origin, sub-cultural styles and professional or technical communities" (Cope and Kalantzis, 1999: 2).

Key Terms

Central to this discussion is the notion of *normativity,* by which is meant the controlling power of ideological beliefs about the need for and insistence on standardized global language usage. This insistence on normativity crystallizes into powerful expectations that influence and shape attitudes and imperatives regarding business communication in transnational contexts. The exercise of this power by Anglophones to assert and demand transnational linguistic normativity is an expression of linguistic hegemony. This is a departure from the debate on the linguistic imperialism or "linguicism" of the English language (Tollefson, 1991; Phillipson, 1992; Pennycook, 1994; Skutnabb-Kangas and Phillipson, 1994). It refers to the cultural hegemony of a particular model of English that has been imposed as a version of linguistic supremacy or "triumphalism" in Malaysian business contexts. This is closer to concerns about the ideological drive for standardizing languages (Milroy and Milroy, 1999; Milroy, 2001).

Through examples of speech data, this chapter argues that, despite the proclamations that English is *the* international language of the globalized workplace, it is being localized. That is to say, despite the fact that English has colonized and is the colonizing language of international capitalism, its global/local dominance is being contested, perhaps most evidently through its appropriation (Singh, Kell, and Pandian, 2002). In Malaysian business contexts, this appropriation is known as *Malaysian English*. The particularity of the localized interactions in global/local business settings contrast markedly with the institutional imperatives which drive language "choice." These workplaces do not represent models of bastions for the use of "international English language."

British colonial administration, the educational and language policies of an independent Malaya and, subsequently, those of Malaysia, have led to the creation of *Malaysian English*. This dialect of English is geographically distributed and socially defined within Malaysia, displaying its own distinguishing features arising from practices of localization. Because English is now taught as a nationally important second language in all publicly funded schools, it cuts across the social divisions that privileged those educated exclusively in English. No longer the preserve of a linguistically empowered social elite, Malaysian English is debated as its speech community expands to include those marginalized by lack of proficiency in standardized English.

Most large Malaysian business houses dictate the use of English as the language of communication. Organizational directives governing workplace adult education inevitably take for granted the use of some imagined standardized version of English. However, these business imperatives and directives have been found to be at variance with the linguistic practices in these workplaces (Morais, 1994; Nair-Venugopal, 1997; Anie Atan, 1998). On the ground research is demonstrating the ascendancy of localized varieties, forms, and styles of Malaysian English. Workers have found other "ways of speaking" in English (Hymes, 1974a and b). As workplace adult education represents a form of *talk-mediated literacy,* this chapter reports on interactions in training sessions that point to evidence of reticence, if not resistance, to linguistic normativity (Nair-Venugopal, 1999).

Here, "ways of speaking" is used to refer to the "relationships among speech events, acts and styles, on the one hand, and personal abilities and roles, contexts and institutions, and beliefs, values, and attitudes, on the other" (Hymes, 1974a: 45). Elsewhere the interdependence between language use, political economy, and hegemonic normativity has been explained as "the relationship between personal economy and the community's speech economy" (Figueroa, 1994: 65). These patterned behaviors or routines are learned within a social matrix through application in particular situations depending on personal economy and the consequences of action. In contrast to the organizational directives, these "ways of speaking" implicate the communicative competence of language users. Localized variations in the speaking of English contrast with and challenge linguistic normativity and its prescriptions governing language "choice." Likewise, contextually prescribed pedagogies for language modeling are contested in the practice of workplace adult education.

Contentious Issues and Data Analysis

There is a linguistically necessary paradox in Malaysian business communication. The rhetoric of the powerful, gatekeeping echelons of senior management is preoccupied with establishing and maintaining "standardized English." Common descriptors of the normative linguistic benchmarks they establish include reference to "good," "proper," "correct," and even "quality" English. However, linguistic normativity is not pedagogically possible to exercise in the everyday work of adult educators. They are much more savvy about the pragmatics of language education in multi-lingual learning and working environments that are their largely mono-lingual, Anglophone gatekeepers.

In practice, it is not possible for adult educators to use the interactional dynamics of training sessions to satisfy the unrealistic expectations of these gatekeepers. For the most, these gatekeepers are firmly wedded to the ideology of linguistic normativity, which they expect to see translated into classroom pedagogies that define and enforce standardized English as the medium for business communication. But adult educators find it linguistically and pedagogically necessary to give voice to priorities that differ quite markedly from those of the gatekeepers. The language "choices" they make in training sessions give expression to asymmetrical power relations governing the authorization and legitimation of linguistic norms, and in doing so both expose and contest the prevailing linguistic hierarchies.

Gatekeepers, particularly "human resource" managers, characterize this struggle by lamenting the decline in the proficiency of new recruits to the workforce, or bemoaning the language competence of adult educators.

Their prescription and mantra exhort the use of "standardized" English. Their linguistic concerns are linked to maintaining a desirable corporate image or brand name in the marketplace. The assumption is that their customers also value standardized English so much so that they take it as a symbol of "good" service. This was equated with an idealized "standard" English variety.

In contrast, adult educators hold different views. They are professionally qualified for their assignments as workplace educators, with advanced education in areas as diverse as total quality management, legal aspects of business practices, computerized operations and applications, banking, and finance. Intent on educating workers as to their roles with respect to these areas of specialization, these adult educators take as their responsibility the transmission of knowledge and skills about these matters. For them, the transmission of the message is the more urgent task at hand. Despite their own preferences for using "standardized" English, pedagogically they find it necessary to engage their workplace learners in the languages, which they find most proficient for understanding the company's approach to quality control or related matters. Which linguistic code and how it is used in the context of an adult education program is subservient to realizing the company's primary training goals. This is a necessary efficiency even in spite of the organizational directives and accompanying rhetoric to the contrary.

While not planned for nor explicitly agreed to by adult educators and workplace learners, standardized English usage is not and cannot be adhered to in the course of classroom training sessions. Although standardized English is frequently appealed too by adult educators, in practice it remains a distant abstraction; insistence on its use would minimize the key learnings required of the session.

On the other hand, adult educators do find it necessary to rely on the communicative resources of Malaysian English for effectively teaching the knowledge and skills required by the company's workers (Nair-Venugopal, 2000; 2001).

Adult educators have to be skilled in mediating localized English diversity that affects and shapes the discourse of Malaysian workplaces, and the limited managerial perceptions that privilege standardized English language use because of its Anglo-ethnic prestige.

These contentious issues can now be illustrated through an analysis of three examples of the verbal interactions between adult educators and workplace learners.

Example 1

The following vignette is taken from a course on Quality Control Awareness conducted by the Quality Assurance Manager of a manufacturing organization. A Bumiputra-Malaysian adult educator (A1) questions trainee K (TK), a Chinese-Malaysian female clerk, about the watch she is wearing. This pedagogical move represents an attempt to mediate between the adult learner's experiential knowledge and the conceptual knowledge to be explored in the training session. This exploration of the reasons or criteria for her "choice," was intended to provide an anecdotal basis for raising the issue of consumer concern about product or service quality, the concept of quality control, and company procedures for delivering on consumer expectations in this regard in order to maintain or secure market share. As in any similar situation extracting the "appropriate" teaching point from the learner is the focus for this exchange.

A1:	What sort of watch are you er wearing?	1
TK:	*Pasar malam* [night market].	2
Others:	(laughter)	
A:	Why...why do you like that one? Why do you prefer that brand?	3
TK:	Doesn't matter.	
A1:	But why do you prefer it?	4
TK:	I just simply choose one because I'm in need of it	5
	so I just er *chin chai [non-fastidiously]* take one only.	6
A1;	I see but how reliable....Is it reliable?	7
TK:	Yes reliable...one and a half years already.	8
Others:	(laughter)	
A1:	Always on time?	9
TK:	It cost me twenty dollars only.	10
A1:	So the word...the key word here is "reliable."	11
TK:	Ya, reliable.	12
A1:	If it is not reliable for example every day, it is five minutes late	13
	five minutes fast....	14
TK:	I would have changed already.	15
A1:	You would have changed already. You are satisfied with that?	16
TK:	Yes.	17
A1:	Good.	18

Trainee K is expected to be proficient in English; this is the language in which the class is conducted. However, even from the outset (line 2), she shifts lexically into Malay in response to the adult educator's question, *What sort of watch are you wearing?* The term *pasar malam* is understood by all Malaysians to refer to the weekly night market held in towns and suburban areas. Moreover, the term carries a particular connotation. Her classmates laugh when K discloses that she bought the watch at the *pasar malam*. This is because it is widely held that goods purchased at these markets are invariably of indeterminate quality or frequently copies of branded products; thereby posing the silently ignored issue of why the company is really interested in "quality control."

The other lexical shift, *chin chai* (line 6), is a local expression. Although derived from the Chinese language, Hokkien, the term is an established feature in the verbal repertoires of all Malaysians. It is understood to mean being non-fastidious or non-discriminating, or even laissez-faire. Besides these linguistic shifts, there are other characteristic features of Malaysian English used by trainee K. Her speech is a good example of the Malaysian English spoken by Chinese-Malaysians because its morphological, phonological syntax adaptations demonstrate the substrate influence of Hokkien. This variant of English is now being acculturated into the Malaysian English language. As an *ethnolect,* K's use of Malaysian English necessarily gives expression to the prosody of her substrate language (Nair-Venugopal, 2000; 2001).

The adult educator, who's also the company's quality assurance manager, uses a subvariety of English, evident in the words *that one* (line 3). The style of discourse he uses is that typically employed by teachers. Dubbed "adult educator talk," it is characterized by certain linguistic routines such as repetition and the use of *good* to signal the end of the exchange. His home language and that of his primary schooling was Bhasa Malay. Professionally qualified as a mechanical engineer from an Australian university, he also has a degree in management from an institution in the USA. However, despite being a fluent speaker of a version of standardized English, he displays considerable competence in being able to engage in communication using variable forms of English. His ability to make these rhetorical and lexical selections is fairly typical for many young male Malaysian professionals. In no way did his use of or engagement with Malaysian English diminish his pedagogical effectiveness in raising and inculcating awareness of the importance of the company's concern for quality control.

Example 2

The following interactive episode is taken from an adult education session on Quality Work Attitudes. The adult educator extols the virtue of having a positive attitude by encouraging worker-learners not to dwell on the past, but to accept workplace changes as inevitable, therefore requiring them to get on with living with and reconciling themselves to the present changes. Both the adult educator (A2) and the trainee (TSM) are Tamil-Malaysians. Trainee TSM, the driver for one of the company directors, is not expected to be proficient in standardized English as his speech indicates. His occupation is likely to reflect the marginalization associated with his linguistic and ethnic background, as much as the fact that he did not complete a full secondary education. Nevertheless, he is able to follow the training session because of the adult educator's mode of presentation.

A2:	...any amount of thinking any amount of guilty feeling...	1
	any amount of regret...it will never change anything.	2
	Now, what has happened before, do you accept that?	3
TSM:	Aah but we got to er change our character what....	4
	Say example, I got some bad habits.	5
A2:	Yes.	6
TSM:	I (2 syllables)	7
A2:	Let's say like...a habit like drinking a lot. Let's say.	8
TSM:	Ah I change. What I means is hundred percent	
	keluhan hati bersih	9
	[come clean with (hundred percent) sincerity]	
	yes (laughter).	10
A2:	Right (laughter).	11
TSM:	Past one year I been drinking.	12
A2:	You've been drinking a lot.	13
TSM:	I stop completely, so I a'ready changing.	14
A2:	Yes now what I said is...Can you change that situation?	15
	Can you go back and say now like... (it) never happen before?	16
TSM:	Yes I change a'ready.	17
A2:	No. No. Now yes. Now you can change. Now, but before...	18

TSM:	Before, aah I cannot.	19
A2:	It's happened isn't it?	20
TSM:	What happen, happen a'ready.	21
	(laughter)	
A2:	Happen, happen already. That's what I'm trying to say	22
	just like what you said. I'm glad M----- you were able	
	to share that with us.	23
	You said that you drank a lot last time.	24
	(turning to the group)	
	dia minum banyak (.) er apa ni erm arak	25
	[he drank a lot of what's this er alcohol]	
	er liquor (.) so he used to take a lot he said...okay	26
	now, he can do a few things. One continue feeling bad.	27
	Drink like mad so that it will...you know, *kelam kabut*	
	[confuse]	28
	you know *semua* [all] and then you feel nice while the	
	liquor is there,	29
	but actually when you take liquor...I have taken	
	liquor before,	30
	so...I will tell you that too. Any amount of liquor you take	31
	only for that moment while the liquor is there, you...	32
	I mean you feel a little better. You can't say that	
	you can erase it.	33
	It's there. You feel a little better but next day...	34
	it gets worse because you go into a depression.	35
	You get worse. Am I right?	36
TSM:	That's true.	37
A2:	So liquor cannot solve the problems.	38

A striking aspect of this interactive episode is the pedagogical efforts made by the adult educator to accommodate to the trainee's language as a means of advancing his learning. This episode demonstrates that linguistic accommodation is a necessary competence required of adult educators operating in global/local multi-lingual contexts. Pedagogically, this involves skill in reducing linguistic dissimilarities between educator and learner by the adult educator paralleling the worker-learner's linguistic features: pronunciation, accent, rate of speech, and content. This skilled adult educator accommodates himself to the worker-learner's needs by "approximating" his linguistic proficiency and idiolect (Coupland, Coupland, Giles, and Henwood, 1988). As Malaysians, these two workers share linguistic repertoires, and an awareness and understanding of the socio-cultural norms of their community. As Tamil-Malaysians, they are able to make a pedagogical advantage of sharing quite similar ways of speaking.

The style shifts, code switches, and lexical changes made by the adult educator serve to enhance his communicative and pedagogical effectiveness. The switch by TSM into Bhasa Malay (line 9) allowed the worker-learner to draw on linguistic resources not available to him in the English language, thereby circumventing any inability at that point to express himself adequately in that language. His confidence in expressing himself in Bhasa Malay means that he does not have to abandon the topic by acquiescing to the linguistic hegemony of English-only politics and pedagogy. Trainee SM is a more balanced Malay-Tamil bilingual; his education does not allow him the same as a Malay-English bilingual. This is illustrated by his switch, *keluhan hati bersih,* which is an idiomatic, culturally salient, Bhasa Malay expression. Unlike *kelam kabut,* it is not a localized expression but functions as a metaphorical switch for rhetorical effect.

The code switch *dia minum banyak* (line 25), leads to a translation by the adult educator of TSM's disclosure that he previously *drank a lot.* The apparent purpose of this translation of personal information is to gain the attention and emotional involvement of the other worker-learners who until then had been merely eavesdropping on the conversation. Lines 25 to 38 are directed to them, although the confirmation check, *Am I right?* (line 36), is specifically addressed to TSM. The adult educator shifts to *kelam kabut* (line 28) and to *semua* (line 29) to strategically accommodate the group's linguistic competence.

The substrate linguistic influence of Tamil was evident in TSM's use of Malaysian English, which, with its audible Indian accent, bore the marks of an ethnolect. His speech is characterized by code switching and mixing (lines 4 and 5). TSM is able to communicate his view that "We do have to change our characters or behavior for the better. What if I have some bad habits, I should be rid of these." The adult learner is parsimonious in his utterances, able to pare down the use of prepositions, articles, and auxiliary verbs to the bare essentials required to communicate a message, the phrase *past one year* (line 12) denoting the substrate influence of Tamil.

Another example of syntactical parsimony is, "Yes, I have changed from what I was in the past year" (line 17). The verb is unmarked for tense and the use of "already" appears in a reduced form. TSM's communication succeeds because the adult educator understands his linguistic repertoire. Line 21 typifies this linguistic variation. The intonation pattern with its extended rise and fall, a substrate influence from Malay, indicates consensual agreement in Malaysian English. In addition to repeating the form *happen* for the past form, the reduced form for "already" is also used. This utterance is mimicked by the adult educator in line 22, generating laughter around the classroom. The pedagogical motivations here are to achieve agreement through convergence, to maintain a positive social identity, and to signal his understanding of TSM's point of view.

The adult educator, a former schoolteacher, was part of that earlier generation of Malaysians who were wholly schooled in English. Depending on the appropriateness of the context, he spoke English, Bhasa Malay, and Tamil, his first language. Being an educated and proficient user of the English language provided the "linguistic capital" he needed in the business contexts in which he worked (Bourdieu, 1977). As the normative code of the organization, his maintenance and vitality in English was assured; from this, he drew his considerable symbolic and economic power. Despite his personal preference for using "standardized" English, he shifted into Malaysian English in this session to accommodate the language uses of his worker-learners. When he was asked to conduct the course on Quality Work Attitudes in English, he held that a dual language approach would be more effective. By this *dual language* method he meant the judicious blending of both Malay and English, noting that *is the trend right through...to use both.*

Example 3

The following vignette is taken from a worker education program entitled *The Legal Aspects of Hire Purchase*. The adult educator (A3) who conducted this session was also the lawyer for this finance company. She is a member of the Peranakan or Baba-Nyonya community, an indigenized group of Chinese-Malaysians and Singaporeans. In this episode, she narrates an encounter with a policeman in order to illustrate the legal implications for the driver of a vehicle-on-hire who is not able to produce the registration card for inspection purposes.

A3:	I want to keep my card. Everybody wants to keep their card.	1
	You see and what happens? I myself was caught in a situation.	2
	My car was uh under financing so they did the the the what you call it?	3
	the finance company said they will renew the road tax for me	4
	and everything. No problem so I gave them the cheque and everything.	5
	It so happened that their runner was late you know	6
	and my road tax was not renewed and the policeman stopped me right?	7
	You see. So I told him *kad dengan kad dengan apa* finance company	8
	duit cek semua dah bayar tapi dia all belum sempat pergi lagi lah	9
	[the card is with what's it the finance company and the cheque for the due amount has been paid but they haven't been able to attend to it yet].	
	You know, I answered him like that and	10
	you know what he answered? What he replied?	11
	apasal kad simpan dengan finance company?	12
	ikut undang-undang engkau yang kena.	13
	[Why is your card with the finance company? according to the law you should have the card].	
	Of course I didn't tell him I was a lawyer *lah* (laughs).	14
	Okay, because I was driving with an expired road tax. Now...	15
	ordinarily how many times it can happen to the ordinary man on the street?	16
	Can you actually guarantee that your runners come back in time?	17
	Can you guarantee that the road tax slip is delivered to the person in time?	18
	So each time one ordinary man on the street gets caught	19

	by a policeman and the policeman doesn't believe his story	20
	But in my case I got out because the policeman	
	believed my story okay?	21
	Tidak [didn't] I didn't have to do anything	
	(much laughter)	22
	(presenter coughs while laughing)	
	Okay, now....If that is the case,	23
	then, you know you can't do this. So you understand	24
	why the consumer association is always making a	
	lot of noise isn't it?	25
	Anyone of you got caught before? Speed trap *ada uh*?	26
	[but you have been by the speed trap, right?]	
T2:	We don't drive without a valid road tax disc.	27
A3:	Ooh! (laughs) You don't have to go to court by nine o'clock	28
	(much laughter).	

The adult educator's chief concern in this episode was to teach the worker-learners about the serious implications of customers not being able to produce the appropriate legal documents for government officials. She matches the language competence of her students by using the range of linguistic resources available within her speech repertoire. She draws on Malaysian English, code switches, and mixes to manage the pedagogic intent of the classroom discourse. The many class participants who spoke Malaysian English proved to be well versed in work-related matters.

In accommodating her students' language repertoire, this adult educator displayed experiential knowledge of Malaysian English and considerable versatility in her own speech repertoire. The code mixes are *finance company* and *all* (lines 8 to 9), while *kad* and *cek* from *card* and *cheque* in English are borrowings, as they have been phonologically adapted into Malay. The contraction *dah* for *sudah* indicates completive action in Malay, while the emphatic particle *lah* is a marker of informality. There is a creative economy in the use of the hybrid form *dia all* (line 9), whereby the third-person singular pronoun in Malay for neuter gender *dia* is used in collocation with *all* to innovatively capture the intended meaning of "all and sundry." It refers collectively to those individuals who were supposedly responsible for processing her application for the necessary road tax renewal.

The code switchings (lines 12 to 13) are direct quotations from the reported conversation between her and the policeman when asked to produce her vehicle registration card for inspection. The adult educator repeats the exchange in Malay in the knowledge that her students are conversant in the language. From lines 14 to 20, the speech is almost bereft of Malaysian English. There is a shift into Malaysian English and the mixed code utterance *speed trap ada uh* (line 26)? This is a very parsimonious expression which means, "but you have been caught in a speed trap before, haven't you?" Here *ada* functions as a confirmation check in Malay, a point driven home by the accompanying acquiescent laughter.

In line 17 there is a socio-culturally marked innuendo that Malaysians would take to mean that the speaker did not have to resort to anything more than a convincing reason to be "let off the hook" by the policeman. That he believed her story and that she *didn't have to do anything* is a reference to the alternative scenario of offering a bribe to be "let off" for the offense. The gale of laughter that accompanies the remark, which was preceded by the sheepishly jocular confession, *of course I didn't tell him I was a lawyer lah* (line 14), confirms the innuendo. However, although the remark is in English, the accent was that of her accented ethnolect. As a Baba-Nyonya speaker of Malaysian English, this contrasted markedly with that of trainee K. Localized language use and accent helped her achieve her communicative goals effortlessly.

This adult educator disclosed that she hardly spoke any Hokkien, although she *understands about 40–50 percent of the spoken variety*. Being of maternal Hokkien and paternal Teochew descent, she also spoke a smattering of Cantonese, the main Chinese language of Kuala Lumpur. English and Malay were her home languages. At home, she spoke the Baba Malay, because of her maternal Baba heritage, as well as Malay and some English to her mother. She spoke only English to her father and siblings. While she was very comfortable speaking English, she did not speak Chinese at all because of her distinctive Baba-Nonya heritage. A product of Malaysia's national education system and a law graduate, she used both Malay and English at work, most of the time switching unconsciously from one to the other in dealings with clients and colleagues. Her fluency in both languages provided her with the pedagogical modus operandi for the adult education sessions she conducted.

The structural and lexical parsimony of the variants of Malaysian English in the speech of the adult educators and the worker-learners is evident in the above examples of speech data obtained from three training sessions in Malaysian businesses. When taken together with its intonation patterns and syllable-timed rhythm, the use of Malaysian English points to its communicative versatility. Its communicative viability in what are putatively formal Malaysian contexts sustains its contestation and appropriation of normative, standardized English.

In keeping with the well-established socio-linguistic practices affecting language "choice" and change, Malaysian English appears to be displacing many standardized forms and patterns of English, even in the face of the powerful prescriptions calling for its use in business communication. To the degree that this continues to occur and gain institutional legitimation, there is the likelihood that Malaysian English will become a localized variation of English, even one recognized as a language option on computer software. The irony is that while the use of English in Malaysian business is still being driven by the ideology of linguistic normativity, Malaysian English is being used as an uncontroversial part of workplace training programs, and no doubt elsewhere (Chitravelu, 1985).

In the dynamics of the classroom, adult educators have little time to heed institutional imperatives and directives regarding the politics and pedagogy of using only standardized English. Their linguistic "choices" in the classroom were shaped, if not decisively determined, by the need to educate, to engage workers in productive learning, and to produce workers more knowledgeable and skilled in company requirements for quality assurance and change than they would otherwise be. The educational reasons for this approach include adult educators' forming their students' identity through acknowledging cultural preferences and marking solidarity among Malaysians through recognizing shared social practice. Further, this approach proved educationally sound insofar as it enhanced communicative effectiveness and pedagogical economy for dealing with work-related topics. Malaysian English provided a comprehensible vehicle for the transactional purposes of transmitting key messages and created a supportive teaching/learning environment in which the adult learners were made comfortable through the use of familiar linguistic codes.

Conclusion

Given concerns about the cultural and linguistic hegemony of a particular version of English, there is a case to be made for language use in workplace education that matches the linguistic repertoires of worker-learners. If adult educators are to realize their pedagogic objectives, then the diverse linguistic resources and communicative designs of worker-learners are very important. David Graddol (1997: 43) argues that in the twenty-first century, workplace Englishes "must service a range of corporate roles and identities and must be usable for both team working and service interactions." Englishes intended for global/local customer-to-service interactions, need to remain routine, conventional and predictable given the range of cross-cultural and intercultural encounters prevalent in these worldwide industries, particularly in tourism and the hospitality trade. Englishes intended to facilitate team working are more diverse because of the restructuring and de-structuring of workplace cultures.

However, the "range of corporate roles and identities" can only be serviced successfully if there is empirically grounded evidence of what happens in workplaces, especially in adult education programs intended to affect worker identity formation. Worker identity formation is embedded in local contexts, and its corporatization cannot override this organic reality by managers singing the mantra "English is the international language of business." Appeals to "global English" or appeals to the traditions of British colonialism reflect an inadequate understanding of language use in local, multi-lingual business contexts. Data obtained from studies of the operations of adult education classes conducted in workplaces may be able to provide a more informed basis for business keen to develop an appropriate and effective multi-lingual communication strategy. Below are several reasons for investigating such an approach to language and communication skills training.

First, one obstacle to successful communication in workplaces is the desire by those in power to maintain the organization's unequal power relations. Corporate public relations are typically exercises in manufacturing management's spin on issues that might otherwise give workers cause for concern. Without such corporate spin, "quality control" might be seen as "worker control," or the injunction to "forget the past" might be understood as workers being asked to reconcile themselves to reduced terms and conditions. Of course, on the other side of the management divide, workers can exercise their power over the communication or non-communication of information or knowledge important for organizational learning. These communication difficulties are perpetuated by the contest over inequitable power relations in the workplace. For instance, gatekeepers inevitably propagate or even unwittingly keep in place the ideologies that reproduce inequitable power relations, necessarily contradicting the corporation's preferred self-image. So communication is never simply or exclusively an issue of language proficiency or expressing oneself in plain language; it is, however, always a matter of inequitable power relations.

Nevertheless, the ability of adult educators to use language that succeeds contextually can facilitate communication that creates improved understanding and insights into organizational power differentials. Where necessary, the dynamics of the educator/learner interactions can be enhanced by drawing on multi-lingual resources, in spite of the difficulties created by powerful directives for communicating in only standardized English. Communicating successfully is certainly not about prescribed usage that promises to work in some mythic way in all contexts. One communicative size does not fit all, nor will one model of English be suitable for all.

Second, there are "ways of speaking" that are context specific and defined by a history of socio-cultural use (Hymes, 1974a and b; Figueroa, 1994). The rise of screen-based labor as a result of the increasing dominance of new media technology in the workplace is making new demands for changing business communication strategies. For instance, the new forms of literacy emerging through the informal conversational language of electronic mail plays a critical role in enhancing organizational productivity. Because of its transnational flows, workplace communication now needs to be sensitive to the different ways members of the organization and its clients speak, write, and interpret communications.

Ways of speaking that actually enhance communication are those in which Englishes and other languages are engaged pragmatically. In multilingual, multi-dialectical contexts, the pedagogical expedience and efficiency of adult educators who are parsimoniously "smart" contests the gatekeepers' insistence on the normative "heritage English." This is a productive pedagogy, legitimizing as it does the work of adult educators who provide workplace teaching/learning that is non-threatening, minimizing adult learner anxieties by drawing on their range of linguistic and communicative resources.

References

Anie, A., *English in Industry: A Study of Language Choice in Two Electronics Firms in Malaysia*. Unpublished PhD dissertation. Kuala Lumpur: Universiti Malaya. 1998.

Bourdieu, P. "The Economics of Linguistic Exchanges." *Social Science Information* 16, no. 6 (1977): 645–68.

Chitravelu, N. "The Status and Role of English in Malaysia." Kuala Lumpur: Universiti Malaya: United States Information Agency, 1985.

Cope, B., and M. Kalantzis. "Multiliteracies: Rethinking What We Mean by Literacy and What We Teach as Literacy in the Context of Global Cultural Diversity and New Communication Technologies." In *Global Literacy: Visions, Revisions and Vistas in Education*, edited by A. Pandian, 1–12. Serdang, Malaysia: Universiti Putra Malaysia Press, 1999.

Coupland, N., J. Coupland, H. Giles, and K. Henwood. "Accommodating the Elderly." *Language in Society* 17 (1988): 1–42.

Crystal, D., *English as a Global Language*. Cambridge: CUP. 1997.

Figueroa, E. *Sociolinguistic Metatheory*. Oxford: Pergammon, 1994.

Graddol, D. *The Future of English?* London: The British Council, 1997.

Hymes, D. *Foundations in Sociolinguistics: An Ethnographic Approach*. Philadelphia: University of Pennsylvania Press, 1974a.

———. "Ways of Speaking." In *Explorations in the Ethnography of Speaking*, edited by R. Baumann and J. Sherzer, 433–51. Cambridge: Cambridge University Press, 1974b.

Milroy, J., "Language Ideologies and the Consequences of Standardization. *Journal of Sociolinguistics* 4, no 5 (2001): 530–555.

Milroy, J., and L. Milroy. *Authority in Language: Investigating Standard English*. (3rd ed.) London: Routledge. 1999.

Morais, E., *Malaysian Business Talk. A Study of the Patterns of Conflict and Non-conflict in Verbal Interactions*. Unpublished PhD dissertation. Kuala Lumpur: Universiti Malaya, 1994.

Nair-Venugopal, S. "The Sociolinguistics of Choice in Malaysian Business Settings." *International Journal of the Sociology of Language* 152 (2001): 21–53.

———. *Language Choice and Communication in Malaysian Business*. Bangi, Malaysia: Penertbit UKM (Universiti Kebangsaan Malaysia Press), 2000.

———. "Talk-mediated Literacy: Negotiating Paths in Training." In *Global Literacy: Visions, Revisions and Vistas in Education*, edited by A. Pandian, 125–130. Serdang, Malaysia: Universiti Putra Malaysia Press, 1999.

———. *The Sociolinguistics of Code and Style choice in Malaysian Business Settings: An Ethnographic Account*. Unpublished PhD dissertation, University of Wales, Cardiff. 1997.

Naysmith, J. "English as Imperialism?" *Language Issues* 1, no. 2 (1987): 3–5.

Pennycook, A., *The Cultural Politics of English as an International Language*. London: Longman. 1994.

Phillipson, R., *Linguistic Imperialism*. Oxford: Oxford University Press. 1992.

Singh, M., P. Kell, and A. Pandian. *Appropriating English: Innovation in the Global Business of English Language* Teaching. New York: Peter Lang, 2002.

Skutnabb-Kangas, T., and R. Phillipson. eds. *linguistic Human Rights: Overcoming Linguistic Discrimination*. Berlin: Mouton De Gruyter. 1994.

Tollefson, J., *Language Planning, Planning Inequality*. Harlow: Longman. 1991.

Chapter 7

Reflexive Theory Building "After" Colonialism: Challenges for Adult Education

Sue Shore

> Living in a nation of people who decided that their worldview would combine agendas for individual freedom and mechanisms for devastating racial oppression presents a singular landscape for a writer.
>
> (Morrison, 1992: xiii)

Theory Building as Problematic Practice

Many adult educators involved in workplace, lifelong, and adult learning have, albeit skeptically, engaged and responded to the agenda of contemporary linguistic:repertoire. To date, however, too little attention has been paid to the connections between the endless promises of enterprising globalization and the historical and material relations of power that are implicated in the making of different possibilities for people. Following Toni Morrison's (1992) insightful remarks on the interrelationship between freedom and oppression, globalization presents enormous challenges for the theory and practice of adult learning. This desire to make a significant difference is even more challenging when it is recognized that these relations of empowerment/dispossession have their roots in the nineteenth-century project of colonialism.

This chapter explores the ways in which theorizing about adult learning is always already implicated in racialized practices. These racialized practices of theory building are not only located in programs designated for "target groups" and "minorities" that are implemented in the hope of disrupting systemic patterns of disadvantage. The interrogation proposed in this chapter unsettles the assumption that racialized theory building is about a "non-white other" whose needs are to be assimilated into an imagined "mainstream," or indeed whose epistemologies of knowing can be used to challenge "mainstream" knowledge practices. Rather, it is argued that theory building about adult learning principles operates to reinscribe racialized differences at the very same moment as it advocates equal treatment, by disavowing differences that count.

What do such claims mean for adult educators? How do adult educators understand the effects of the contradictory racialized discourses of contemporary globalization on the production and disciplining of knowledge? How might adult educators engage in a critical reading of the theory that informs their work in order to recognize the presence of colonial legacies in that work?

Rethinking "the Problem"

The theories informing adult education have been limited by discourses of individualism and which in turn have constrained and limited our understandings of social change (Bright, 1989). The influence of these conservative discourses in adult education sees their normative claims being recycled without challenge. Kathleen Rockhill (1996) argues that this is so despite their limited explanatory power for the everyday work of adult educators.

The taken-for-granted features of adult learning principles are a consequence of the tightly structured processes of knowledge production. They are also indicative of the manner in which theory building about adult education disguises racialized practices of writing as part of the disciplinary production of knowledge *and* the role of scholars in producing that knowledge at the same time as "we" claim an equal space for all learners. By drawing attention to routine recycling practices, my aim is to foreground the explanatory limits of critical reflection as an adult learning method.

Toni Morrison's (1992) insights suggest two possible ways forward with this project. First, she offers an entry point in providing evidence of the racialized nature of knowledge production. Second, she details how such claims are met with a resiliency that is part of the racializing process itself.

Representing Adult Education

"Difference" is a familiar organizing concept in adult education. It is through "difference" from schooling that adult learning programs define their aims and purposes, the distinctive qualities of participants (educators, learners, and scholars), their distinguishing pedagogical qualities, and the educational possibilities they claim for students and society. Paradoxically, it is this legacy of difference that assists in understanding how theory building is premised on and at the same time dissipates difference through generic adult learning principles which provide the mooring points for what adult learning programs can be. It is also paradoxical that frameworks of difference are what make identification of the problem—in this case, reflexivity "after" colonialism—something of a challenge. The claim that we have moved on from a colonizing moment is questionable, hence, "after" colonialism is itself a problematic term.

Drawing on "Deleuze-Bergsonian problematics," Dorothea Olkowski (1999: 91) argues that "stating a problem *correctly* and not simply in terms of the order-words handed down to us requires invention...[to give] being to what does not already exist." Of course it is not merely a matter of stating a problem "correctly." Rather, what Olkowski offers adult educators is a way to understand the possibilities and limits of theory building given the discursive tools at our disposal.

Calls for invention, innovation, and imagination are not new to adult education. Increasingly, global responses to social inclusion/exclusion call on the human imagination to help solve the problems of inequality (Australian National Training Authority, 2000; Department of Trade and Industry, 2001). However, notions of imagination and invention are more commonly related to reductionist processes of entrepreneurial innovation that are central to the development of contemporary adult education and training policies. Rarely do they address the market's failure to provide for an equitable distribution of and access to the resources required for a healthy life and the increasing levels of violence visited upon citizens.

My response is to resist calls for a new, and equally problematic, "oppositional pedagogy" which has every possibility of continuing to frame intractable socio-economic problems as problems of "difference." This ignores the extent to which these pedagogies are already located in representations of social change premised on the enterprising individual agent of liberal humanism. The requirement to use these discourses as a means of stating the problem is critical in consolidating their resilience to interrogation. At the same time, they are made inseparable from the very hierarchical relations of adult education that need unsettling.

Discursive practices of representation are premised on hierarchical notions of difference. In *Difference and Repetition*, Gilles Deleuze (1994: 137) argues that "difference becomes an object of representation always in relation to a conceived identity, a judged analogy, an imagined opposition or a perceived similtude." Accordingly, representation invokes a set of comparisons, judgments, resemblances, and evaluations that provide the grounds for knowing the agentic self and fashioning supportive and nurturing processes of adult learning. What is not made apparent in conventional discourses on adult learning is that the selves it is possible to fashion are created *in relation to a conceived identity* that is produced via liberal pedagogic discourses saturated with assumptions of Whiteness.

Such criticisms of adult learning principles are not new. What is different about this chapter is the direct connection made between the notion of Whiteness and the imagined "mainstream." While the latter term is problematic, it is widely used in education. "Mainstream" is a code word for the White, agentic, masculinist values which adult learners, educators, and researchers—men and women, White and non-White—experience differentially as a function of their participation in adult education.

Studies of Whiteness are not new. People of color have long known the power of Whiteness as a system of pressures and forces underpinning adult education and the subsequent effects on knowledge production, participatory learning, and educational outcomes (Said, 1993; Holt, 1999; Moreton-Robinson, 2000).

Research on Whiteness is becoming more visible. Of particular importance is that research which challenges representation as the unproblematic portrayal of the "real" and engages in the "ruin of representation" (Olkowski, 1999). Edward Said, Ann Stoler, and Toni Morrison's investigations of the co-implications of Whiteness and colonialism are especially relevant to theory building in adult education. However, not all research can be transferred seamlessly into theory building about adult learning. Rather, invention and imagination are required to judge which links provide useful articulations and which are likely to consolidate and work counter to a social and political project of "ruin." Toni Morrison (1992: xii–xiii) understands this complexity well when she asks:

> When does racial "unconsciousness" or awareness of race enrich interpretive language, and when does it impoverish it? What does positioning one's writerly self, ... as unraced and all others as raced entail? ...How is "literary whiteness" and "literary

blackness' made, and what is the consequence of that construction? How do embedded assumptions of racial (not racist) language work in the literary enterprise that hopes and sometimes claims to be "humanistic"?

Such questions go to the heart of theory building in adult education for and in global/local contexts. These questions invite adult education *scholars* to make visible the practices involved in weaving discourses of liberal humanism and empowerment with discourses of agency and enterprise via the claims for endless, unrestrained possibilities for all human beings. These questions gesture towards interdisciplinary projects that foreground how (White) European-ness is created through diverse practices that evaluate and discriminate according to privileged representations of "White European bourgeois civility."

At the same time these judgments collapse class, race and sexuality across a grid of differences, producing culturally hybrid selves that count less when compared to selected representations of bourgeois Whiteness. The contemporary challenge for adult educators and scholars is to investigate the ways Whiteness collapses judgments in adult learning principles through theorizing and practice. The following section illustrates however, that this requires careful scrutiny given the embeddedness of such practices in liberal pedagogic discourses.

The "Invisibility" of Whiteness in Adult Education

Analysis of contemporary research in adult education provides evidence that theory building is constrained in its capacity to inform and equip adult educators, policy makers, and other researchers. The prevailing emphasis on decontextualized practice is a barrier in this regard. I use three examples of theory building to disrupt the effects of Whiteness that anchor adult education within a highly problematic set of discursive relations that are silent about their racialized underpinnings. I then move to a perspective that suggests that these effects on theory building combine with neoconservative globalism and its project of internationalizing of adult education to obscure the extent to which "Western" theory building about adult learning reinscribes the project of colonialism in this field.

Self-reflection and the "Knowing" Self

Reference to critical reflection is ubiquitous in adult education. Jack Mezirow (1991; 1999) rests his theory of transformative learning on critical reflection, claiming that it is a means of moving from the unexamined to the examined. Much advocacy of critical reflection assumes that adult educators are able to know, however tentatively, their values make them explicit, and "see" how they affect practice (Brookfield, 1995).

In contrast, research on Whiteness suggests that many White people are unaware of how Whiteness permeates the daily lives of both White and non-White people. Mike Hill (1997) argues that calling Whiteness an invisible norm enables White people to claim they have engaged with the issue and then do nothing. As will be seen below, others turn to teaching strategies in domains where race is marked and visible, in the belief that playing down the complexity of pedagogy is a helpful step for adult educators. In this chapter, I explore the nuanced ways in which Whiteness materializes in writing about adult learning.

Reflective practice provides a useful starting point, as it insists that innovation and improvement in adult education can be realized through investigating one's own practices. In contrast, I contend that normative versions of critically reflective practice obscure adult educators' understandings of the effects of Whiteness. I use a practical example from adult education to illustrate this point.

While Stephen Brookfield (1986; 1987; 1995; 1999) has written extensively about reflection and critical practice in professional development and adult education, he does not necessarily see the operations of Whiteness in his own theory building. In many of his works, Brookfield draws on personal diaries to describe his learning in action as an adult educator. While arguing for the importance of critical reflection, he notes the problem of individual and collective reflection in practice, the difficulty of exploring one's own experiences, and the challenge of *starting* with experience and ensuring one moves on to multiple understandings rather than merely redescribing events.

Brookfield's personal reflections are quite courageous as they demonstrate his willingness to expose his own vulnerabilities as an adult educator learner. However, on another level they can be seen as problematic. The model of critical reflection he offers is embedded in theories of adult learning that center an enterprising, knowing, and agentic self, yet, rarely acknowledges this. Consider Brookfield's (1995: 57) exploration of his experience as a member of a conference session on diverse learning styles:

> I was in P's session today on attending to diverse learning styles and found it very interesting. I liked the discussion time that was allowed and found my interest level to be much higher during this part of the session. However, there were lots of people

in the room who wanted to say something and they were all trying to get into the conversation. I must have raised my hand to signal I wanted to say something at least six or seven times but was never called on. P. got into intense conversations with two or three people in the group that were interesting but I felt shut out. I wonder if anyone else had this feeling? When I did force myself in on the discussion I felt a bit as if I was throwing my weight about.

This journal reflection describes, from Brookfield's standpoint, the interactions in a conference setting, which could well represent any number of adult learning settings. As Olkowski (1999) has noted, the reflections possible on any practice depend on the "order-words" available to frame interpretations of practical problems of adult teaching and learning. How then do Brookfield's reflections on this incident "distort" his understanding of this dilemma as a learner in this class (for we are not clear that the presenter has a dilemma at all), and hence limit Brookfield's understanding of the restraints on his involvement in the session? To follow his own text, what order-words might help to "coax" Brookfield beyond this experience and imagine other ways of reading the event?

More details about his reflections are needed here. To help his reader understand the possibilities of reflection, Brookfield mobilizes "fair play" as a means of enacting inclusive practice in large groups. His reflections on the conference session lead him to posit a way of using his experiences of feeling "Othered" to ensure his own teaching does not reinscribe the same problems for students in his classes:

> My classes aren't power-free vacuums. Students bring in habits of conversation and interaction they have learned, or been inducted into, in the wider society. So, I need to make some effort at positive discrimination, to find a way to establish a procedure for calling on people that's perceived as fair. (Brookfield, 1995: 57)

Marginalization of adult learners is a key theme in this account. Many adult educators have to deal with issues of who speaks, when, for how long, what about, and with what effect. As a learner, Brookfield felt the need to "force myself in" in order to have a voice. Of course, creating space for marginalized voices is a hallmark of adult learning principles. However, *self-reflexive* practice, that understands how theory is located in historical practices of enterprising agency (for White people in particular), could provide a different way of reflecting on this incident. What is it that prompts Brookfield to force himself into this discussion? What is driving the persistent need to "say something"? What is behind the speaker's practice of *not* calling on Brookfield to speak? Why does this leave Brookfield feeling Othered?

What is missing from Brookfield's analyses is the possibility that the practice, as experienced, may well have been constructed as fair play by other adult educators. This possibility is unlikely to be identified by versions of critical reflection constructed using the dominating discourses of adult learning.

Brookfield's journal responses reveal the degree to which he is unaware that his practice of critical reflection is embedded in ahistorical notions of fairness and the extent to which this subsequently influences how he theorizes practice. To suggest that particular forms of pedagogy will render these differences immaterial is as remarkable as it is questionable.

The incongruities here are significant. Brookfield does not portray the adult educator as all-knowing. However, in this instance, the adult educator *will* know the stories of the classroom in such a way that they *will* be explained to the adult learners, who *will* in turn "know" and accept them and act on them appropriately.

One of the difficulties with my reading is that it challenges adult learning principles which claim the right for all to speak equally, for all to have a say. Put another way, adult educators need to consider how reflection on practice disrupts this claim with another, which asks participants to be more cognizant of the forms of power operating on learning settings and the extent to which theories about adult learning reinscribe these forms of power in classroom interactions. Brookfield's reflections illustrate the difficulty in seeing multiple possibilities in a learning setting, especially when the forms of analysis available have already framed the problem as one of fair play.

Self-reflection and Discourses of Possibility

Another example of adult education practice illustrates that inadequacies in "order-words" available to frame a problem is not an issue of liberal humanism alone. Michael Newman's (1994) view of adult educators recognizes the complex roles and positions they occupy in educational practice: as actors; a collection of decentered others; a collage of selves who experience historical, institutional, and embodied forces that tug and pull their practice. Newman's notion of the adult educator's decentered self helps to move away from the rescuer, "hero", savior, all knowing position adult educators are often assumed to occupy. Nevertheless theorizing such a decentered self is fraught, especially when it comes to the task of reflecting on our pedagogy and the manner in which multiple subjectivities influence our capacity to critique our pedagogies.

In exploring the notion of "oppressor," for example, Newman observes the potential of liberal discourses to be overly attentive to individual behavior resulting in the tendency to blame the victim for their own oppression. Nevertheless, Newman's analysis largely ignores the Whiteness of the adult learners with whom he works. Analyses of White subjectivity suggest that White adult educators may have trouble doing what Newman advocates, namely, connecting personal stories and structural oppression (Dyer, 1997; Moreton-Robinson, 2000). By invoking the notion of the enemy as oppressor, Newman secures the meaning of oppression within structural relations of power. However, he also locates oppression within White discourse, which *differentially* confers privilege and at the same time masks the differential benefits to those who seek to generate social change.

Differential privilege is important here. Adult educators could have some resistance to the idea that "we" are the benefactors of White privilege. Adult education has a low status in most academic institutions, with programs being poorly funded under short-term contracts. Women and community members who are active in articulating concerns about inequity and the need for systemic changes in adult education manage many programs. However, most adult educators have limited capacity to change the erratic industrial conditions under which they labor. How then is White privilege conferred on the union members in Newman's stories, who struggle against greed and corporate capitalism? What of the women involved in community literacy programs whose work is never fully acknowledged with appropriate funding? Much of this work involves a problematic alliance with government and its funding programs, which frame the intractable contradictions of capitalism as "literacy problems" or "youth at risk." This structures avoidance of questions concerning the political and moral will of the state to address racialized privileges that are rarely linked to Whiteness.

By securing the idea of social injustice beyond educational practice, oppression is placed beyond the embodied action of the adult educator. In this way, Newman closes off the possibilities for exploring the support and collusion White *educators and scholars* provide as we engage in the ritual habits and procedures of pedagogy/writing about pedagogy that is saturated by liberal humanistic discourses. This reinscribes the "all-knowing" certainty of adult educators at the heart of practice. At one level this is precisely what Newman is saying that as adult educators we are not "free." But critical reflection in its normative form is unable to recognize the complexity of power relations of adult educators who are not "free" and those who are differentially privileged by the racialized discourses of adult learning principles that disavow difference, especially Whiteness.

Normative forms of critical reflection represent a missed opportunity for reconfiguring the problems of practice in adult education. For Michel Foucault (1977: 139), the microphysics of power provide an entry point for identifying how "[s]mall acts of cunning endowed with a great power of diffusion, subtle arrangements, apparently innocent, but profoundly suspicious" are always at work. Although deemed to be ordinary, their effects can be otherwise. Portrayed as trivial, banal, even boring, the everyday culture that dominates the world does not have to be invisible to those who identify as White adult educators. By not racializing oppression, adult educators (especially those who make formal theorizations of policy and practice) offer limited access to interdisciplinary understandings of Whiteness. These interdisciplinary insights could provide accounts of the articulations between the enterprising character of liberal humanism in contemporary notions of lifelong adult teaching and learning, and the workings of everyday Whiteness.

In raising these issues, adult educators must avoid demonizing individual White people in isolation from wider systems of colonialism and imperialism. Yet the opposite effect, disconnecting these "small acts of cunning" from structural relations of power is also a concern. It is important to consider such "acts of cunning" as integral to reproducing the White colonialist legacy in contemporary theory and practice of adult education, even when it seems that its purpose is to disrupt this questionable heritage. Moreover, as with any set of complex power relations, attachments are contingent, hence privilege is not simply aligned in a causal way with "Whiteness." Nevertheless, concerns to resist a causal relation between Whiteness and privilege can also emanate from a reluctance to see "Whiteness" as discursive and material. Whiteness is part of the system of knowledge production which manages and organizes the ways in which adult educators construct the social world, and how they can take educational actions in that world.

Self-reflection and Deflecting the Gaze

Analysis of Whiteness and its effects on theory and practice in adult education does not always have to be undertaken in settings that are tagged as "raced." When racially "fixed" in this way, such analyses can be reduced to a simplistic reading of Whiteness against the cultural norms and practices of Others—that is, non-White people. On the other hand, White supremacist frameworks are not the only perspectives available for illuminating the workings of White identity formation and privilege. For many adult educators "doing something" in terms of educational activism is a problematic but not completely hopeless task. Mechthild Hart (1998: 190) explains:

> Visiting the mothers living in Chicago's public housing has taught me to see that my skin and class privilege is a form of deficiency because it is part of my ignorance concerning vital experiences of people who live there. I can only partly improve this ignorance by recognizing the many concrete obstacles in the way of my own true learning about the situation, background, or histories of the people living in public housing, and by overcoming some of these obstacles. Many of them will remain intact. To enter a world which is different from the one I am more familiar with therefore requires a tremendous effort on my part to realize and learn more about the scope of these differences and the many reasons for their existence, and to acknowledge how, despite these efforts, I can only gain a certain amount and a certain kind of knowledge.

In the work of Hart and Newman (and, although less so in the work of Brookfield), there is an underlying concern that focusing on "practical strategies" will result in bleaching the sharp edge of educational action to re-inscribe a racialized order. In the above quotation, Hart alludes to the partiality of knowledge gained from such strategies. However, the implications of partial knowing have little effect on normative versions of critical reflection. Adult educators are rarely advised that the aim is "knowing differently," an outcome that could potentially destabilize every existing premise currently held about adult education policy and practice. Many critical pedagogies rely on a knowing agent, the adult educator, to reveal the failings of systems to unknowing adult learners, who will then come to awareness and be situated as knowing subjects of their own disadvantage.

While Hart's work does not present this problem, it does raise other dilemmas for adult educators involved in thinking through the implications of racialized (White) lives. Hart's entry point to awareness of partial knowing is in "entering a world which is different from the one I am more familiar with," suggesting that White adult educators move to those spaces that are marked by the presence of non-White people to reflect critically on the power and privilege of Whiteness. The partial analysis of Brookfield and Newman's work offers a way of exploring the impact of racialized theory building in adult learning by using a supplementary set of "order words," a different kind of imagination invoked by contemporary policies of lifelong adult teaching and learning.

"After Colonialism": Knowing Otherwise

Dorothea Olkowski (1999) reminds adult educators that we are immersed in representations of adult learning that are both the problem and the condition against which we struggle. Imagination, invention, and self-reflexivity are central to processes for understanding and improving theory and practice in adult education. Nonetheless, self-reflexive work cannot be reduced to a set of Advanced Reflection techniques, or a course taken by adult educators after an introduction to basic facilitation methods. Nor is it a self-indulgent practice that reinscribes conventional power relations via acts of cunning, the effects of which are largely "invisible" to many adult educators.

The self-reflexivity I advocate undermines the desire to be able to understand and explain social relations, a stance central to the practices of critical reflection described by Stephen Brookfield and Michael Newman. The resultant uncertainty need not diminish political commitment to political or social change, nor does it need to produce political or pedagogic paralysis.

Pedagogies of certainty are rooted in discursive systems of knowledge production derived from enterprising colonialism. That adult education is part of the practices of colonialism is no accident. The challenge is to identify the workings of colonialism in adult education theories, even when they appear to be absent or consigned to history. When theory claims racialized difference is not an issue by virtue of treating all people equally, this disavowal that differences count needs close investigation.

By calling for greater self-reflexivity in the production of theories about adult learning, the ahistorical character of theory building may be rendered problematic. The purpose is to investigate what reading and writing practices might be developed in order to make explicit racialized processes in the theory, policy and pedagogy in adult teaching and learning. Of course many already notice these problems through discrete lenses of gender, sexuality and class. Here my aim is to provide a way to render visible another way of approaching this task.

By renaming the problem as racialized theory building, my intention is not to center and isolate race as an exclusive category of analysis. Rather, I attempted to show the embedded nature of adult learning principles in a form of theory building that is premised on differential privilege born of discriminations about "White European bourgeois civility." These discriminating practices were evident in nineteenth-century theorizing of subjectivity (Stoler, 1995) and continue to be articulated in and through theory building that produces representations of "the adult learner," "progressive reflective practice," and "socially critical educational action."

This chapter provides one way of investigating the ordering and structuring of the "problem" of adult education and the processes by which it is enacted. The taken-for-granted naming of a problem by the available order words is not something which can be separated from history. Being reflexive in this context refuses complicity with over-determined practices of White identity formation and difference. From this perspective, globalization is as much about capitalist enterprise as it is about the continuing legacies of Western European colonialism, which together generate the mechanisms for contemporary racial distinctions.

Investigating adult education theories, policies, and practices for their complicity with historical practices provides an opportunity to render visible the influence of Whiteness within this field. The challenge is to understand that the global/local practices of adult education are not simply about exploring offshore delivery, or critiquing First/Third World relations. Rather, for White adult educators, the problem is much closer to home than we thought.

References

ANTA. *The National Marketing Strategy*. Australian National Training Authority, Brisbane, 2000 [cited 30 March 2000]. Available from http://www.anta/gov/ au/lifelong/ STRATEGY/ Default.asp.

Bright, B., ed. *Theory and Practice in Adult Education*. London: Routledge, 1989.

Brookfield, S. "Reclaiming and Problematizing Self-Directed Learning as a Space for Critical Adult Education." Paper presented at the Standing Conference on University Teaching and Research in the Education of Adults (SCUTREA) 29th Annual Conference, University of Warwick 1999 cited 30 June 2002. Available from http:// www. leeds. ac. uk/ ducol/ documents/ 000000977.

———. *Becoming a Critically Reflective Teacher*. San Francisco: Jossey-Bass, 1995.

———. *Developing Critical Thinkers: Challenging Adults to Explore Alternative Ways of Thinking and Acting*. Milton Keynes: Open University Press, 1987.

———. *Understanding and Facilitating Adult Learning: A Comprehensive Analysis of Principles and Effective Practice*. San Francisco: Jossey-Bass, 1986.

Deleuze, G. *Difference and Repetition*. New York: Columbia University Press, 1994.

DTI, Department of Trade and Industry. *Opportunity for All in a World of Change: A White Paper on Enterprise, Skills and Innovation*. 13 February 2001 cited 30 June 2002. Available from www.dti.Gov.uk/opportunityforall/index.html 30.

Dyer, R. *White*. London: Routledge, 1997.

Foucault, M. *Discipline and Punish: The Birth of the Prison*. Ringwood: Penguin, 1977.

Hart, M. "The Experience of Living and Learning in Different Worlds." *Studies in Continuing Education* 20, no. 2 (1998): 187–200.

Hill, M. "Introduction: Vipers in Shangri-La. Whiteness, Writing, and Other Ordinary Terrors." In *Whiteness: A Critical Reader*, 1–18. New York: New York University Press, 1997.

Holt, L. "Pssst ... I Wannabe White." In *Unmasking Whiteness: Race Relations and Reconciliation*, edited by B. McKay, 39–44. Nathan, Brisbane: The Queensland Studies Centre, Griffith University, 1999.

Mezirow, J. "Transformation Theory—Postmodern Issues." Paper presented at the 40th Annual Adult Education Research Conference 1999 cited 30 June 2002. Available from http://www. Edst .educ.ubc.ca/ aerc /1999 /99mezirow.htm.

———. *Transformative Dimensions of Adult Learning*. San Francisco: Jossey-Bass, 1991.

Moreton-Robinson, A. *Talkin" up to the White Woman: Indigenous Women and Feminism*. St Lucia, Queensland: University of Queensland Press, 2000.

Morrison, T. *Playing in the Dark: Whiteness and the Literary Imagination*. Cambridge: Harvard University Press, 1992.

Newman, M., (1994). *Defining the Enemy: Adult Education in Social Action*. Sydney, Stewart Victor Publishing, 1994.

Olkowski, D. *Gilles Deleuze and the Ruin of Representation*. Berkeley: University of California Press, 1999.

Rockhill, K. "Challenging the Exclusionary Effects of the Inclusive Mask of Adult Education." *Studies in Continuing Education* 18, no. 2 (1996): 182–94.

Said, E. *Culture and Imperialism*. London: Vintage, 1993.

Stoler, A. *Race and the Education of Desire. Foucault's History of Sexuality and the Colonial Order of Things*. Durham: Duke University Press, 1995.

Chapter 8

Performing Identities: A New Focus on Embodied Adult Learning

Gayle Morris and David Beckett

Taking Intentional Actions Seriously

With the dawning of the twenty-first century, there are no shortages of hopes for adult learners. They are expected to be creative and decisive, yet compliant and mindful of the precarious and contingent political economy governing their employment. They are meant to pursue "lifelong learning." Consequentially a strong element of self-direction and experiential sensitivity, both within and beyond work, is well regarded. At the same time, it is thought that "people-soft" capabilities—being able to learn in and from groups (such as work-based teams), and to participate in leadership and solve conflict—are essential. Catching oneself not learning something economically worthwhile is no longer acceptable.

Amidst these desiderata, we want to take an approach which starts from the premise that adults are *ineluctably embodied and are, therefore, active, that is to say, they act with intelligence in the world* (Beckett and Morris, 2001). We are serious about embodied learning and skeptical about the perpetuation of Cartesian models of learning. We want to show empirically and conceptually the extent of this skepticism. In the empirical section of this chapter, we draw attention to the ways adult literacy students may have their needs under-recognized by well-meaning teachers. In the conceptual section of this chapter, we draw attention to the way "understanding" can be achieved through the articulation of inferences.

What is common to both parts of this chapter is the centrality of *performance* in the formation of adult identity. Whilst there is a keen interest in the formation of adult identity through education, we argue that this is more significant when this formation is regarded as a *self*-construction of identity. By this we mean that adults' intentionality is a key to successful learning in this new century. Whether it is in classrooms or the life beyond, adult intentions are articulated through embodied actions, including, but not reducible to, speech actions. It is this point that the wish lists of adult educators and lifelong learning desiderata allude to, but leave unexplored. We investigate this issue herein.

Embodiment

Why have bodies become important? Since the Enlightenment, and due largely to Descartes, the triumph of the mind over the body has shaped Western European learning in terms of mental rather than physical criteria. Learning in general, and education in particular, has, in the Western European tradition, been regarded as successful if understanding something in a new way can be inferred from behavior (such as in an examination, or in writing an essay). The focus is on the targeting of a change in a mental state from one of ignorance to one of knowledge. Of course, bodies are essential in that targeting, since the adult learner has to be present in an examination room, or seated at a desk to write an essay.

However, the relationship between the body and the mind remains dualistic, thanks to the Cartesian tradition. In Western European education, the highest status is reserved for the most abstract and immaterial learning, irrespective of its utility. The lowest status is accorded to concrete, material learning, much of which we acquire in daily, embodied actions. The utility of this latter learning has hitherto been under-recognized, although with "lifelong learning" there is a chance for giving it greater prominence in adult education pedagogy and policy. We intend this chapter to contribute to that prominence.

The Cartesian perspective is well entrenched, even if many adult educators feel it to be unsatisfactory. In Western European educational epistemology, entire school systems have been built on a Cartesian ontology, whereby physical criteria of understanding are parasitic upon mental criteria. The "grammar" school offers a more highly esteemed model of understanding than the "technical" school. Differentiated forms of schooling shape teaching and learning for life by and for adults. Our very beings are shaped by the Enlightenment epistemology of education. Many new expectations are made of adult learning, so much so that old approaches are less than convincing and, for many of us adult educators, ideologically unsupportable.

It is time once again to confront this dualistic epistemology by showing how valuable (that is to say, educative) knowing arises in daily life experiences. We want to deal with the body partly as philosophers, namely, through argument and conceptual analysis, but we also want to bring some empirical evidence—actual reports of embodied experiences—to round out this approach. After all, it is important to stay close to the best evidence we have for the centrality of embodiment in our human experience, namely, people's reports of what they are doing.

In presenting both empirical and conceptual evidence that brings the body back into adults' learning, we hope to subvert the outcomes-driven commodification of knowledge. Outcomes show up in the panoply of "performativity" criteria such as those of standardization, outcome criteria, credentials, registrations, quality assurance, and appraisal mechanisms (Blake, 1998). In this sense, what adult learning does is summative—as an end, or as a product—calibrated. To target those actual performances at and through workplace learning is rendered insignificant or invisible. In the rush towards the homogenization of outcomes in adult education to produce convergent performances in adult learners, the diversity of and sensitivity to human experiences is the first casualty. Those human experiences which can be "commodified"—slimmed down, packaged, and calibrated for the performativity"—are represented as the educational outcome.

Attention to embodied performance does not only confront prevailing policy enthusiasms (such as competency-based training and government fixation on "training packages"), but also the prevailing education theorization of these enthusiasms: namely, that these policies are merely contentious *discourses*. Because discourse theory downplays human agency and socio-economic contexts, it is implicated in perpetuating the passivity of adult learners. O"Loughlin (1998: 290) argues that "discourse is employed as a kind of one way process in which discourses construct subjects and in which bodies are "normalized" though discursive intervention, such that the bodies can no longer speak or have their experiences heard or interpreted." Hager (1999: 67) nails home the point:

> It is not enough to simply assert that this discourse creates the objects of which it appears to speak. What is needed is some convincing demonstration that this lan-

guaging and being languaged is a sufficient account of the variety and depth of our encounters with the world around us.

Anything less than accounts of adult learners' encounters with these discourses fails to attend to the complexities of adult education practices. Crossley (1995: 51) says it well:

> Discourse itself is a fleshy process.... It is produced through the work of the body. Moreover, one of the chief characteristics of the body, qua active body, is that it speaks and listens, and reads and writes. There is and can be no choice between discourse and fleshiness then. They belong to each other as do legs and walking.

Discourse-driven analyses of adult learners and educators are susceptible to problems. They are reductive, in that "conscious action" (the cognitive) is minimized, and actual social and affective experiences of adult learners and teachers are similarly ignored. However, this is not to deny that discourse-driven analyses are helpful up to a point. They inform and critique dominating research constructions of workers in these "Post-Fordist/Neo-Fordist" times. Prominent amongst these are creative/self-directed workers (Beckett, 1992); compliant/humanly "resourceful" workers (Butler, 1999; Garrick, 1998), and workers-as-victim (Gee, 1990). Discourse analyses also inform debates about adult learners, drawing attention to the constitutive role of discourse in the production of knowledge, pedagogical relations, and identities, as well as in the flow of ideological approaches to adult literacy education (Fairclough, 1992; McKay and Wong, 1996; Thesen, 1996).

These constructions present varied implications for adult teaching and learning at, for, and through work. This is despite the widespread and legitimate interest in the adult learning needs thought to be inherent in various kinds of workers. We want to explore the embodiment of adult learning. That is, our research is a departure from projects that address questions such as the following: What would an epistemology of practice/skill/professionalism for various kinds of workers look like? How, if at all, does lifelong teaching and learning relate to vocational education and training? In particular, we want to give attention to human agency (the cognitive: "What I/we want to happen here") and to emotions in social experiences (the affective: "what I/we feel about what is happening here"). We are undertaking an ontological enquiry about the life-worlds of work and learning for adults. First, we will show how selfhood ("identity") grows out of adults' everyday actions and, after a brief conceptual discussion, suggest a model of adult teaching and learning which is based on the whole person. By "holism" we mean the whole person as an identity displayed in *practical, performative, material (embodied) actions-in-context*.

Adult Literacy Learners and Their Lifelong Learning

Locating the body at center stage, we would like to direct the attention of adult educators to the complex realities of the embodiment of adult learners in discursively constituted settings. We draw upon evidence from fieldwork conducted at two metropolitan institutes of Technical and Further Education (TAFE), where we examined how adult learner identities are enacted in the context of an adult English literacy classroom. We have left the analysis of teachers' identities and their propensity for intelligent action for another time and place.

The evidence below is used to illustrate that placing the body at the center of an analysis of subjectivity and literacy allows different questions to be raised about the self, the individual in relation to others, and literacy as socio-cultural practice. If embodied selves shape and are shaped via adult education policies and practices, it is important to attend to the performative aspects of teaching. An awareness of how our adult teaching practices elicit or construct identities may well lead us to perform differently.

The Limits of Inscription

In the first data extract, a teacher reflects on the challenge of working with a diversity of adult learners in her daily practice:

> So this Muslim woman, she would wear the hijab. She didn't wear anything across her face, her face was exposed and we went, as I said, used public transport and everything was fine. Several months later, she has become more and more strict, and now she wears a full veil, right over the top of her face, you can't even see her eyes. It's just black gauze right over the top, she wears gloves as well. ...One day when we were walking down the stairs and I was just next to her, and I thought I could ask her. I said, "Look, how come only six months ago you came with me on public transport and you showed your face. That was no problem. Now, you've got it totally covered?" And she said, "Well, I'm closer now to my religion, I'm more...I'm a better person now because I do this." Now for someone like you and I, that is just...how on earth can we possibly understand what stage each of these people are at and how do you know you're offending people. I said to her, "Aren't you worried about what people think of you?" I mean I could, because she knows me very well, so I could push the limits a little bit. I said to her, "Look, to look at you, you are very frightening. If someone on the street looks at you they would be very frightened and if there's anybody that doesn't like Muslims you're the person they're going to at-

tack" I said, "Aren't you worried about that?" She said, "Oh no." I said, "You could have something underneath your dress, you could have a weapon and people would be frightened of that." And she was totally; she just thought there was no need for her to worry. (Interview, 7.12.99)

Of importance here is the tension that the female Muslim body evokes in the female Anglo-teacher's secular Christian body. It works at a number of levels. At the surface, the body is inscribed with meaning, quite literally "written on" by gender, ethnicity and culture. In this instance meaning for the teacher is tied up in an external representation, and therefore the swapping of a hijab for full veil is implicated in how the learner is constructed. The data extract gives us some indication that this "material" transformation represents a challenge to a teacher, whose very comfort with and understanding of the adult learner, comes from a construction of that learner's identity as one that is enduring in nature: stable, continuing and unitary.

But the body can also be more powerfully understood as a seat of subjectivity, where the "self" is held to be an integrated being and the body as a lived structure and locus of experience. Here, the adult learner (re)presents a very different version of culture, one that is lived, where knowledge, beliefs, and experiences are located in the body, where the body is the medium for having a world. The discourse that the teacher employs makes it difficult for her to understand the learner's individual bodily practices. It is as though the body is treated obliquely as a symbol for something else, which acts to distance the teacher from the individual's everyday embodied experiences. Davis (1997: 14) argues that understanding embodiment requires of adult educators an ability to work out "how differences intersect and give meaning to their interactions with their bodies and through their bodies with the world around them."

Rules of Engagement

This section explores shifting identities and the work of identity construction as evidenced through classroom discourse. On the day of the observation, the adult learners were preparing for a two-week work experience placement. This is the final lesson drawn from a course manual designed to systematically prepare adult learners of English as a second language (ESL) for work experience. What follows is part of a discussion between Elaine, the teacher, and Hawa, Abshiro, and Bedria, her students (not their "real" names). The objective of this lesson was to foster an enhanced awareness of what was expected of the students while on placement."

Performing Identities 127

Elaine   What's a positive attitude?

Hawa   It's a...

Before Hawa finishes her response, Elaine continues...

Elaine   Not negative, you smile. If the man asks you to do something you smile, look happy. They are doing you a favour. Look happy, look excited!

Abshiro   Do I have to go? (on work experience)

Several other students almost in unison make similar requests.

Elaine   You have to. You have no choice.

Hawa   Why no pay? Why not $1 for 1 hour. I don't care. 20 cents.

The teacher doesn't respond and continues the lesson by having individual students read line by line characteristics associated with "good worker" from their course book.

Bedria   Do learn and absorb as much as possible and always keep your goal in mind.

The teacher interjects.

Elaine   You all have hopes and dreams. Think of this as one way of meeting it.

Students continue to read. This time the "Do" refers to "not getting involved in office politics." Several exchanges in first language, a few shrugs and shaking of heads. The teacher "senses" that perhaps the meaning isn't clear and attempts to clarify.

Elaine   Office politics, you know, "he said, she said..." don't get involved. Keep your private lives private. No one wants to hear about...maybe a little is okay.

(Fieldwork observation, 1999)

Lankshear (1997) argues that adult education is a modernist institution characterized by "spaces of enclosure"—the book, the classroom, and the curriculum. These spaces work to enclose meaning and experience through a fixed curriculum that is transmitted in classrooms and where the book is the paradigmatic embodiment of truth. In the data extract above, the teacher provides the students an opportunity to participate, but does so through mandated forms of activity, requiring these adult learners to represent the singular, definitive, and reified version of the "good worker" contained in the course manual. The teacher's task, as the representative of state authority, is to ensure the "accuracy" of their interpretation of what it means to be a "good worker." This process discourages participation from Bedria, as it fails to recognize or engage with her substantive understanding, experiences, knowledges, and skills. Both text and teacher work to ensure that these adult learners are "kept in their place."

In this instance, the learners call this "space of enclosure" into question. They question the assumption about the fixity of the text and the teacher as authoritative bearer of meaning. For these women, learning flourishes in the interstices of family, community, and work life and is shaped by their cultural, socio-economic, and historical circumstances. These adult learners do not re-present meaning, but rather collaborate in creating meaning, thus opening up the possibility of determining their own learning paths. They actively draw on knowledge and experiences beyond the walls of the classroom, disrupting the normalizing tendency of teacher and text. Where acknowledged, such embodied learning offers a means to move adult learners to fuller engagement and valued participation in their own literacy education. In other words, a re-reading of this classroom story opens up a space through which to do pedagogy differently—one that does not close off the women's efforts to insert themselves and their own meaning-making into the text.

What arises from these stories and resurfaces throughout the fieldwork are "active bodies" constructing and reconstructing their sense of self and occasionally resisting "other" constructions of them. Grosz (1993: 199) reminds adult educators that such "bodies" can become "sites of struggle and resistance, actively inscribing themselves on social practice." They are not merely subject to external agency, but are simultaneously agents in their own social construction of the world. We begin to see how different components of identity can be understood as dimensions of existence expressed by an active body. In the data extracts above, the adult learners' embodied or experiential knowledge challenges the universalizing impulses of pedagogies that privilege representational epistemology.

By attending to the adult learners' identities that are constructed through pedagogical interaction in the classroom, adult educators may better understand how the meanings adults make of literacy education and literacy are influenced by their agency. We may begin to construct adult learners' embodied knowledge not as distractions from language learning but rather as constituting the fabric of learners' lives. This is where the opportunity for doing pedagogy differently lies. The challenge, however is in being attentive to embodied differences in ways which do not simply "other" those bodies that are marginalized by a reliance on markers of difference.

Recall that we also wanted to establish a "holism," whereby the whole person as an identity is displayed in *practical, performative, material (embodied) actions-in-context*. So far we have shown empirically how certain adult learners actively construct their identities in literacy classrooms. This data analysis is based on the assumption of embodied learning, in contrast to Cartesian dualistic learning. Our claim of holism now turns to a conceptual discussion.

We make an identity claim: that *(embodied) ontological performance* of the practical, purposeful and contextually sensitive kind outlined above is a sound way to approach adult teaching and learning "for," "through," and "at" work. Of course, we acknowledge the view that humans have bodies which are active in some learning experiences. At the outset we stated this—but we have advanced the stronger claim that putting bodies at the center of adult learning corrects the Cartesian emphasis on mental criteria for knowing or understanding work experience and workplace culture. From an ontology that takes embodiment seriously, it is possible to construct a post-Cartesian epistemology centered upon a community of practice (that is authentic, embodied work); a dynamic (Aristotelian meansends) engagement with diversity, power, and a variety of discourses; and a context which is well integrated with the wider environment.

In terms of adult education policy, the future of lifelong teaching and learning is bound up with *what it is to be a whole person*. This is because the experience, knowledge, and skills adult learners already possess range over all of a person's life, not just that part of it in paid employment. Adult learners bring to work and learning their entire experiential selves, and so it would be very odd indeed to shape workplace learning only around the propositional knowledge that the workplace requires. But, as noted, this formal knowledge has high status in adult education. Although workplaces provide powerful contexts for purposive experiential learning, reflecting the veracity of the tripartite model outlined above, they confront the educational epistemology which most adult educators have grown up with, and with which we have the most comforting investments.

Performing Identities in an Age of Lifelong Teaching and Learning

Traditionally, under a Cartesian epistemology, mastery of propositions of the form "knowing *that* x" has characterized educational success (Ryle, 1949). Essays, examinations, and impeccable scholarship in both are hallmarks of that success. These are behavioral manifestations of inner, mental states. Once initial formal studies had been completed, it was thought that life at work was the successive refinement of this propositional knowledge by the amorphous and ephemeral alchemy of "experience." Thus, the Cartesian dualism was represented through formal education and its separation from daily work life. Nowadays, following Schön (1983; 1987), we give greater and long overdue attention to "knowing *how* x." Recognition of know-how gives adult workplace learning experiences an explicitness which adult educators are finding quite productive. We have tried to show two examples of that here. If lifelong teaching and learning can be regarded as a policy area with this potential, we argue that it does indeed have a transformative educational significance beyond the rhetoric currently so prominent.

Concepts like Giddens' (1979) "practical consciousness" and tacit knowledge draw attention to significant human experiences, but do not demystify those experiences. On the contrary, to claim "consciousness" or "intuition" of something which is embodied in activities is a Cartesian response, reinforcing the dualism that preserves the mystery of the intelligently practical act (Beckett and Hager, 2000; 2002).

With the empirical evidence from adult literacy classrooms, we have engaged in an ontological exploration of the construction of adult learner identity through embodied action. The intentionality of those actions (the expression of a "knowing *why* x") seems to be a logical consequence of this ontological exploration. In that very intentionality are the seeds of a new educational epistemology.

Coming to know or understand something has typically been an achievement brought about by formal, abstract and immaterial means. For this, we have the Cartesian tradition to thank. Whilst its legacy is rich, it no longer serves as an adequate basis for the educational expectations generated by changing workplaces and life experiences. Instead, starting with the view that the embodied actions of adults are the raw material for powerful learning, we have trawled that materiality for its epistemological significance. How does it reshape the achievement of understanding?

Basically, adult educators acknowledge that adult learners, whether in classrooms or workplaces, bring their propensity for intelligent actions with them: it is the heart of their embodiment as humans. However, this is under-recognized both pedagogically and conceptually. Understanding something is not the arrival at a state of mind (as Cartesian ontology and epistemology would have it), rather, it is evident in its emergence in articulated inferences, always embodied often in speech acts. The case for this self-construction of learner identity sees the emergent of "understanding" in daily adult experiences (Beckett, 2001).

Articulating Inferential Understanding

How does learning through experiences help our understanding of "understanding"? Instead of asking how learning through essays, examinations, and formal training is *represented* to the adult learner, there is a need to ask—has there been a change in the state of the adult learner? There is a more important question. What *inferences* can the adult learner articulate?

If we focus not on the outcomes but on the inferences drawn from them, then we have a different indicator of a change in some internal state of the learner. By focusing on the pro-activity and creativity of intentional action itself we open a space for this new "inferential understanding." Schön (1987: 36) argues that practitioners make and re-make their "practice worlds." Likewise we argue that all adults, not just professional practitioners, make and remake their worlds by intelligent and self-constructed action. Understanding is an inferential phenomenon, it arises from the fluidity of actions and achievements which constitute the daily life of adults across routine and contingent situations.

Notice, however, that this inferential understanding is *articulated*. This is crucial. Whereas representational understanding tries to map itself through the identification of mental states such as "mechanisms," "ideas," "mental models," "learning loops," "pictures," "images," "maps," "metaphors." In contrast, inferential understanding is manifest in public, socially located justifications. These are warranted assertions of how experience is proceeding: they are the "whyness" of practice.

This interpretation of "understanding" requires not just one embodied learner but a whole community of them, because these experiences are "assertoric" practices. Justifications of how one proceeded, or intends to proceed, or (more commonly) finds oneself proceeding are articulated in ways that depend on the values and norms of one's community. The warrant for proceeding is embedded in the "assertoric" practices of which one is a member.

In the daily life of all adults there will be a range of these practices all overlapping from a household, a workplace, a profession, a citizenry, and even humanity itself. Boundary crossing and multiple memberships of communities provide the diversity for the construction of rich identities for those who claim various sorts of memberships in them. Right across this range, inferential understandings and the assertoric practices in which they are embedded are normative. The public, socially located articulation of justifications reveals understanding. When an individual engages in these overlapping series of reason-giving exercises for her or his actions—and this occurs in normal daily conversations, embodied in speech acts—the individual self-constructs her or his identity and co-constructs her or his communities. The empirical sections of this chapter brought this to our attention. Adult ESL learners bring their assertoric practices to the classroom and, of course, to all their lifelong learning experiences.

In other words, as we "stand up to be counted" when we articulate through our bodies and our speech, where we stand on all manner of justifiable matters, we are literally standing up to be counted—as identities with certain ontological and epistemological claims. As our "understandings" are made explicit when these are articulated in embodied action, we not only "know where we stand", others can tell where we stand. And we can co-locate others in this way.

This analysis is Wittgensteinian (1963), in that it fits with his constructivist "language-game" metaphor about the meaningfulness of human actions. The metaphor, which is representational, points to his insight that our rule-governed capacities are entirely due to our socio-cultural and not our private self-interested reality. The significance of Wittgenstein for adult educators is that he re-presents his insight into the relationship between language and the experienced world. His argument against the possibility of a private language is central to that insight, not the metaphor in itself. The practice of assertion is ineluctably public, he argues. This is a formidable assault on the Cartesian *cogito*. But inferential understanding has many supporters based on a rich and contemporary legacy that includes Frege, Kant and Leibniz. Perhaps Rorty and other Deweyians fit well with this tradition? What is especially noteworthy for adult learning in this philosophical tradition is the significance of *judgement*, which we can find as far back as Kant:

> The unquestioned assumption before Kant was that an explanation of linguistic meaning must begin with a theory of terms or concepts, both singular (e.g. "Socrates") and general (e.g. "human"). Their meaningfulness would be grasped independently of, and prior to, the meaningfulness of anything else. They are representations. (Mackenzie, cited in Beckett and Hager, 2002: 193)

It was through the combination of these linguistic assertions and the inferences produced, that the truth of which is based on what is combined and how. For Kant,

> the fundamental unit of awareness or cognition is the *judgement* (assertion). "Now the only use which the understanding can make of these concepts is to judge by means of them".... Since this was the *only* use, it followed that "...we can reduce all

acts of *understanding* to judgements...." To understand something as a singular or general term presupposes its role in judgement. (Mackenzie, cited Beckett and Hager, 2002: 193)

In all of this, the enemy is, and ought to be, any Cartesian assumptions that understanding is represented mentally, that is, divorced from embodiment. But it is also unhelpful to regard understanding as represented *discursively* (as only a linguistic phenomenon), or as represented *logocentrically* (as only a syllogistic phenomenon).

Conclusion

In both the empirical and conceptual sections of this chapter, we have argued that the whole person presents as an identity displayed in *practical, performative, material (embodied) actions-in-context.* We have argued for an approach which starts with the act of human judgement and its embeddedness in embodied human actions. Attention to specific adult learning processes in workplaces is intended to give substance to learning outcomes. The social construction of the adult learner is counterposed by her or his intentional self-construction through experiential learning. Teachers in adult classes can enhance learners' propensity for embodied action through their teaching/learning experiences. But this is a reflexive relationship. In the talking, communicating, and acting the adult learner is making and remaking her or his identity. Of course, what the *substantive worth* of these (re-)constructions amounts to will vary depending on the depth and breadth of the learning that is gained and upon the value-ladenness of these pedagogical interventions. A focus on the performance of identities—an adult's self-construction—through embodied actions and the emergence of articulated understanding in judgements—is a fruitful way forward for adult education in this new century.

References

Beckett, D. "Hot Action at Work: Different Understandings of 'Understanding.'" In *Sociocultural Perspectives on Learning through Work: New Directions in Adult and Continuing Education Series*, edited by T. Fenwick, 73–84. San Francisco: Jossey-Bass, 2001.

———. "Straining Training: The Epistemology of Workplace Learning." *Studies in Continuing Education* 14(2), no. 2 (1992): 130–42.

Beckett, D., and P. Hager. *Life, Work and Learning: Practice in Postmodernity, Routledge International Series in Philosophy of Education.* London: Routledge, 2002.

———. "Making Judgments as the Basis for Workplace Learning: Towards an Epistemology of Practice." *International Journal of Lifelong Education* 19, no. 4 (2000): 300–11.

Beckett, D., and G. Morris. "Ontological Performance: Bodies, Identities and Learning." *Studies in the Education of Adults* 33, no. 1 (2001): 35–48.

Blake, N., P. Smeyers, R. Smith, and P. Standish. *Thinking Again: Education after Postmodernism*. Connecticut: Bergin and Garvey, 1998.

Butler, E. "Technologising Equity: The Politics and Practices of Work-Related Learning." In *Understanding Learning at Work*, edited by D. Boud and J. Garrick, 132–150. London: Routledge, 1999.

Crossley, N. "Merleau-Ponty, the Elusive Body and Carnal Sociology." *Body & Society* 1, no. 1 (1995): 43–64.

Davis, K. *Embodied Practices: Feminist Perspectives on the Body*. London: Sage, 1997.

Fairclough, N. *Discourse and Social Change*. Cambridge: Polity Press, 1992.

Garrick, J. *Informal Learning in the Workplace*. London: Routledge, 1998.

Gee, J. *Social Linguistics and Literacies: Ideology in Discourses*. London: Falmer, 1990.

Giddens, A. *Central Problems in Social Theory: Action, Structure and Contradiction in Social Analysis*. London: Macmillan, 1979.

Grosz, E. "Bodies and Knowledges: Feminism and the Crisis of Reason." In *Feminist Epistemologies*, edited by L. Alcoff and E. Potter. New York: Routledge, 1993.

Hager, P. "Robin Usher on Experience." *Educational Philosophy and Theory* 31, no. 1 (1999): 63–76.

Lankshear, C. *Changing Literacies*. Philadelphia: Open University Press, 1997.

McKay, S., and S. Wong. "Multiple Discourses, Multiple Identities: Investment and Agency in Second Language Learning among Chinese Adolescent Immigrant Students." *Harvard Educational Review* 66, no. 3 (1996): 577–608.

O'Loughlin, M. "Paying Attention to Bodies in Education: Theoretical Resources and Practical Suggestions." *Educational Philosophy and Theory* 30, no. 3 (1998): 275–98.

Ryle, G. *The Concept of Mind*. London: Hutchinson, 1949.

Schön, D. *Educating the Reflective Practitioner: Toward a New Design for Teaching and Learning in the Professions*. San Francisco: Jossey-Bass, 1987.

———. *The Reflective Practitioner*. New York: Basic Books, 1983.

Thesen, L. "Voices, Discourses and Transition: In Search of New Identities in Eap." *TESOL Quarterly* 31, no. 3 (1996): 487–511.

Wittgenstein, L. *Philosophical Investigations*. Oxford: Blackwell, 1963.

Part Three

Practitioner Development

Chapter 9

Adult and Vocational Educators: Their Changing Work and Professional Development

Roger Harris and Michelle Simons

> Governments have great expectations for the vocational outcomes of their adult education and training systems. Their policies are intended to deal with unemployment, skills shortages, deficits in basic skills, reducing the burden on universities, attracting full fee-paying students from overseas, reducing inequality and enhancing access. All these require responses from adult and vocational educators. The variety of policy agendas has often resulted in high levels of government intervention in the provision of vocationally oriented adult education and training. This has, in turn, impacted on the extent and pace of change which the sector is expected to manage. Within the current context, adult and vocational educators occupy a unique position. They are both *subject to* the dramatic changes that have impacted on the workforce in the last decade, while also being expected to *support and facilitate* the change process.
>
> (Waterhouse, Wilson, and Ewer, 1999: 1)

Drawing on Australian experience, this chapter argues that the work adult and vocational educators now confront, and the demands for managing both the scope and nature of change, far exceed previous experiences in the sector. Data from three Australian studies are used to elucidate this changing context and to present a case for conceiving of new ways to meet the professional development needs of adult and vocational educators.

The Changing Context

During the last twenty years, there have been a number of significant global trends that have impacted on adult education provision. The dramatic restructuring of the global economy with its concomitant social processes now permits greater flows of information and capital across national boundaries than ever before (Seddon, 1999). This has been promoted by the internationally competitive state where intervention by governments has been supplemented by market forces as combined steering mechanisms. In Australia, these two trends have manifested themselves in the rise of economic reductionism and corporate managerialism that have transformed the way in which states operate and their relationship with adult education institutions. Within this changed economic and social context, strong claims have been made for the links between economic prosperity, international competitiveness, and the development of human capital. Adult education serves global/local interests by the development of human capital as a means of gaining a competitive advantage in a global marketplace.

There is a growing recognition of the importance of knowledge and knowledge creation in many types of work. Likewise, the growth in information technology has also impacted on the way in which workplaces are organized. New technologies have altered the "temporal and spatial organization of work, the nature of manufacturing systems, the professional identity of employees and in-company human resource development" (Young and Guile, 1999: 204–205).

Within this context, governments have sought to realign adult education and training systems to ensure that appropriate policy responses can be formulated. System-wide reforms, including, *inter alia,* the introduction of competency-based training and more flexible responses to the ways in which VET (vocational education and training) qualifications might be developed and implemented, have changed the way adult education and training providers do business. These training reforms have resulted in significant decentralization and the assertion of customer choice, but all increasingly regulated through the use of centralized purchase/provider agreements and compliance regimes (Kell, Balatti, Hill, and Muspratt, 1997; Seddon, 1999). New technologies and curriculum frameworks have significantly changed what pedagogical practices and teacher identities are valued. Altered industrial relations laws have given rise to the development of new ways to meet industry's skill requirements (Attwell, 1997).

In 1996, the election of a neo-conservative Liberal Coalition government in Australia changed the industrial relations environment with a strong push beyond enterprise bargaining to achieve increased labor flexibility through individual workplace agreements (Billett, McKavanagh, Bevan, Angus, Seddon, Gough, Hayes and Robertson, 1999: 25). This has been justified as supporting the decentralization of decision making away from large bureaucracies in favor of arrangements that improve the capacity for local decision making as close as possible to the point of delivery. These changes towards increasing labor flexibility have seen a rise in the employment of part-time and sessional adult educators and of paraprofessionals, such as assistant lecturers (Harris, Simons, Hill, Smith, Pearce, Blakeley, Choy, and Snewin, 2001; Malley, Hill, Putland, Shah, and McKenzie, 1999).

These changes pose major challenges for adult educators in terms of the nature of vocational teaching/learning that they need to promote, as well as the ways in which they might design teaching/learning experiences to equip workers for their emerging but uncertain roles. The ways in which adult educators think, feel, and carry out their functions as adult educators are undergoing substantial transformation. The changing scope and construction of their work and their identity has given rise to debates regarding the "professional" nature of their work and how it has been affected by these reforms. Additionally, the characteristics of VET providers have been challenged with the work of training being dispersed across a range of occupations, giving renewed value to the workplace as an authentic teaching/learning environment (Harris, Simons and Bone, 2000). These changes have given rise to a number of issues relating to the increasingly diversified VET workforce and the divergent ways of understanding their role in facilitating learning. These themes are examined in more detail in the following sections.

An Increasingly Diverse Adult Education Workforce

A significant feature of the VET workforce is its diversity. Several groups of adult educators can be identified, differentiated primarily by three key factors—function, qualifications and affiliation (see figure 9.1). Location also plays its part, although it may be becoming less of a distinguishing feature. In the center are adult educators with a full-time VET role—teachers, trainers, and managers. While they are located in public and private adult education institutions as well as larger business enterprises, their work often takes them outside their organizations. They have responsibility for managing delivery and assessment processes; developing curriculum materials, especially for online learning; as well as taking the lead in entrepreneurial activity. Often, they possess higher education qualifications, from diplomas to postgraduate degrees in teaching, education, human resource development, or management.

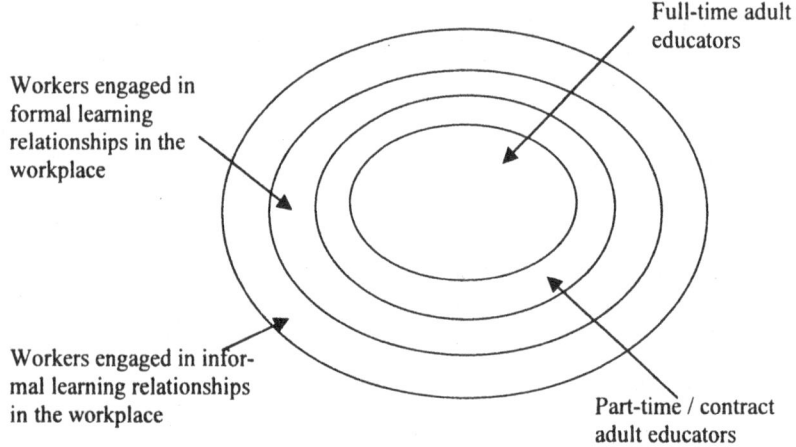

Figure 9.1: Conceptualizing the adult education workforce

In the second circle are those with a part-time role in adult education or, increasingly, several part-time roles across more than one provider of adult education. They are found mainly in industry, schools, and as part-time staff in both public and private training providers. Their primary role is teaching and assessing VET students. Characteristically, they have credentials in assessment and workplace training, and a proportion is currently upgrading their certificates to higher education degrees in hope of full-time positions. The growth of this group of adult educators is occurring at a time when overall employee costs within public adult education providers have fallen. Employee costs have gone from 68.4 percent of expenditure in 1994 to 60.8 percent in 1999. This is despite substantial increases in student numbers (Kronemann, 2001: 4). This trend represents government and employer preferences for a flexible, casualized workforce as a response to and expression of pressures from the competitive globalized market for adult education. Leaving adult educators grappling with uncertain employment prospects affects both their personal lives and their ability to provide quality teaching/learning experiences for VET students.

The third category comprises workers in industry who assist with adult vocational education in their organization. Although primarily involved in the core business of their organization, they help with the assessment of apprentices and trainees. They may be involved with an external provider and some have a relevant credential such as a "train the trainer" course.

The fourth group includes those in industry who are full-time workers in the core business of their enterprise but who, in the course of their regular work, informally help others learn in the workplace. Their learners may be in formal programs such as apprenticeships and traineeships, but often are likely to be fellow workers who need on-the-job training. For this group of adult educators, work and learning are inextricably intertwined. They are skilled, experienced, and qualified in their work discipline, but may well have no formal training qualifications. It is by inclination that they develop an interest in and gravitate towards helping others learn on the job.

Figure 9.1 connotes a dynamic interrelationship between the concentric circles. As contexts and situations change, so too do adult educators move between circles. Adult educators in each of these groups play an important role in the valuing of the workplace as a teaching/learning environment. This focus on industry-relevant qualifications emphasizes the application of flexible policy frameworks that validate multiple learning pathways. The work of the third and fourth groups is different from classroom-bound conceptions of adult teaching and training, and reminds all adult educators of different ways of understanding how adult learning might be facilitated in these environments.

Adult Education Practitioners in Workplace Environments

Training reform in Australia has meant a shift from a supply- to a demand-driven adult and vocational education system, and a move from off-job to on-job training. In this context, the workplace-based adult educator is assuming an increasingly important role in the provision of adult education opportunities. The critical issue is to what extent workplace trainers (especially in small enterprises) are ready, willing, and able to meet this enhanced commitment in their changing role. Although a considerable amount of informal training is occurring in small businesses, it is largely unrecognized and not structured in ways that "count" in VET statistics or accreditation (Harris, Simons, and Bone, 2000). Work and teaching, learning are inextricably intertwined and shape each other in a dynamic interrelationship, as, for example, when trainers structure work processes to accommodate employee learning.

There are five functions central to the role of the workplace trainer. These include fostering an environment conducive to adult learning; working and learning with co-workers; structuring and shaping work processes to accommodate adult learning; promoting independence and self-direction in adult learners; and linking external learning experiences with work and learning in the workplace. Workplace trainers experience considerable challenges in juggling the twin tasks of doing their own work and assisting others to learn. Various strategies are employed to juggle these conflicting demands. These include working longer hours; planning and prioritizing work very carefully; supervising "at a distance"; continually judging the abilities and competence of workers and how these might be matched with requirements of the task at hand; and using other workers to supervise by delegating training tasks.

Notions of the "workplace trainer", which assume formality, structured contexts, and large business environments, are questionable. Increasingly, every worker is potentially an informal trainer. For those who, as part of their work in formal adult education institutions, go into the workplace, it is not a matter of simply transferring classroom-based techniques. Rather, they must develop fundamentally new ways of conceiving and carrying out their roles. In a similar vein, the changes in the work of adult educators within VET institutions are placing new demands on them.

Adult Educators in Institutional Settings

A study of adult educators in both public and private training providers across five Australian states/territories revealed considerable shifts in their roles (Harris, Simons, and Clayton, 2003). These shifts have occurred in role expansion, diversification, and balance. This has resulted in role tensions and considerable ambivalence on the part of adult educators in their feelings towards these changes and their perceptions of their place within the VET sector.

"Role expansion" arises from additions to existing workloads. Adult educators are now required to work in different contexts and have a strong "outward focus." They work in such places as institutes, schools and a wide variety of other workplaces. They build industry links and develop relationships with a range of specialist service providers now operating in the provision and administration of the VET system (for example, Na-

tional Apprenticeship Centres). The emphasis on vocational outcomes has resulted in adult educators developing skills in career advising and work placements. Role expansion has also manifested itself in greater time and energy being spent on administrative and management functions that have been devolved down to them. Adult educators now have to take increased responsibility for administrative functions, such as managing budgets and being more focussed on financial issues than ever before. They have to be more aware of funding opportunities, costs of training, and the need to generate surplus income. These changes have been especially significant for adult educators in senior positions who have been given the added responsibility of supervising the work of colleagues to ensure compliance with increasingly stringent accountability requirements.

The passion of adult educators for teaching is being eroded by administrative battles, as they take on more administering work rather than interacting with students. Role expansion has occurred alongside a contraction in the numbers of permanent teaching and administrative staff. This reflects the preference by employers to increase the number of part-time or contract staff. The result has been a concomitant increase in the work associated with recruitment, staff training, and industrial relations. The cost of this work has been hidden by means of devolution. While sessional or casual staff have the content knowledge, considerable time has to be spent in explaining new delivery systems and accountability requirements. This creates substantial managerial work for the shrinking core of permanent staff who have to carefully supervise sessional staff to ensure that audit requirements are met. This adds to the pressure for ensuring compliance.

"Role diversification" results from the broadening of work responsibilities, and for adult educators, it has been even more dramatic than role expansion. Role diversification for adult educators is underpinned by growing corporate managerialist rhetoric about training adult students to learn how to learn. The ability to deliver a fixed amount of content is no longer the critical factor. Rather, the future of adult education is in developing a self-pacing, self-reliant, independent learner. Many adult educators now "facilitate" learning rather than undertake face-to-face teaching. In the press to minimize the need for employing adult educators, there has been a shift away from teaching, towards facilitating student learning. There are increased demands for adult educators to be effective communicators, to have relevant and up-to-date content knowledge, and to have the skills for classroom, workplace, and on-line delivery and assessment.

Developments in the use of new technology require adult educators to develop skills for training and assessment on-line, with demands for twenty-four hour, seven day access by students. "Clients" often expect immediate responses, and, as a result of competition, adult education providers are always struggling to provide quality services and more than the minimum requirements, keep up-to-date with the requirements of industry, and maintain a watch on what competitors are offering. Adult educators are not only expected to adopt these different practices, they are also expected to apply them across a range of geographical locales, and spend greater time working in industry monitoring progress of adult learners in workplaces. Adult educators are often working with industry personnel who do not own the training agenda and are having difficulty with the demands placed on them for workplace assessments. They are also increasingly expected to take on the roles of educational designers, or to work collaboratively with specialists to create materials for on-line delivery and for use in workplaces.

"*Role balance*" has arisen as an issue for adult educators as a result of the expansion and diversification of their work responsibilities; in particular, there has been a shift in emphasis from teaching/learning to assessment and the administration of compliance. There is more pressure on staff when determining whether a student has achieved "competency" or not, despite questioning the validity of demonstrable outcomes. This is problematic at diploma and advanced diploma levels where verifying "competence" takes a long time on the job. Time and cost of assessments and compliance are issues yet to be adequately resolved. Likewise, because assessments and audits often have to be "signed off" by a number of people, there are unresolved problems of ensuring that they have a shared conceptualization of competency or quality.

An accompanying shift has been a decreasing emphasis on adult educators as creators of curriculum and an increasing focus on them being receivers and interpreters of the wishes of industry within received training frameworks. In Australia these take the form of Training Packages that represent the current government's preference for "flexibility." The adoption of these frameworks aids concomitant shifts to enterprise-based, market-oriented training that is claimed to be responsive to the needs of enterprises. Training Packages are intended to bring together a "set of tools" as "new formal reference points" for the VET system (Misko, 1999: 13). These tool sets consist of endorsed components (competency standards, assessment guidelines, and qualifications) and support materials (learning strategies, assessment tools, and professional development materials). These packages replace the previous requirement for the accreditation of national curricula by providing industries with the means to direct the development of flexible training pathways that lead to nationally recognized qualifications.

In order to interpret the requirements of these training frameworks, adult educators are required to hold certain capabilities in teaching, learning theory, curriculum development, and content expertise. In a context where public resources are diverted to other agendas and outcomes are paramount, adult educators are often faced with ethical dilemmas. They have to wrestle with decisions that require them to ensure that students have a sufficient base of knowledge and breadth of experience against cost-efficiency considerations.

"Role tensions" occur as a consequence of changing expectations on the part of government, industry, and employers about the work of adult educators. These tensions are experienced in various ways. There has been a major shift from what adult educators were originally employed to do, namely, teaching and training. The competitive funding regime has now redirected their efforts away from teaching and into other areas. Such dilution of effort has become a cause for concern among adult educators who warn about threats to the efficacy of adult education and training. These concerns have fuelled changes in the professional preparation of adult educators. In Australia, the *de facto* qualification for adult educators is now the Certificate IV in Assessment and Workplace Training. This situation is not conducive to quality education and contributes to tensions around the status and functions of adult educators.

The composition of the student population has changed, and so too have students' relationships with adult educators. This has created additional workplace tensions. Students, now constructed as consumers and clients, are more assertive, holding higher expectations and wanting "value for money." Students also have increasingly complex lives, and therefore a greater range of factors affecting their capacity to learn. With few increases in full-time staff, increases in part-time staff mean that the remaining full-time staff have more work to do with respect to student counseling and complaints, such that trying to squeeze in educational work can be very problematic.

Government accountability controls, along with the competitive market in adult education, have heightened tensions around legal responsibilities. The burden of accountability is not carried equally, particularly in relation to part-time and sessional staff. Adult educators are increasingly aware of their competitors and are constantly called upon to appraise and justify their work in order to maintain a competitive edge. They also experience tensions in their changing relations with their colleagues and working conditions. For some, this has meant increasing demands for teamwork; for others, it has meant increased isolation, with fewer opportunities to meet with like-minded colleagues. Increased pressure to deal with issues relating to budgets, performance, and competitors leaves little time and energy to invest in networking and learning from colleagues. Changes to industrial relations, including the introduction of enterprise bargaining, have led to the erosion of working conditions, with concomitant falls in morale and job satisfaction.

Professional Development for Adult Educators

Within this climate of re-ordered relationships, newly emerging patterns of work, and constant change by employers, industry, and different levels and agencies of government, the position of professional development for adult educators is especially important. The changing work of adult educators arguably has a decreasing effect on those less affiliated with the core functions of vocational education and training. This looser connection reflects (a) smaller chunks of VET work, (b) a weaker degree of affiliation with VET, and (c) a lessening in formal certification for training. A key issue, therefore, is that in such a differentiated adult education workforce, professional development also needs to be differentiated. What is needed will differ as a result of an individual's function, affiliation with the VET system, and existing qualifications. Questions of location and function, however, are only one of a number of factors that could influence the professional development made available to adult educators. As in industries, key stakeholders within the VET "industry"—specifically employers and policy-makers—also have a significant input into shaping professional development activities for the sector.

Only about half of the current adult educators throughout Australia possess the necessary skills, knowledge, and capabilities needed to meet the challenges ahead (Harris, Simons, Hill, Smith, Pearce, Blakeley, Choy, and Snewin, 2001). Moreover, these capabilities are not uniformly distributed across the workforce, with part-time, older, and casual staff having less expertise. Less than half the current adult educators are considered to have the attributes required to improve the quality and cost-efficiency of

VET provision. To the extent that these judgments have validity, they hold significant implications for professional development over the coming years.

The combined impact of the changes in the VET sector is causing increased pressures on the work of adult educators. This pressure itself is a critical factor preventing many from undertaking professional development. Nevertheless, there are indications that a substantial amount of formal and informal professional development is happening. Three key trends are evident, namely, a shift in the balance of professional development activities away from individual to corporate concerns; greater differentiation in the roles of teachers and trainers; and an increasing diversity in the way professional development needs are addressed.

There are tensions between meeting corporate priorities and staff needs within the VET sector. Typically, corporate stakeholders identify current challenges for professional development in terms of compliance with the agendas of external agencies to whom adult education providers are accountable. The needs of adult educators themselves are considered as secondary. The corporate managerialist assumption is that students' needs will be best served by organizations demonstrating compliance in the areas nominated by the state. On the other hand, when key stakeholders were asked to identify future professional development challenges, they nominated enhancement of the professional expertise of adult educators. There would appear to be a realization on the part of stakeholders that quality VET delivery requires teacher expertise to be of a high order. There is an issue here about the appropriate balance between compliance-driven and capacity-building professional development.

The roles of adult educators have become more differentiated, so they need to be appropriately skilled in order that their practice reflects the changes arising from the new sectoral requirements and the increasingly differentiated workforce in VET. For some adult educators, the focus of their contribution to VET delivery is very narrow; some are employed solely for their technical currency and have minimal training in instructional techniques. A differentiated workforce implies that professional development requirements will vary. However, those with higher responsibilities are just as unlikely to have greater access to relevant professional development opportunities.

Adult education providers have little professional development opportunities beyond initial qualifications (which in the case of a majority of teachers and trainers is the Certificate IV in Assessment and Workplace

Training). Many contract and part-time adult educators are upgrading qualifications in order to seek permanent teaching positions, despite such opportunities becoming less common. This invites the question of what constitutes an adult educator when the teaching role is being broken down, with many undertaking the task of training as just one part of their job. Career paths are becoming fragmented, if not disintegrating, thus making a costly investment in professional development a problem for many adult educators.

Increasingly, professional development has come to mean, from a naïve corporate managerial perspective, information downloading from above. This reflects the compliance pressures on adult educators driven by uncertain and contradictory "top-down" changes. Such an environment increases the tensions between the compliance demands and adult educators' focus on teaching, learning, and education. This approach is increasingly problematic, given the insistence by VET providers that adult educators market their programs to international students and organizations where demands for new knowledge and skills are greater. Furthermore, there are important differences between public and private VET providers in their approaches to ongoing professional development (Harris, Simons, Hill, Smith, Pearce, Blakeley, Choy, and Snewin, 2001). Far more VET institutions have specialist structures for professional development than do private training providers. This, coupled with the trend for adult educators to contribute to the costs of their initial and ongoing professional development, is resulting in responsibility for their education being unevenly distributed across providers.

Professional development programs frequently use action learning, work-related learning, and flexible on-line delivery as core pedagogies. In effect, the provision of professional development is moving towards knowledge being generated by adult educators as part of their work practice and bound by the situation in which it is produced (Hoban, 1997). This trend is in keeping with broader initiatives promoting situated learning for many occupations. Professional development takes on an *ad hoc,* and possibly parochial, character. Learning is structured by the workplace, and, in particular, the work undertaken there, its organization, and people's ideas about both. Learning in the workplace takes multiple forms; learning is embedded in policies and formal learning programs; learning occurs in groups; external bodies such as professional associations drive learning; and individual workers are initiating learning (Van der Krogt, 1998; Poell, Van der Krogt, and Wildemeersch, 1998). All of these forms of learning are valuable and together comprise the rich and varied mosaic of adult learning that can support adult educators in their various roles.

However, whatever the model of professional development that is supported, it must address the issue that all adult educators work in complex and dilemma-ridden environments. It is not enough to provide them with information or opportunities to solve the immediate problems presented by the implementation of the latest in ever-changing policy mandates. Professional development needs to enable adult educators to develop a sense of coherence and self-efficacy in an environment riddled with the uncertainties manufactured by constant crisis-driven, crisis-making change. These changes and the crises they manage to engineer are systemically directed to challenge the norms, beliefs, values, and practices of adult educators. This can only happen if professional development opportunities acknowledge the lived realities of adult educators across a range of contexts.

In the absence of spaces for critique, acknowledgement of adult educators' accumulated expertise as the basis for change, and recognition that change is experienced in very individualized ways, adult education is problematic. In current circumstances, the pressure is for professional development to be reduced to an exercise in substituting, eliminating, and extinguishing advances made in adult education theory and practice, rather than providing opportunities for new ways of working to emerge from adult educators' theories and practices. At the heart of dilemmas relating to the provision of professional development for those for whom adult education is their career is the degree to which adult educators are vested with the autonomy and power to be able to view themselves as professionals. This contrasts markedly with notions of professional development with adult educators as technicians who work within limited contexts with lessening degrees of autonomy. Professional development to support the extension and deepening of their professionalism recognizes that adult educators need the knowledge to work in complex and unpredictable environments. As professionals, adult educators need the skills to be reflexive and critical to fulfill the role of transforming adult education.

Conclusion

The role of adult educators in the vocational education and training sector is expanding and diversifying as the opportunities for a full-time career contract. Arguably, there are more "adult educators" now concerned with the task of building the skills of the workforce than ever before. All are subject to different contextual factors that shape the degree to which they can attend to the task of developing vocational competence. The previously separate occupations of human resource developers, training and development specialists, schoolteachers, technical teachers, and university academics are now converging around vocational education creating possibilities for collaboration and the opening up of new ways of working. Potentially, every worker in an enterprise is a trainer, facilitator, and mentor involved in supporting adult learning.

There is a complex web of adult educators who now form the VET workforce. The changing VET sector is creating considerable challenges. The roles of adult educators vary considerably depending on where they work, the nature of work in their workplaces, their functions, and their degrees of affiliation with the VET system. There is emerging a differentiated workforce that comprises a small core of permanent adult educators alongside growing "peripheral" groups of other workers with varying degrees of attachment to the VET sector. There is also an evident shift in balance of professional development activities away from educational to corporate concerns and an increasing diversity in the ways development needs are addressed. Pushing through the possibilities beyond the limitations of this system is a challenge for adult educators.

References

Attwell, G. "New Roles for Vocational Education and Training Teachers and Trainers in Europe: A New Framework for Their Education." *Journal of European Industrial Training* 21, no. 6/7 (1997): 1–12.

Billett, S., C. McKavanagh, F. Bevan, L. Angus, T. Seddon, J. Gough, S. Hayes, and I. Robertson. *The CBT Decade: Teaching for Flexibility and Adaptability.* Adelaide, South Australia: National Centre for Vocational Education Research, 1999.

Harris, R., M. Simons, and J. Bone. *More Than Meets the Eye? Rethinking the Role of Workplace Trainer.* Adelaide, South Australia: National Centre for Vocational Education Research, 2000.

Harris, R., M. Simons, and B. Clayton. *Shifting Mindsets: Impact of Changes to Work in the VET Sector on the Roles of VET Professionals.* Adelaide, South Australia: National Centre for Vocational Education Research, 2003 (in press).

Harris, R., M. Simons, D. Hill, E. Smith, R. Pearce, J. Blakeley, S. Choy, and D. Snewin. *The Changing Role of Staff Development for Teachers and Trainers in Vocational Education and Training.* Adelaide, South Australia: National Centre for Vocational Education Research, 2001.

Hoban, G. "Opportunities for Knowledge Building in Professional Development Models." In *Exploring Professional Development in Education,* edited by R. King, D. Hill and J. Retallick. Katoomba, N.S.W.: Social Science Press, 1997.

Kell, P., J. Balatti, A. Hill, and S. Muspratt. "Mapping Teachers' Work, Charting New Futures." Townsville, Queensland: Institute of Interdisciplinary Studies, James Cook University of Northern Queensland, 1997.

Kronemann, M. *TAFE Teachers: Facing the Challenge.* Southbank, Victoria: Australian Education Union, 2001.

Malley, J., R. Hill, C. Putland, C. Shah, and P. McKenzie. "Trends in the TAFE Institute Workforce and Their Implications for the Training and Development of Staff 1998–2008: Report Prepared for the Office of Training and Further Education." Melbourne, Victoria: Monash-ACER Centre for the Economics of Education and Training and Chisholm Centre for Innovation and Research, 1999.

Misko, J. *Competency-Based Training. Review of Research.* Adelaide, South Australia: National Centre for Vocational Education Research, 1999.

Poell, R., F. Van der Krogt, and D. Wildemeersch. "Solving Work-Related Problems through Learning Projects." *International Journal of Lifelong Education* 17, no. 5 (1998): 341–51.

Seddon, T. "Capacity Building: Beyond State and Market." *Pedagogy, Culture and Society* 7, no. 1 (1999): 35–53.

Van der Krogt, F. "Network Learning Theory: The Tension between Learning Systems and Work Systems in Organizations." *Human Resource Development Quarterly* 9, no. 2 (1998): 157–77.

Waterhouse, P., B. Wilson, and P. Ewer. *The Changing Nature and Patterns of Work and Implications for VET.* Adelaide, South Australia: National Centre for Vocational Education Research, 1999.

Young, M., and D. Guile. "New Possibilities for the Professionalization of UK VET Professionals." *Journal of European Industrial Training* 21, no. 6/7 (1997): 203–12.

Chapter 10

The Work of Adult Literacy Teachers

Bobby Harreveld

Introduction

Teachers' work in adult education has been appropriated by the neo-conservative agendas of governments seeking to position their states for political and economic survival in the twenty-first century. Central to this appropriation is the alignment of adult vocational education and training to the production of human capital for a globalized labor market. Governments mediate as much as they mitigate the effects of globalization on the economic and social demands of everyday life. With respect to the provision of adult education, this has been achieved through policies that have reframed the work and organization of adult literacy teaching. The Australian National Training Authority's chief executive officer observes that adult vocational education and training (VET) has been positioned at the "point of convergence for almost all aspects of Australia's society and economy" (Scollay, 2002: 3). Adult literacy education previously existed on the margins of formal education, however, this convergence of the social and economic has seen it repositioned closer to the center of the vocationally oriented adult education and training system.

Rather than being passive victims of this change, this chapter argues that teachers actively broker their compliance with these neo-conservative imperatives from within the system in which they work. Findings from research into the work of twenty-three adult literacy teachers in rural, regional, and remote communities throughout northern western Queensland (Australia) between 1996 and 2001 are used to contextualize this analysis.

These teachers were participants in a professional development course in adult literacy teaching. They were also employees of registered training organizations that are struggling to survive in Australia's competitive, contractual vocational education and training marketplace.

The first section of this chapter explores the notion of globalization used in this research. The second section explores the concepts of "compliance" and "brokerage" that informed this research into teachers' work and its organization. In the third section, examples of adult literacy teachers brokering compliance with both their students and the VET system are presented. Consideration of the implications of these findings for theorizing global/local futures in adult education is offered in the final section.

Dimensions of Globalization

Globalization is a process that has become known as much by its effects as by its causes. As financial and social capital has moved out of country towns throughout regional Australia, associated public infrastructure and private institutions have mutated, shrunk or disappeared altogether, resulting in high mobility rates and demographic shifts in populations. In an earlier research study that focussed adult literacy education and new technologies in outback Australia, it was found that such relationships were

> not only embedded in broader organizational dimensions governing changes in vocational education and training, but in quite complex ways, they are also connected to the development of information industries covering computers, telecommunications, publishing and broadcasting. (Singh, Harreveld, and Hunt, 1997: 158)

The processes of globalization are multidimensional, complex, and interconnected. While "globalization" is the subject of contested interpretations, it is characterized by an integration of economies across nation-states that facilitate flexible markets for products and human capital, which in turn are dependent upon and responsive to continually evolving information technologies (Edwards, 1997). Crucially, these processes of globalization involve inequitable and changing power relations, identities, and networks across "the dimensions of communications technology, ecology, economics, work organization, culture and civil society" (Beck, 2000: 19).

Prakash and Hart (2000: 5) argue that globalization is "a process of market integration, primarily through the establishment of value chains that are increasingly dispersed geographically." For adult literacy teachers in rural, regional, and remote communities, the geographical dispersal effected by globalization is an important consideration when interpreting the "value chains" of individuals and groups with which they work. Smyth, Dow, Hattam, Reid, and Schacklock (2000: 147) argue that in this context, teachers' work necessarily has "political-economic, socio-cultural and technological dimensions." Across all these dimensions of globalization, adult educators' engagement with such processes calls for a strategic repertoire of socially and culturally responsible teaching practices.

Adult Educators' Tactics of Engagement: Brokering Compliance

While adult literacy teachers are positioned at the extremities of Australia's adult vocational education and training (VET) system, they are pivotal to the operationalization of the system's policies at the "coal-face." If the system really wants its literacy policies enacted, then it has to rely on educators to do the work of adult literacy teaching in local communities.

In the nomenclature of the VET system, the term "compliance" denotes unquestioning submission with systemic imperatives, with conformity effected through a demanding surveillance regime. If they wish to have a job, adult literacy teachers must comply with the VET system's nationwide competency-based curriculum frameworks that have constructed literacy as "communicative competence" (ACTRAC, 1994; Coates, Fitzpatrick, McKenna, and Makin, 1995). In Foucauldian terms these "institutional practices have a primacy over forms of knowledge" (Macdonell, 1986: 90). Such is the case in adult literacy teaching where the VET system assigns limits on what is adult "literacy," determines who can or should engage in teaching it, and restricts the conditions for doing so.

Through its regional, state, and national structures, Australia's VET system has inscribed discursive practices with which adult educators are expected to comply and audit mechanisms have been institutionalized to effect their submission. Nevertheless, these practices are open to challenge and disruption by adult educators committed to their profession, discipline, students, and community. de Certeau (1984) talks of "tactics" in relation to resistance and subversion. Teachers' choices of tactics for their engagements with the system depend upon how they construct "compliance." From the study's evidence, compliance is not unquestioning submission. Compliance is not configured either as uninformed obedience or as a cover for alternative spaces where clandestine and creative ruses are coordinated. It is reliant upon context to give it meaning.

Depending as it does upon socio-cultural, economic, political, and technological imperatives, compliance is a contingent practice. It is mobilized when adult literacy teachers' actions are seen and believed to be in alignment with systemic expectations. Registered training organizations interpret teacher compliance in terms of: (1) their pre-service and in-service qualifications; (2) competency-based training and assessment processes; (3) fulfilling the terms and conditions of policy-dependent funding; and (4) audit requirements under the Australian Quality Training Framework (ANTA, 2001). When teachers coordinate the power of the system in ways that fulfill their professional responsibilities, values, and beliefs, they are also complying. In such instances, they are complying with their own interpretations of what it means to be an adult educator as much as the normative expectations of students, their community, and their discipline. This means that compliance can be traded or brokered depending on the situation and the people involved.

Brokerage involves buying or selling something on behalf of others, usually, though not necessarily, for a fee. Teachers broker "learning" for those who wish to sell it (their employers) and for those who wish to buy it (their students). However, this dichotomy does not capture the intricate, ideologically based economic and political mechanisms by which some adults are positioned as sellers and others are positioned as buyers of adult literacy education. Brokerage is a contingent and contextually dependent practice that is allied with compliance to enable it to function in full view of the system's surveillance and control structures. Brokerage is dependent upon the multi-dimensional professional commitments of adult educators. When mobilized at the policy-practice interface in the context of adult literacy teachers' communities of practice, the brokerage/compliance relationship coordinates diffuse power relations through individuals and groups within those communities. In the following section, the practices of adult literacy teachers brokering compliance with both the system and their students are presented through their own words. While their own words are used here, their names have been changed.

Adult Education Brokering Compliance

None of the adult literacy teachers in this research worked at the core of the VET system's decision-making processes that ultimately impacted upon their work. Given the positioning of teachers within the political, economic, and social structure of the VET system in which these changes were enacted, this is understandable. It was not until the course design, delivery, assessment, and evaluation stages that these adult literacy teachers entered the VET system at the policy-practice interface. These teachers brought with them their own school or industry-based identities as adult educators, together with their specific ways of using language, objects, tools, and technologies from the sites and institutions for which they worked (Gee, 1996; 1999). Here, the power of the VET system was mediated and mitigated by the power of these teachers. Their power increased because the VET system itself could not do the teaching; it institutionalizes the structures within which the work of teaching occurs.

In this section, evidence of teachers brokering compliance is analyzed. Policy-induced and bureaucratically administered funding processes engaged teachers in technologies of power and language that framed six key aspects of their work. These include: (1) the particular curriculum focus as per syllabus or training packages; (2) the timing of teaching/learning, by day and night, and across the year; (3) the duration of teaching/learning; (4) the location/s in which teaching/learning could take place; (5) the availability of teachers and/or tutors whose qualifications meet human resource requirements; and (6) the reasons why adult learners participate in literacy courses. From their lived experiences with the tensions and dilemmas emerging from these aspects of their work, it was found that teachers brokered compliance with their students and the system. Concomitantly, they "became" new types of adult educators.

Teachers brokered compliance with their students' perceptions of literacy and the particularities of their learning in at least two ways. Initially, they identified what their students wanted from this learning. Secondly, they clandestinely subverted the VET system's power to determine what that adult learning would be. This meant that these teachers' foregrounded their students' learning as the primary focus of their professional work and identity, while systemic imperatives were positioned as secondary to their focus on adult learning.

Catherine articulated her commitment to a teaching-learning relationship that was "student centered—starting with students, their experiences and their profiles." Because of the VET system's compliance requirements, Maggie believed that she had to "force the students continually into learning outcomes—that are not necessarily what they want." Her experiences with adults' reactions to the systemic expectations that they achieve literacy as "communicative competence" were disorienting because:

Many were amazed at the sheer number and scope of the learning outcomes. One man wailed, "but I just want to learn to read." He could not perceive the connections between speaking to a group, taking telephone orders or filling in forms and reading.

Terry's response illustrates her tactics of engagement as she brokers compliance with such tensions and dilemmas:

I just say, well, I think this equates. I don't take it as purely prescriptive, I just take it as a guide and I then introduce a whole range of different things. People usually choose what they like the best and what's going to suit them. Then I see where that's going to fit in. I don't use it as "must do." Sometimes I prefer to be creative rather than just follow. I don't like following rules particularly.

In these instances, teachers were faced with students' expectations that they would be learning a "literacy" that was meaningful within the contexts of what they, as adults, understood literacy to be. This means that there are contexts-of-relevance that are dependent upon adult students' wants and needs. This finding supports Walters' (1997: 10) contention that, "globally, the majority of people manifestly engage with learning for their own purposes and interest when it is to meet a social, economic, political or technical need." If they wished to remain "student centered" teachers, then Catherine, Maggie, and Terry's compliance with their students' conceptualizations of literacy had to be brokered against both their own and the system's different, if not conflicting, conceptualizations of adult literacy and adult literacy education.

Teachers brokered their compliance with the VET system in four ways. First, they identified complexities within the VET system's curriculum frameworks, not only for their students, but also for themselves, their employers, and other stakeholders. Second, they questioned the relevance of these complexities for their own work and their students' lives. Thirdly, they made connections to their knowledge and understandings about the VET system. Finally, based upon prior knowledge and understanding of adults as students and their reasons for wanting to learn, teachers "traded off" decisions of what would and would not be implemented from the VET system's curriculum policies.

First, from transcripts of professional development sessions with adult literacy teachers the complexities of curriculum frameworks were identified. For instance, working through policies such as the National Reporting System (Coates, Fitzpatrick, McKenna, and Makin, 1995), teachers identified a range of issues. These included the physical layout of the policy, in particular, each of the five level descriptors and the discourse of the text (i.e., the "language bits" that carry a high lexical density and nominalization). There were also concerns about the lack of clear statements about what literacy is understood to be and the relationship between six aspects of communication and five levels of competence. To these were added each level of competence, the relationship between five indicators of competence plus three conditions of performance across three workplace and social contexts, six assessment principles, together with four language and literacy features and performance strategies, as well as four numeracy features and performance strategies.

Second, teachers asked questions of these curriculum policies. As Peter pointed to a page of the syllabus that listed learning outcomes, he asked his colleagues, "Having done this, is that going to make them really any more literate than they would be?" Rebecca wondered, "What room is there for me in my teaching?" Denise later echoed Peter's concerns when she posed the question, "Can such a complex web of skills, meaning-making, and individual differences be adequately slotted into a framework of levels and performance criteria?" The VET system constructs adult literacy within competency-based training and assessment frameworks. This framework was found to be both conceptually incoherent and contentious to implement. Significantly, these teachers questioned the relevance of the superordinate fragmentation of adult learning represented in these policies. The teachers also indicated their unease with the contentiousness that this reductionist, piecemeal conception of adult education brought to teacher-learner relationships.

Third, making connections with their existing knowledge and emerging understanding of the VET system was a feature of brokering compliance, with its competency-based curriculum frameworks. Because of his trade background, Kerry was familiar with outcomes-based education in the form of training packages. However, he acknowledged that, "I'd imagine someone who hasn't come across learning outcomes before would find them to be rather constraining." Chris knew enough about the VET system to understand the National Reporting System (NRS) to be a "very very powerful document—gives the standards." For Ed, this meant "getting the linkages together with all that paperwork—there's a vast quantity of paperwork to get a handle on...just getting the whole philosophy of the different—NRS to the AQF and Mayer key competencies." While "getting the linkages" was identified as a complex task for teachers because of the system's conceptual incoherence, tensions and dilemmas remained because they believed that adults in their local communities would neither be able to, nor want to make these linkages with such constructions of "literacy." During professional development sessions, Peter and Kevin shared this view:

> even someone who worked at the Commonwealth Employment Service [now known as Centrelink] or the Department of Education, Science and Technology or the local office—who's going to have access to that knowledge? (Peter)

> It begs the question, doesn't it—we talk about—transparent curriculum and sharing the curriculum and empowerment and student-centred learning—if they're level 1, they're not going to be able to read that document. (Kevin)

Here, concern is expressed that adults in local communities may not be able or want to engage with the language used to talk about literacy. Nor may they believe that such a framing of literacy is worthwhile to either their learning needs, or those of their clients (in the case of employment agency staff) or employers. For these teachers, the tenets of adult education were being breached because, professionally, they believed that they could not use these VET system curriculum policies in a transparent process, in which they shared with their adult students the joint development of their curriculum.

Fourth, trading off what will and will not be implemented from a syllabus to report against levels of competency always involved the teachers using their knowledge and understanding of their students as adults who may or may not want to learn. Eleanor was familiar with the syllabus' compliance requirements and its conceptualization of literacy, but she did not let it constrain her into making decisions prior to working with her students because, "You wait really until you see—*who* you've got—and then *what*." This iterative curriculum development process, through which she brokered compliance between the syllabus and her students, continued throughout their time together.

Robyn argued that this dialogic process constituted a challenge for adult literacy teachers in their relationships with their students because "understanding the adult learner is not a static activity that is fixed at the beginning of an adult literacy program." It is "an ever-changing, fluid component" of adult literacy teaching. From his own experiences, Kerry supported this position, since, "you can't size everyone up straight away—you learn all the time." Together with the students "We build on knowledges—we move out from there." From this study, the research data suggests that brokering compliance is not a "one-off" activity. It is part of a continual dialogue involving the teachers, their colleagues, and the VET system's policies, as well as their students.

Socializing Global/Local Futures in Adult Education

These adult literacy teachers neither slavishly complied with the VET system's requirements for literacy teaching/learning, nor did they fully comply with their own or their students' expectations for teaching and learning. In their tactics of engagement with both the system and adults as students, the teachers brokered compliance through varied, contextually contingent practices. Through compliance brokerage, they engaged in what Giroux (1990; 1992) termed a "border pedagogy." They decentered the competing interests created by the VET system as they remapped their relationships and interactions across adult education. As a feature of contemporary globalization, border pedagogy is characterized by brokering compliance through the creative appropriation of spaces in which alternate readings of ideologies and power are framed, debated, and coordinated.

Central to this proposition is Edwards' (1997: 182) contention that "society is not a bounded entity, but an interactive space of multiple shared sentiments, collective bonds and customs, of sociality." Global society is characterized by heterogeneity, reflected in and responded to through adult education. Yet when working with the homogenizing potentialities of social and economic globalization as interpreted by Australia's VET system, it is the unbounded incoherence created by institutionalized education, harnessed through brokering compliance as part of teachers' work.

Adult educators in this study are working with "power at its extremities, in its ultimate destination, with those points where it becomes capillary...in its more regional and local forms and institutions" (Foucault, 1980: 96). At its extremities, in its regional and local forms, the VET system's power is met with the heterogeneous power of local communities. One risk in brokering compliance with this power is that adult educators may be de-professionalized. Wickert (1997), Kell (1998), and Chappell (1999) warned that as the VET system has been entrenched throughout Australia, adult educators were at risk of working in contradiction to their professional ethics, beliefs, knowledges, and values. This remains an inherent danger when engaging in the pedagogical work of brokering compliance within and across the complex and contentious power relations prevailing in adult education.

Conclusion

The tenor of these research findings is marginally optimistic. At the interface of policy and practice, these adult literacy teachers have retained a sense of professional identity and a fulfilling sense of a worthwhile role in society. The weight of the VET system's ideology centers on the economic imperative for adult education while marginalizing its social imperatives. This poses challenges for adult educators' engagement with the VET system's coordination of power as expressed through its organization of teachers' work. This chapter explored adult literacy teachers' creation of spaces for their practices; spaces that were not acknowledged by their students, the VET system, or the organizations which employed them. In these spaces, they brokered compliance with the system and students as a means of engaging with both dimensions of their work as teachers and employees. Through their compliance brokerage practices, these adult educators were engaging with the economic, social, technological, and political dimensions of globalization as enacted locally. The future of adult education is not entirely within the purview of nation-states, nor its integrated economies and technologies. It lies within the multi-dimensional, complex, and connective relationships between people as they establish networks, coordinate power relations, and reconfigure identities as their work changes.

References

Australian Committee for Training Curriculum ACTRAC. *National Framework of Adult English Language, Literacy and Numeracy Competence.* Frankston, Victoria: ACTRAC, 1994.

Australian National Training Authority ANTA. *Australian Quality Training Framework.* cited 31 October, 2001. Available from http://www.anta.gov.au.

Beck, U. *What Is Globalization?* Translated by P. Camiller. Cambridge, UK: Polity Press, 2000.

Chappell, C. "Identity, Location and the Making of Adult Educators." Paper presented at the SCUTREA, 29th Annual Conference, University of Warwick, U.K., 5–7 July 1999.

Coates, S., L. Fitzpatrick, A. McKenna, and A. Makin. *National Reporting System.* Melbourne: Language Australia, 1995.

de Certeau, M. *The Practice of Everyday Life.* Translated by S. Rendall. Berkeley, CA: University of California Press, 1984.

Edwards, R. *Changing Places? Flexibility, Lifelong Learning and a Learning Society.* London: Routledge, 1997.

Foucault, M. *Power/Knowledge: Selected Interviews and Other Writings 1972–1977.* Brighton, Sussex: Harvester Press, 1980.

———. *The Archeology of Knowledge.* London: Tavistock, 1972.

Gee, J. P. *An Introduction to Discourse Analysis: Theory and Method.* London and New York: Routledge, 1999.

———. *Social Linguistics and Literacies: Ideology in Discourses*. 2nd ed. London: Taylor and Francis, 1996.

Giroux, H. *Border Crossings: Cultural Workers and the Politics of Education*. London: Routledge, 1992.

———. *Curriculum Discourse as Postmodernist Critical Practice*. Geelong, Victoria: Deakin University, 1990.

Kell, P. "New Challenges and New Futures for VET Teaching." *Literacy Link*. (1998) 2–5.

Macdonell, D. *Theories of Discourse: An Introduction*. Oxford, U.K.: Basil Blackwell, 1986.

Prakash, A., and J. A. Hart. "Coping with Globalization: An Introduction." In *Coping with Globalization,* edited by A. Prakash and J. A. Hart. London: Routledge, 2000.

Scollay, M. "CEO's Message." *Australian Training* (2002): 3.

Singh, M., B. Harreveld, and N. Hunt. "Virtual Flexibility: Adult Literacy and New Technologies in Remote Communities." Rockhampton, Queensland, Central Queensland University, Research Centre for Open and Distance Learning: Queensland Adult English Language, Literacy and Numeracy (QAELLN) Council, 1997.

Smyth, J., A. Dow, R. Hattam, A. Reid, and G. Schacklock. *Teachers' Work in a Globalizing Economy*. London: Falmer Press, 2000.

Walters, S. *Globalization, Adult Education and Training: Impacts and Issues*. London: Zed Books, 1997.

Wickert, R. "Where to Now for Adult Literacy?" *Literacy Link*. 1997 cited 5 August, 2001, Available from http://www.acal.edu.au/publications/papers/occasional/rosie_wickert_article.html.

Chapter 11

Educating Adult Researchers: Mitigating Neo-conservative Globalism and Mediating Eco-cultural Sustainability

Michael Singh and Lynne Nengying Li

Introduction

The "enterprise" of adult education now provides the parameters governing research education in nation-states throughout the Minority World. An overly deterministic view of this enterprise holds that it is a monolithic and invariable state apparatus. However, such a description can only reproduce the very structures that many, if not most, adult educators seek to displace. It is also at odds with evidence of the enterprise of adult education as being unstable, if not crisis ridden, due to its embodiment of both repressive and dangerous attributes, as well as enabling characteristics (Bourdieu, 1998).

Taking as its point of reference as the struggles over innovations in post-industrial education for eco-cultural sustainability (Oviedo, Maffi, and Larsen, 2000; Singh, 2001), this chapter conceptualizes a framework for tactically engaging the shaping the training—and education—of adult researchers. As will become evident, this has implications for extending and deepening the professional repertoire of adult educators responsible for mentoring research students. Considerable effort is being invested in rethinking the education and training of adult researchers in, for and against the contradictory currents that are constituted by competition among the powerful forces imposing "globalization from above." This includes the resistant forces of global/local civil society seeking "globalization from below" as well as the agents of innovative projects that treat the "global" and "local" as problematic. Tactically, the struggle is to identify the contradictions arising from the negative moments in critiques and to build on the positive potential of resentment so as to engage the nodes of hope glimpsed in between.

Weighted down by the intensification of work and faced with the weakened collegial structures of unions and professional associations, often all that seems possible for some adult educators is finding ways of surviving in the interstices between whingeing passivity and the slow, relentless pursuit of neo-conservative globalism. However, Walters (2000: 197, 206) has suggested developing students' research strategies to help disaffected and alienated adults survive the harsh conditions created by the local/global capitalist economy. This includes developing their research capabilities for participating in the multicultural and political global/local civil society, as well as research skills for working in the informal economy and engaging in the transnational labor market.

This position holds that adult educators work the gaps in the boundaries between competing orientations arising from the transitions in globalization. By questioning unsustainable economic consumerism and overdevelopment, adult educators can point to the threats to the global/local sustainability of democracy, economic well-being, and ecological and multicultural diversity. Translating the dangerous opportunities provided by the enterprise of adult education means drawing out—and drawing adult educators' attention to—new and, albeit limited, spaces of freedom. The cost of this freedom requires innovative tactics for engaging this enterprise and the ideology of neo-conservative globalism that drives it. Adult educators variously experience this relentless, thirty-year-old ideological project as cult of franchise management, economic reductionism, or as a seductive third way to neo-conservative globalism (Singh, 1990).

Neo-conservative Globalism and the Enterprise of Adult Education

The enterprise of adult education is a productive site of incitement, interdiction, and contradictions. For instance, while this enterprise insists on the exotic project of globalizing English, the multiple languages spoken by its transnational students express the complexity of the human minds it claims to be educating. There are uncertainties in this enterprise's use of multiple languages to construct itself as a global institution, to negotiate transnational business deals, and to weave staff and students into its cosmo-political fabric. Despite public relations fantasies of a singular, unified "global English," this instability precludes attempts to give the enterprise of adult education the appearance of unity. This is especially so given the multiple languages by which it targets markets in different cultures. Rather than being totalizing in its constraints, the fragmented, stress-ridden politics of this enterprise makes it constitutive and enabling of productive, innovative possibilities for educating adult researchers. Admittedly, these innovations are as limited, compromised, and constrained as educational reforms have always been. Public goods such as research knowledge are open to expropriation by the powerful agents of neo-conservative globalism for private purposes neither anticipated nor intended. Four practices are integral to the manufacture of neo-conservative imaginings of what and how to constitute adult education.

Reconstituting Mechanisms of Governance Using Quasi-economic Models of Regulation

The first practice for the manufacture of neo-conservative imaginings of adult education as a "business enterprise" involves disciplining research education through the regulatory mechanism of quasi-economic models. The ideology of neo-conservative globalism is being used to reduce government responsibility for citizens' social and economic security. Instead, government disinvestment in research education is forcing people to deal with risk management as a personal rather than a collective undertaking. Adults are being pressed into being flexible enough to willingly submit to the compulsion to be forever reinventing themselves by paying for reeducation throughout their lives. The privatization of risk management is evident in efforts to lower citizens' expectations regarding the state's provision of public goods such as adult education. Research education is being incited into intense competition by setting loose the regulatory power of global/local market forces. However, power is unevenly and inequitably distributed among participants in the global/local marketplace. For instance, in publicly acknowledging this, the World Wide Fund for Nature (WWF) recognizes the crucial role of, and difficulties inherent in forming coalitions committed to education for, and the sustainability of ecological and multicultural diversity, but accepts the need

> to support Indigenous and traditional peoples in finding ways to develop and strengthen their cultures and societies while sustainably managing their resources.

> This is a difficult and complex challenge in times of globalization and expanding economic and market forces; a task that requires cooperation and alliances, both locally and globally. (Oviedo, Maffi, and Larsen, 2000: 1)

The state is still a key actor in the market, creating legislation to de-structure the common wealth and providing huge private sector subsidies. For over three decades the state has been ever so gradually de-structuring the very public goods established to provide citizens with the socio-economic security necessary to counter market inefficiencies and failures. The underwriting of public social and economic security through the creation of common wealth or public goods one provided the vehicle by which the state has secured its legitimation within civil society. Departing from this social contract, the state continues to willfully create a meaner, profit-driven corporatized system of adult education enterprises. Given this ideological commitment to institutionalse the regulatory force of global/local markets, neo-conservatives work to convert research education into transnational franchises that provide mass and niche business lines ostensibly determined by market need.

Adult education institutions have been invited as often as they are forced into the global/local market as "for-profit ventures." They are expected to generate a multi-million-dollar budget surplus to compensate for government dis-investment. This has bow become an imperative driving some senior managers keen to secure the pay rises, bonuses and other privileges their power makes it possible for them to demand. The competitive struggle over economic, socio-political, and multicultural resources means only the fittest—or most corrupt—are likely to survive without state intervention. Notable exceptions to regulation by market forces include political patronage, in the case of regional education institutions and privileged research fields, such as biomedical technology. The latter offers aging elites the promise of an even longer life, perhaps even a cure for death, the former provides much needed political legitimation.

The goals of this neo-conservative project are to transform research education into corporately managed, moneymaking enterprises governed by the businesses rules used to control the knowledge, "owners" and work practices of many franchises, and to create a consumer culture among adult earner-learners gratified by market-driven desires. Fee-paying students (mostly from overseas, and therefore mostly bilingual) are "simply seen as present and future consumers by people who only care whether a profit is made off of them" (Apple, 2001: 184). The business rules focus on the "flexible accumulation" of credentials via "reusable learning objects" and the use of parental concerns about "economic and political insecurity" to market education as a vehicle for entering the mobile global/local labor market.

Increasingly, the local/global market in English-only pedagogy and politics is becoming the arbiter of worthwhile research education and a contributing factor to the unsustainability of the world's eco-cultural diversity (Oviedo, Maffi, and Larsen, 2000). For the adult education enterprise, this means that commercial issues, including the commodification of English language teaching, are very important determinants in research education. Increased productivity and a substantial return on investment, in terms of research project completions, income-generation, and refereed publications, are expected from the market-driven allocation of declining public funds. Much of Australia's public budget is being devoted to the program of global/local militarization sponsored by the not-so-united States of America and the want-to-be great again Britain.

Despite rhetoric to the contrary, there has been no reduction in or minimization of state activity or retreat from its role in the governance of adult education. There has been a shift in the state's controls for putting into effect franchise management to produce an improved "bottom line." As Williamson-Fien (2000: 45) argues, neo-conservative politics has reinvented and repositioned the state within new problematics of governing.

On the one hand, neo-conservativism is a bipartisan political intervention by the parties of both labor and capital which problematizes all aspects of public education, including the education of adult researchers. It rejects the funding needed to produce researchers and dismisses the productive pedagogical relationship between adult educators and research students. On the other hand, this governmental coalition multiplies the domains of research education that are being de-structured by market forces, as well as intensifying the surveillance technologies designed to effect changes in research education. Neo-conservative state extensions of the regulatory power of market relations to create an enterprise of adult education has induced exclusionary forms of governance. However, as argued below, this may also open up possibilities for the exercise of new (but nevertheless limited) forms of freedom for generating innovative approaches to the education of adult researchers.

Calculative Regimes of Performance and Valued Expertise

Marketing and legitimating reductionist "fast-research training" agenda to those who exist in and live day-to-day with its effects is but one strategy in the omnipresent political work of neo-conservative globalism. A compliance regime is also used to contain those adult educators who express alienation or resistance, as much as those who see merit in promoting alternative ideas, relationships and work practices by investing their passion and effort in creating innovative initiatives. The franchise managers have expropriated a disproportionate amount of funds provided for the research education of adults to recruit the consultant courtiers and complaisant technocrats used to make the audit tools for effecting the de-structuring of innovations in research and research education (Strathern, 2000). They give affect to the techniques of neo-conservative control via regimes of reductive accountability, high-stakes measurement, tight product control, ideological assessment of corporate loyalty or "value fit". There is a naïve security found in dealing with abstract figures in preference to the lived realities of adult educators. They develop centrally prescribed and controlled techniques using ever-advancing technologies as tools for privatizing public assets, for sponsoring competition between and within adult education enterprises, and for corporatizing the procedures governing research education.

Franchise managers work to enhance both state control and market-based regulation by developing disciplinary mechanisms for evaluating the success or failure of these enterprises in educating adult researchers. This involves "importing business models and tighter systems of accountability into education [and by] giving new meaning to the lives of managers" (Apple, 2001: 30). This includes mobilizing such control mechanisms as the triple-chin bottom lines, benchmarks, best practice assertions, ivy-league tables, imbalanced scorecards, productivity targets, and performativity indicators. These technologies are used to measure the ideological submission of adult educators to the agenda of neo-conservative globalism, in much the same way as "kill ratios" and "body counts" were used to "win" the US/American war against Vietnam (Singh, 1989).

Rather than rolling back the power of the state, the pedagogical work of adult educators is now subject to its increasing intervention. State regulation and scrutiny is effected via practices that test document control regimes and compliance procedures: this "regime of control is based not on trust, but on a deep suspicion of the motives and competence of teachers" (Apple, 2001: 51). These increasing forms of performance surveillance created by the evaluative state intensify adult educators' never-ending experience of perpetual manipulation. This punctures the very trust on which all multicultural enterprises operate, replacing the pursuit of truth with the public relations cult of image management. The problem for the ideologues of corporate managerialism is that original research is an open-ended undertaking that necessarily generates novel contributions to theory construction, provides for the thorough analysis of existing knowledge claims, and tests the defensibility of interpretations against empirical data.

The pedagogies of adult educators are wedded to their students' interests, their changing discipline, their professional community, and the sustainability of the research education system they helped to build. However, because they are keen to publicly discuss dangers to global/local public goods, they are no longer trusted by neo-conservative ideologues. Those who ask questions without prior notice, make critiques, of the incompetence and deceitfulness of some senior managers or register dissent are attacked and vilified, just as were those citizens who did likewise with respect to the USA-UK-Australian wars of vengeance (Silberstein, 2002). Likewise, any public debate engendered over corporate managerialism and the nightmares created by its impact on the education of adult researchers, or knowledge producers, are held to be disloyal, if not treacherous. Nevertheless lapel buttons carry the slogan: "Neoconservativism is anti-educational!"

This low-trust environment arises from the unreconstructed professional identity, skills, and judgments of adult educators, and their lack of desire to legitimate and protect the neo-conservative project of imposing globalisation from above (Walters, 2000: 199). In response, the neo-conservative regulatory state and its apparatchik demand "the constant production of evidence that one is in fact making an enterprise of oneself" (Apple, 2001: 75). Because not every adult educator can be trusted to be continually making entrepreneurial researchers of themselves, the tools of franchise management are used to reduce their academic freedom and to constrain their power for professional discretion.

The manufacture of successful imaginings of the adult education enterprise relies on the establishment and deployment of new calculative regimes. This repertoire of monocultural technologies of power embodies forms of expertise which have a myopic focus on constructing supposedly measurable outcomes that give emphasis to the production, management, and assurance of control. It is these technologies of auditing which now have a high status in the hierarchy of political values privileged by some senior managers in adult education enterprises. Through these technologies, adult educators are now being continually monitored and evaluated. Their pedagogical work is reduced to a series of (inconsequential) indicators of performance, with unpredictable and unjustified business judgements being made about how "appropriate" forms of conduct can be induced. Adult educators are now held responsible to the contestable claims of these accountancy criteria.

This means that the claims to truth and expertise valorized by adult educators have been breached so that their work is now opened up to programs of neo-conservative governance (Williamson-Fien, 2000). The ambiguous and insubstantial concepts of "work-related learning" and "lifelong learning" have been mobilized to remove teachers, community formation, knowledge production, and the public good from considerations of research education. These concepts have been mobilised to de-emphasize government responsibility for the institutional provision of education for its citizens and to use advancing technologies to challenge the pedagogical and disciplinary knowledge of adult educators. Such technologies are advocated as the means whereby adult learners will have individualized, teacher-less access to information, so as to privatize different aspects of adult education provision. The expertise and identities of adult educators as mediators of adult learning is being devalued as those charged with surveillance contend for the key role in adult education.

Each adult is expected to engage in her/his own individualized learning: "As the state retreats from responsibility for provision the onus is on individuals to engage in lifelong learning to keep abreast of developments in the marketplace" (Walters, 2000: 201). Moreover, any positive value attached to the centering of adult learners in the economic reductionist policies driving adult education merely add to "the pressure placed on people to continue learning while existing in vulnerable work situations" (Walters, 2000: 208). Within this meshwork of power, experts who assure these controls have been made crucial to the hegemony and ideology of corporate managerialism. These calculative regimes are now a key site of expert power in the adult education enterprise, not the adult educators.

Legitimizing and Naturalizing Adult Education as an "Enterprise"

The third practice used in the manufacture of imaginings of an adult education enterprise involves generating neo-conservative frameworks that make highly selective meanings of the dis-ordering that has been imposed on the very bodies of adult educators and their research students. The elaboration of this enterprise involves the legitimation and naturalization of the practices of technologization, commodification, and globalization of research education. In this regard, much effort has been devoted to the development of an entrepreneurial and competitive corporation delivering reusable learning objects via distributive digital technology.

The relentless de-structuring of the common wealth—the local/global public good—being effected in the interest of neo-conservative globalism is done by disguising this ideological project in the language of liberal progressivism. This creates the ambiguities franchise management requires to undermine the formation of creative and innovative alliances from below. Here, its quest for power is concealed in "accords" or "enterprise bargains" between management and unions that trade salary indexation for work intensification, job dissatisfaction, and insecure employment. Over there its coercive force is deceptively shielded behind the compensatory empowerment of (Anglo-ethnic) women carefully selected for their ability to wear the mask of "reasonableness" and their capacity to willfully manage the franchising of the adult education enterprise. Everywhere it has involved the de-structuring of the work units of adult educators in order to marginalize their positioning within hierarchies of power, and to de-structure their professional identity.

The neo-conservative vision is to institutionalize the extension of the market throughout the fabric of the adult education enterprise. This means structuring the game of enterprise, and commodifying the whole assemblage of adult research education, from recruitment, retention, and completion through funding and pedagogy, to publications. Neo-conservative governance operates through the institutionalization of the regulatory force of the market to ensure the optimal operation of self-disciplinary technologies. While these technologies suggest individual autonomy for both research students and adult educators, the reconfiguring of governance into market forms greatly enhances the possibility the state has for manipulating these individuals. They are rendered perpetually responsive to shifts in the politics of the world's multilingual knowledge economies.

Neo-conservative governance constructs research students simplistically as self-interested consumers seeking to maximize their individual welfare by optimizing their research education through their own supposedly "free" choices. Here, there is no appreciation of the structuring of people's decisions or interests by multicultural norms or socio-economic conditions of possibility. Within this mode of governance, the point is to use the English language, for instance, as an anti-market mechanism to mobilize research students to equate their interests with those of business and technology, as well as to construct and understand themselves as members of an English-only global economy. Battles in the adult education enterprise around languages are being fought over whether research students can use their first language, and under what conditions. Given the bilingual abilities of research students from around the world, the adult education enterprise claims it has the unilateral right to decide which language can be used in producing meaningful knowledge. Likewise, the capacity of international students to make meaningful contributions to research has been invested in one powerful language, English, which is now the focus of an education industry of global proportions (Singh, Kell, and Pandian, 2002).

Appropriating Critiques of Neo-conservative Globalism

The marginalization, if not exclusion, of adult educators from processes of governance in the adult education enterprise, and the capture and deployment of the research agenda by corporate managerialism, offers a focus for critique. But, perhaps surprisingly, a fourth practice in the manufacture of imaginings of adult education as a shared-holder controlled business enterprise is the use of ideological critiques of research education to construct models for neo-conservative governance (Williamson-Fien, 2000). Critiques pointing to past research as the reason for the current lack of business and technological innovations are used to construct research education and adult educators as the source and cause of this problem. Expressions of frustration, despair, and stress among adult educators are interpreted by corporate managerialists as indicators of their success in destructuring the public good and effecting the losses privatisation seeks. Such critiques are read as signs of the very success of the neo-conservative attack on adult education, thereby reinforcing the project that adult educators least desire.

Critiques are either used to provide a resource to serve the neo-conservative agenda or otherwise ignored. This provides adult educators little more reassurance than "feel-good" diversionary therapy. For instance, critiques of the performance indicators now used to revalue and redirect the research of adult educators by recreating publications as the marketing tool for securing competitive funding from external sources have long been silently overlooked as distracting irritations (Singh, 1990). What is criticized as a narrowing of adult research education to instrumental, reductionist goals is celebrated by neo-conservatives as enabling the undercutting of the unified system of adult education via competitive segmentation within and across different institutions.

Those who produce the critiques of the adult education enterprise are made objects neo-conservative repression. They necessarily find themselves unavoidably implicated or otherwise involved, the neo-conservative agenda. For this reason, if for no other, it is important not to foreclose fruitful investigations into the productive possibilities created by the emergence of this enterprise and its new technologies of adult research education. This tactic recommends itself for another reason, namely, that contemporary regimes of adult education may not be any more instrumental than they were in the past.

Despite claims to autonomy, adult education has consistently been breached by governmental technologies across a range of issues, such as curriculum relevance, its insistence on graduating students with stronger bilingual potential, and many more technical, work-related skills. Neo-conservative irrationalities merely represent new forms of continuity in governance. In some respects, this may not be quite so radical a departure from the past as some critiques suggest. There is evidence from early in the twentieth century of adult education being pursued in the interests of national industry, economic prosperity and security (Meredyth, 1998).

Hostile takeovers of the curriculum and pedagogical work of adult educators makes asset stripping—especially the de-skilling of the profession—integral to efforts to institutionalise franchising as the new business model for adult education enterprises. This involves combining a corporate brand name and marketing scheme with the centralization of the control and management of knowledge through the packaging of formulaic, reusable "learning" objects, and then licensing clusters of adult education functionaries to compete as surrogate small businesses for short-term, rigid, and de-limiting contracts. Old Macdonald no longer wants to own a farm, but prefers instead to make more money from mass marketing images of success through a regime made up of dependent franchisees over whom ever more encompassing power and excruciating controls are enacted.

Further, attempts to depict adult education institutions as idealized sites for the training of adult researchers are also questionable. Any suggestion that they were or should constitute the one—best—site for perfecting the production of researchers is misplaced. Research education has always combined, somewhat problematically, the means of ensuring the social and economic security of the state by training productive and linguistically intelligent researchers and by disciplining the nation's morality through the surveillance audits researchers undertake (Meredyth, 1998).

Stand-alone adult education institutions have always provided an assemblage of contingent and limited solutions for dealing with the nation-state's grab bag of moral and material exigencies.

Neo-conservative globalism has sanctified the geopolitical interests of the powerful Anglophone coalition of the willful and their corporations. The questionable claim they make is that there are no viable alternatives to the intensification of globalized market competition, ecologically unsustainable policies of destructive overdevelopment, and the continuing marginalization and deprivation of billions of people in the Majority World (Walters, 2000: 199). This project also involves exporting the blame for the detrimental consequences of neo-conservative decisions onto research education and adult educators for refusing to make entrepreneurs of themselves. Dominating economic interests blame the state for recurring market inefficiencies and failures, such as the creation of excessive salary packages for franchise managers. In turn, the neo-conservative state deals with its own legitimation crises in a similar manner. The state exports the blame for its privatization of the risk management associated with the education of a new generation of researchers onto adult educators and adult education enterprises. With the four practices reviewed in this section in mind, what possibilities present themselves for innovative approaches to educating adult researchers?

Educating Adult Researchers for Making Innovations in Enterprising Eco-cultural Communities

The adult education "enterprise" itself enables a range of research education opportunities to be identified and valued. It also points to ways in which the expertise of adult educators might be extended and deepened to address the problems of continuity and change in the transition from industrial to post-industrial education and work (http://www.iah.bbsrc.acuk/TAPPS/). Where economic reductionism is privileged and economic irrationalities are left unquestioned, this enthrones some areas of research concentration and disqualifies others. Specifically, research education in the humanities is now research in, about, and for technology and business. It is now these latter research fields that claim to represent the "real world" and which most easily secure financial resources and status.

In these circumstances, if despair can no longer mobilise the heroism of collective resistance, then we seem to be left with frighteningly ambivalent questions. How, might adult educators working in the humanities achieve (political and economic) status as well as (state and business) support through the integration of adult research education into this agenda? Is this a defensible aspiration? Could the need for adult educators and their newly corporatised institutions develop innovative approaches for their mutual survival by marshaling the productive moments of resistance to engage gaps in the neo-conservative armor?

No doubt adult educators will continue to debate whether research education in humanities should use abstract, positivist forms of inquiry. Otherwise, we could be left with drawing on survey techniques to conduct market research in order to secure status and financial survival. This is a crucial question given the marginalization of research and research education that the state superficially judges to be technologically irrelevant or lacking economic utility. It also suggests concerns about the degree of control adult educators have over the circumstances under which they display their expertise as research supervisors and mentors. At the very least, this raises questions for research students to investigate:

- How might research in the humanities be tactically articulated as part of an economic and technological matrix?
- What can students engaging in humanities research learn from research undertaken in the fields of business and technology?
- How might research, which is demonstrably of real multicultural, socio-political, economic, and technological value to the world be evaluated?
- What tactical adaptations need to be made to the "use value" for research in the humanities relative to that in business and technology?
- How might research students in the humanities tactically adapt to the shift in the balance of power towards technology and business?

While adult education enterprises may think they have achieved control of the language of pedagogy, they are increasingly being asked by research students to make provisions for languages "othered" by English. This is also disorienting for those Anglophone adult educators who believe that they control the language/s used in educating researchers. For instance, "blurring of boundaries" has been captured as a slogan to create the complexities and ambiguities needed to legitimise the de-structuring research education in order to establish franchisees. This stands in opposition to Indigenous and environmental struggles to use multiple knowledges for sustaining ecological and multicultural diversity:

> Flexibility across boundaries of established knowledge domains is increasingly accepted globally as necessary as new economic and social problems are addressed. Global competitiveness is driving a growing number of corporations around the world to adopt approaches to "risk management" that require them to have more holistic and integrated approaches to adult education and training. ...companies are "managing risks" [by] working with Indigenous people and managing the environmental impact.... This leads to agreements with local populations, which build on Indigenous knowledge [and languages] and incorporate some of the best participatory practice of community adult education...the importance of affirming Indigenous knowledge [and languages is that] it affirms human and environmentally sustainable values. (Walters, 2000: 206)

Consider for a moment the following practices as dynamic components in the education of research students for the multilingual knowledge economies and ethically responsible investment in the sustainability of ecological and multicultural diversity.

Learning from Problem-posing Feedback: Innovations Need Dissent

Refusal to engage and efforts to escape the neo-conservative illogics of the adult education enterprise now seem less likely, if not almost impossible. Nevertheless, a diverse and conflicting array of research programs struggle for power and influence to guide business and technological engagement in, with, and throughout the world. Given that research students in the humanities are expected to translate their interests into the needs for innovation in the business and technology sectors in this multilingual world, they could explore the possibilities for macro-socio-cultural innovation evident in the dissent which neo-conservative globalism has stimulated. Because further contestation can be anticipated, it could provide a focus in the education for innovation in eco-cultural sustainability.

Consider for a moment the "solutions" offered by the founder of the Body Shop—a transnational business corporation—to the market inefficiencies and failures of neo-conservative globalism, especially the dramatic erosion of "social capital." Anita Roddick (2001: 10) advocates an enterprising research program that is in direct competition with and is intended to create problems for the "secretive system of impersonal, international committees and cabals," which she sees as "competitive globalization from above." Roddick (2001: 10) characterizes this neo-conservative globalism as "the conspiracy of the rich against the poor," and she sides with the latter in their struggles to access resources for innovations in their lives.

Likewise, consider researching the business risks that might be more effectively managed through "change/continuity honesty." Evidence could be collected on the congenital inefficiencies, ineffectiveness, and huge costs of corporate change mismanagement and compared with "activist change/continuity management." These could include documenting evidence of suspicion and distrust; rumors and gossip; the waste of the knowledge, skills, and energy of adult educators; and student dissatisfaction. A well-researched account of problem-posing dissent could identify the contradictions and consequent gaps that offer nodal points for promoting bottom-up organizational learning about what an adult education enterprise might be in this post-industrial era:

> We who protest are recognized as powerbrokers in the globalization race. Change activists impact the value of your pension funds by highlighting moral gaps in some trade activity. Change activists are evolving as joint term setters for future market growth. ...Who wrote the rule saying when you sign the contract of employment you waive all rights to question company objectives? ...we need honest dissent at work—dialogue aimed at raising problems in order to fix them. ...how free are you to give honest feedback to the people who pay you? Feedback-rich firms/ teams/ individuals tend to be successful because learning happens with feedback. (McConnell, 2001: 8, 84, 85)

What opportunities exist for research students to explore the links and gaps between "change/continuity activist management," relevant moral or ethical principles, the development of compliance tools, and the success or failure of the adult education enterprise? Is it possible for research students to help the adult education enterprise to investigate ways of trading with trust; adding value to eco-cultural diversity as a means of strengthening its reputation; generating profits from morally responsible practices; or making the sustainability of eco-cultural diversity a source of competitive advantage?

Given the possibilities of bilingual and dual language education, students speaking languages "othered" by English in adult education enterprises understand themselves as being denied multicultural empowerment. Because language is part of students' social identities, to demean a student's first language by marginalizing it reflects a harmful prejudice. We know that "international students" have more difficulties in accessing and experiencing the pedagogy of research education than do many of their domestic counterparts (Deem and Brehony, 2000). The adult education enterprise has not, as yet, reconciled itself to the appreciation, integration and learning of different languages, let alone the world's multilingual knowledge economies. Nor has it engaged strategically with the complex and multi-layered understandings of the economic, political, multicultural, and localising practices of globalization from above and below.

Tactical Innovation: Reshaping the Education of Adult Researchers

Not withstanding the dominance of neo-conservative globalism, and given that projects of governance are not singular constructions, the elaborated repetition and reconfiguration of neo-conservative rhetoric does create opportunities for tactical innovations. Such tactics may lead to the dispersal and possible displacement of this agenda that constitutes the education for adult researchers, as much as they are open to containment through cooption. However, Spivak (1993: 65) suggests that there are "catachrestic spaces" wherein "words and concepts are wrested from their proper meaning" in ways that recode their value; this tactic for innovation interrupts dominating neo-conservative discourses by "tampering with the authority of the story lines." Thus, while one answer may lie in producing alternative forms of humanities research education, there may be another in practices of critical corporate literacy: mimicry, counter-construction, contrapuntal re-writing, and strategic reinterpretation (Singh, 1998). This involves unsettling, reconfiguring, and elaborating the dominating discourses that privilege the education of adult researchers in the fields of technology and business.

Appropriation is a tactic for innovation that recognizes the contestation, ambivalence, and uncertainty that prevails in the adult education enterprise in the desires of corporate managerialists to control every aspect of the research process, and in neo-conservative globalism more generally. Tactical innovation sees the research education agenda as unstable and not necessarily settled (Walters, 2000: 201). Therefore, it can be read (and rewritten) as open to recuperation and reformulation in a range of innovative ways, without necessarily reproducing or reinforcing it in any consistent or coherent manner. However, these re-workings do not offer any promises of escape from being compromised by the hegemonic project of neo-conservative globalism. Adult educators know the complex terrain over which students' research projects are constructed. Adult educators understand flexibility in work and workers, as well as appreciating that instrumental intentions are not always realized. This raises the possibilities to explore ways to analyze, translate, and elaborate, if not subvert, the economic reductionism driving the education of adult researchers.

Humanities researchers have used "appropriation" as a tactic for innovation by locating themselves within and accessing governmental resources in order to secure disciplinary survival, if not expansion. These tactics could prove preferable to either acquiescing to co-optable displacement or succumbing to the romance of resistance. Adapting to or resisting the demands of the new hierarchy of power governing research education are two contextually specific responses; "elaboration" is another tactic that offers possibilities for innovation (Singh, 2002). An in-depth study conducted over an extended time frame no longer suits the multi-tasking involved in adult education, let alone the short time horizon within which adult educators have to reconstitute themselves. If people are to survive, to live their lives through reinventing themselves by finding or taking on new tasks, then a mode of research education that enables them to document this multiplicity and then retrospectively produce an overarching meaning for it, could offer new "work"-related research.

A multi-task-based approach to research education could involve an adult educator investigating ethical investment companies via the collection of their publicity material and newspaper reports in order to contribute to teaching about eco-cultural sustainability. A subsequent project undertaken to inform the teaching of business marketing strategies could analyze the claims transnational corporations make about their ethical principles and assessing how financial commentators view them (Lewis, 2002). A third project, designed to contribute to teaching about justice and security, could examine the role of protests against corporate irresponsibility and unsustainable overdevelopment. A fourth project, built around the teaching of consumer education, could compare the information services provided by companies to ascertain their contribution to citizens' understanding, debate, boycotts (avoidance), and lobbying (active engagement). Constructing a narrative that gave new meaning to these disparate tasks in the work-life of a flexible adult educator would be undertaken retrospectively. Producing theoretical insights grounded in these disparate accounts could provide a scaffold within which to locate conclusions to this multi-task, evidence-rich research.

In this way, adult educators might bring their expertise to bear, acting as "appropriation devices" in reshaping the pedagogies of research education. This might be done by re-framing students' particular research concerns in terms that engage, but beat less totalizing, one-dimensional drums. This could include researching the calculative regimes being used and their role in the managerial crises now confronting the adult education enterprise. These crises are not just manifested in financial mismanagement and the failure to manage socio-technological changes, but, more importantly, in the "learning attention deficit" syndrome that afflicts senior management. For example, this could involve the inclusion evidence of deficiencies in the franchise managers of adult education enterprises to attend to "learning" as their core business, or the role international education is playing in knowledge death and language extinction. The World Wide Fund for Nature, for instance, is increasingly

> concerned about the loss of cultures and knowledge among Indigenous and traditional peoples. Traditional peoples have accumulated vast amounts of ecological knowledge in their long history of managing the environment. Such knowledge is embodied in languages. However, as languages become extinct, so associated traditional ecological knowledge is lost. (Oviedo, Maffi, and Larsen, 2000: 1)

Similarly, there is mounting concern over the loss of deep knowledge among the senior managers of adult education franchises about learning and teaching. This concern reinforced by managerial deficiencies in understanding the changing multuiculture and political economy of both learning and work (including teaching) in this post-industrial era.

Enterprising Partnerships: Assembling and Enlisting a Functioning Meshwork

It is as important as ever for adult educators to assist their research students in assembling a functioning mesh-work in and through which they learn that their interests can be construed as communal concerns and develop a shared discourse that constructs a basis for binding them together. For instance, there are many nodes in the ethical investment movement for making such alliances. These include seeking research (and employment opportunities) with companies that avoid: the manufacture of weapons, polluting the environment; testing of ephemeral products on animals, producing tobacco and alcohol, operating gambling houses, exploiting labor, including children in the Majority World, and supporting oppressive, anti-democratic regimes (Lewis, 2002: 4, 19, 59).

The point is for adult educators to assist students in exploring and developing ethically informed criteria for creating an alliance wherein they can increasingly frame their research as an apparatus for addressing problems of global/local significance. For example, Indigenous struggles over their intellectual property rights and entitlement to benefit from being made the "objects" of others research has given significant robustness to research ethics and associated knowledge claims. If nothing else, adult educators who have taken for granted their power, but now find their privilege being undermined by corporate managerialism can learn from Indigenous peoples. The Majority World generally have struggled to transform themselves from being the savagely abused victims of colonialism, and sought to disentangle the contradictions in a world that has brought them so much grief in order to make their lives worth living. Moreover, the marginalised have much to teach those who expect their colonizers to willingly forgo their power.

In developing an ethical framework for their research, students need to engage the debates over what it means to avoid harm and wrong (Miles and Huberman, 1994: 288–297). Likewise, research students need to be made aware that there are others who will be working to reformulate research ethics in ways that point to different, if not conflicting possibilities for practice. Nevertheless, adult educators can help students to associate their research projects with having potentially socially just benefits for a range of socio-cultural and ecological interests. This, in turn, means engaging industry, government and community partners in ways that enable recognition of research as an ethical undertaking especially when tactically translating these interests into students' research efforts.

A focus on innovation in and through research—in other words, a focus on critical in(ter)vention—could include the translation of openings in these mesh-works into career opportunities, as much as the articulation of shared vocabularies and the establishment of alliances around points of congruence (Miller and Rose, 1990). For instance, a positive moment in the ethical investment movement is its active engagement with companies making productive contributions to the sustainability of ecological and multicultural diversity (Lewis, 2002: 98–101). Thus, a second and interrelated dimension to developing and testing an ethical approach to the interdependencies inherent in their research sees students contributing to public discussions over what multicultural reciprocity means in everyday practice (Miles and Huberman, 1994: 288–297). Adult educators have the capacity to position research students in a loosely coupled, mobile, and indeterminate alignment with such partners, while taking responsibility for actively contributing to the public discussions about corporate ethics.

Through engaging with these mesh-works, it is possible for students to learn to give form to a common language about ethical partnerships and any long-term program of ethical research that might emerge. The expertise of adult educators is especially useful to accessing and learning how to operate and mesh-work industry partners that do business without doing eco-cultural harm (Suzuki and Dressel, 2002). Students can learn the skills needed to align their research objectives with partnerships in the agriculture, forestry, fishing, housing, and tourism industries that are working to restore eco-cultural diversity. These skills are important for translating mesh-work goals into their research interests.

The capabilities of adult educators are also useful in creating specific research projects that have the credibility of disinterested truth and offer possibilities for achieving timely outcomes. That is to say, adult educators have the know-how to generate and deploy conceptual tools, research methodologies, a rich range of evidence that speaks to various policy actors, and project management skills to meet regulatory requirements and carry authority with partners or stakeholders involved in any given industry. These include organizations and corporations as diverse as those working in public relations (www.adbusters.org); wildlife conservation (www.panda.org); predatory-friendly, holistic, and organic farming (www.lambandwool.com; www.phdc.com/wwoog), multicultural globalization strategies (www.crossculturalsolutions.org); fishing (www.conservefish.com; www.ecofish.com); and restaurants (www.whitedog.com; www.chefnet.com).

Researching the Problems of Governance: The Shifting Politics of State Intervention and Market Failures

The practices of governing the adult education enterprise are messier than the neo-conservative mind-set asserts. This is especially so given the constitutive role of resistance from below as well as transformative projects of innovation. But the governance of adult education institutions is perhaps more complicated due to inefficiencies, failures and errors steeped in the arrogance of some corporate managers. There is growing evidence of their false appraisals arising from superficial understandings, of government efforts to regulate education via a competitive trans-national market forces, as well as their faulty financial calculations due to what might be called a "learning deficit disorder" among senior franchise managers (see for example www.audit.vic.gov.au). This inability to understand education, research and research education is compounded by an incapacity of increasing numbers of corporate managers to understand the complexities of teaching/learning processes they seek to control. This reflects their lack of experience as academics; to few have any real world experience as lecturers, of engaging in academic debates or in testing their ideas via refereed publications.

This "learning deficit disorder" is evident in the undermining of the financial viability of adult education institutions. A case study of one organization found that this included the disastrous effects of mismanaging changes in its complex socio-technological systems; along with the failure to create organisational arrangements for producing a vibrant culture of scholarship and securing research funding (Hayes, 2003). Added to these was the mishandling of its multi-million dollar property portfolio; repeated failures in extremely risky international ventures, and the imposition of severe restrictions on communications about its operations in the face of popular democratic expectations for public openness and transparency. This included prohibiting students from its home-base visiting one or more of its offshore campuses. To date the outcomes of these business plans include a loss of at least $US 40,000 resulting in budgetary cuts, and reinforcing a mono-cultural business ethos of blaming the victims of senior management's incompetence. Those middle managers and innovative staff concerned about the organization's good name as a corporate citizen, its long-terms horizons, and the need to enhance its reputation, were rejected for promotion, and charged with not being "loyal" corporate players. Related outcomes include damaging the institution's brand name and diminishing its reputation internationally thereby undermining its own relative advantages; intensifying pressure on academics to raise revenue from full-fee paying overseas students, and resignations from academics concerned about the serious consequences of bad governance.

Because managerial plans of all sorts regularly fail to match the programmatic ambitions that informed them, at a huge emotional cost to adult educators and their students, governance can be seen as a practice that is marred by congenital failures (Rose and Miller, 1992). For instance, while White ethno-nationalist, English-only politics may secure the electoral capital government requires to press forward with neo-conservative globalism, neither are accepted by all Anglo-ethnics, Indigenous-, Asian-, or African-American, Britains on Australians. This inter-ethnic collaboration is manifested in civic opposition to the neo-conservative state's mandatory internment of asylum seekers. Not only does this contribute to their efforts to create alternative projects, even those seduced by them find little comfort from either the forces of neo-conservative globalism or White racism. Even efforts by migrants from the Majority World to acquire the attributes of "White-ness" are perceived as an unsettling menace by Anglo-nationalists. The state's mobilization of societal fears around anti-Asian and anti-Moslem prejudices offers nothing to redress the economic marginalization and social alienation created by government pursuit of neo-conservative politics (Singh, 2001).

With regard to the English language intensive courses for students from overseas, their graduates have been ambivalent when recommending research education programs offered in the Minority World to peers in their homelands (Li, 1999). They are often fulsome in their praise for teaching staff as well as those productive pedagogies and informal educational experiences that enhance their growing cosmopolitan identity. Their reticence is due to the revivification of White nation, English-only pedagogies and politics, and their exploitation by the neo-conservative political economy that uses full-fee paying students from overseas to compensate for government dis-investment in the research education, and thus the knowledge producing capacities of its own citizens. Thus, a multitude of small, apparently insignificant, disparate, and diffuse, interventions from below can affect the undoing of the deliberately meaning less dot-points franchise managers use to chart the de-structuring of adult education enterprises. The struggle by corporate headquarters to control the labor of its workforce, to appropriate and manage the knowledge of adult educators, and to effect the transition from one discursive formation to another is contradicted by the neo-conservative state as often as it is by the quavering uncertainties of corporate managerialism.

Given that the terrain of neo-conservative globalism is itself uncertain, contingent, and shifting, it is necessary to avoid conceptions of the adult education enterprise in terms that suggest it has well-thought-out and unified political ideals, economic doctrines, or managerial know-how. Given the problems of governance in this enterprise, it is important to recognize that the neo-conservative project has never been constituted as a comprehensive package. It has yet to demonstrate that it is destined to emerge as the preeminent political project for governing adult education, let alone society. Corruption, incompetence, and evasion of corporate responsibility, as well as the growing socio-economic inequalities produced by neo-conservative globalism continue to be met with protests.

There is no necessity for things being the way they are—it was not a matter of course or self-evident that the adult education enterprise should emerge. It is not necessary that it will stabilize in its current form. However, it is important for adult educators to identify those factors that enabled a given research education system to be imagined as "inevitable." The insistence on English as "given forever" as the global/local language is not without resistance. English-only pedagogy and politics is no longer just a unilaterally declared "normal" activity for this transnational enterprise. Increasingly, this linguistic prescriptivism is being commented on and criticized in the competitive adult education market.

Conclusion

In spite of the adult education enterprise being a corporate institution for dominating, de-structuring, and having authority over the education of adult researchers and their mentors, it is not a totalizing, invariable monolith. This enterprise is a hybrid field of diverse and complex representations with shifting and uncertain boundaries. The tactics proposed here do not seek to resolve tensions between the monoculture of research education and the politics of this enterprise. What is offered is a practice where different—marginalized—knowledges are tactically entered into the dominating discourses of business and technology.

The pluralization of the language of neo-conservative globalism and the elaboration of the franchise model of business may go some way to estranging the basis of their authority. At least the intention is to unsettle some of the contemporary certitudes that find expression in this ideology. By inciting the tactical use of the technical arts of governance in multilingual knowledge economies, through which neo-conservative irrationalities are initiated and deployed, new and educationally sound innovations in the education of adult researchers may be possible. Admittedly, these ideas have been developed retrospectively. Perhaps these ideas are not too late as neo-conservative governance promises to continue its function of inciting problems rather than being an expression of their resolution.

References

Apple, M. *Educating the "Right" Way: Markets, Standards, God, and Inequality.* New York: Routledge Falmer, 2001.

Bourdieu, P. *Acts of Resistance: Against the Tyranny of the Market.* New York: The New Press, 1998.

Deem, R., and K. Brehony. "Doctoral Students" Access to Research Cultures—Are Some More Unequal Than Others?" *Studies in Higher Education* 25, no. 2 (2000): 149–65.

Lewis, A. *Morals, Markets and Money: Ethical, Green and Socially Responsible Investing.* London: Pearson Education, 2002.

Li, L. "Grouping Practices and Individual Differences in Adult Esl Programs—with Special Reference to High English Language Achievers." Unpublished PhD Thesis, RMIT University, 1999.

McConnell, C. *Change Activist: Make Big Things Happen Fast*. Harlow: Pearson Education, 2001.
Meredyth, D. "Corporatising Education." In *Governing Australia*, edited by M. Dean and B. Hindess. Cambridge: Cambridge University Press, 1998.
Miles, M., and A. Huberman. *Qualitative Data Analysis*. 2nd ed. Thousand Oaks, CA: Sage, 1994.
Miller, P., and N. Rose. "Governing Economic Life." *Economy and Society* 19, no. 1 (1990): 1–31.
Oviedo, G., L. Maffi, and P. Larsen. *Indigenous and Traditional Peoples of the World and Ecoregion Conservation: An Integrated Approach to Conserving the World's Biological and Cultural Diversity*. Gland, Switzerland: WWF-World Wide Fund for Nature, 2000.
Roddick, A. *Take It Personally: How Globalization Affects You and Powerful Ways to Challenge It*. London: Thorsons Harper Collins, 2001.
Rose, N., and P. Miller. "Political Power Beyond the State: Problematics of Government." *The British Journal of Sociology* 43, no. 2 (1992): 173–205.
Silberstein, S. *War of Words: Language, Politics and 9/11*. London: Routledge, 2002.
Singh, M. "Re-Writing the Ways of Globalising Education?" *Race, Ethnicity & Education* 5, no. 2 (2002): 217–30.
———. "Advocating the Sustainability of Linguistic Diversity." In *Australia Policy Activism in Language and Literacy*, edited by J. Lo Bianco and R. Wickert. Melbourne: Language Australia, 2001.
———. "Critical Literacy Strategies for Environmental Educators." *Environmental Education Research* 4, no. 3 (1998): 341–354.
———. *Performance Indicators in Education*. Geelong: Deakin University: 1990.
———. "Measurement of progress: "Kill Ratio," "body Counts" and Other Performance Indicators." *The Australian Administrator* 10, no. 5 (1989): 1–7.
Singh, M., P. Kell, and A. Pandian. *Appropriating English: Innovation in the Global Business of English Language Teaching*. New York: Peter Lang, 2002.
Spivak, G. *Outside in the Teaching Machine*. New York: Routledge, 1993.
Strathern, M., ed. *Audit Cultures: Anthropological Studies in Accountability, Ethics and the Academy*. London: Routledge, 2000.
Suzuki, D., and H. Dressel. *Good News for a Change: Hope for a Trouble Planet*. St Leonards, N.S.W.: Allen & Unwin, 2002.
Walters, S. "Globalization, Adult Education, and Development." In *Globalization and Education: Integration and Contestation across Cultures*, edited by N. Stromquist and K. Monkman. Llanham: Rowman & Littlefield, 2000.
Williamson-Fien, J. "Constructing Asia: Foucauldian Explorations of Asian Studies in Australia." Unpublished PhD thesis, University of Queensland, 2000.

Part Four

Adult Learning, Technology, and Work

Chapter 12

Technological Literacy for Adults: Insights from Malaysia

Ambigapathy Pandian and Shanthi Balraj Baboo

Information and communication technologies (ICT) promise to educate and empower societies, being widely promoted as indispensable tools for individuals to lead their learning, economic, and social life and to participate as active citizens of local/global society. The rapid acceleration in the development and cross-border use of information and communication technologies has created many challenges in the field of adult education. Malaysia has taken heed of the importance of ICT. Many grand programs like Vision 2020, Smart School Integrated Solution, and the Multimedia Super Corridor have been advanced to transform Malaysia into a "knowledge economy."

One of the key areas experiencing major challenges is the education of adult educators in Malaysia being in the midst of dramatic transformations. This involves the teaching and learning activities of a large number of young adults who in turn will engage in the processes of lifelong teaching and learning. This chapter offers an analysis of education students' perceptions of teaching in this era of ICT. The first part of this chapter outlines the major movements in education in Malaysia. The second part examines the knowledge and practices of adult education students in relation to ICT. This focus on adult education students is important, as the development of ICT literacy among these young adults will contribute to the essential changes needed in adult education to shift Malaysia towards a knowledge-driven civil society. The final section raises some of the key challenges that need to be confronted. Programs for adult education are to contribute meaningfully to this shift.

The Changing Teaching/Learning Settings in Malaysia

The term "new times" (Hall, 1996) signals shifts in the social, cultural, economic, and political movements that shape education, work, private interests, and public life. In addressing these new times, adult educators have to ensure that adult education goes beyond technological advances that are linking the world ever more closely to focus on knowledge and issues around its creation. These dimensions are linked to challenges in economics, politics, culture, religion, the environment, social justice, and peace to ensure the well-being of each nation and the wider world (Pandian, 2001). The roles and capacity of adult education institutions are being re-engineered to manage the reality of new times and provide openings for employment, cultural and spiritual activities, as well as involvement in political processes. This task demands that contemporary societies be active in designing teaching/learning processes and living environments that promote participation and active interaction.

The teaching/learning settings in Malaysia are undergoing major alterations—changing the culture and practices of Malaysia's schools and adult education programs. There is a move away from memory-based learning to an education that stimulates critical thinking, creativity, and caring in all learners, that caters to individual abilities and learning styles and is based on more equitable access. This requires learners to exercise greater responsibility for their own education, while seeking more active participation by employees and the wider community. Preservice programs for adult educators in Malaysia are built upon the aspirations of the National Philosophy of Education, which states

> Education in Malaysia is an on-going effort towards further developing the potential of individuals in a holistic and integrated manner, so as to produce individuals who are intellectually, spiritually, emotionally and physically, balanced and harmonious, based on a firm belief in and devotion to God. Such an effort is for personal wellbeing as well as contributing to the betterment of the society and the nation at large. (Ministry of Education, Malaysia, 1997)

As evident in the blueprint for the Smart Schools Program (Ministry of Education, 1997), education institutions are being reinvented in terms of teaching-learning practices and management in order to prepare adult learners for the "Ideas and Imagination Age." These institutions are continuously developing their professional staff, their educational resources, and their administrative capabilities. This is enabling these institutions to adapt to changing conditions, while continuing to prepare adult learners for life in a new world (dis)order. This new learning setting is marked by dynamic interaction with ICT, which is not only a means of communication or a source for accessing information, but integral to adult learners' knowledge creation and dissemination.

In driving these new learning settings, the Malaysian Government is transforming its educational system to work towards a teaching workforce that is capable of critical thinking and is prepared to participate in the global economy of the twenty-first century. Teacher education programs are experiencing major changes within their cultural practices, especially through engaging in active participation by the wider community in the exercise of greater responsibility for education. As an initial step, it is important that adult educators are aware of these dramatic shifts and the purposes of these transformations throughout the education sector.

The focus of this chapter is on adult education students, in the process of reflecting upon their knowledge and practices in relation to the use of ICT activities. These graduates will play a major role in sustaining conventional practices as much as they will be involved in the work of the remaking of adult education in response to and as an expression of the demands of an ICT-"driven" era. This is an era in which governments and ICT corporations have decided that education is the area where huge amounts of public taxes will be invested.

Focusing on Students of Adult Education

Students of adult education constitute an important part of the structural setting for educational reform in Malaysia. In order to advance ICT as a medium to enhance the teaching/learning process, changes in students' roles and interests is most important. Examining their perceptions of ICT is valuable, because professional development is critical to the success of the reform agenda, delivering new learnings to students and communities.

Given that many students of adult education have limited ICT experience, intensive education in the use of information technology and in its integration into classroom activities in ways that enhance thinking and creativity is necessary. These students also need to learn to facilitate adult learners in taking charge of their own learning. In order to produce competent, caring adult educators, their professional development programs are being reworked. The aim is to ensure that they are taught how to regularly enhance their teaching skills so that they can stay abreast of developments in their profession and remain confident in their abilities in applying new technology creatively in teaching/learning settings.

There is a strong correlation between the literacy development in ICT among adult educators and its contribution to the ICT education of their students (Chan and Cheah, 1999; Norizan, 1999). The expertise of adult educators is a very important factor in determining students' achievement. Adult educators who have an in-depth knowledge of ICT, what this means for teaching/learning, and who work in environments that allow them to know their learners well are critical to the success of adult learners.

The quality of teaching and learning is dependent upon, albeit not exclusively, teachers' conceptualization of education, subject knowledge, pedagogical skills, appreciation of adult learners, and contextual understanding. What teachers know and can do affects the core tasks of teaching. For example, what the teachers understand about subject content and their students shapes how judiciously they select curriculum materials and how effectively they present these materials in their lessons. Their skills in assessing their students' progress depend also on how deeply they themselves know the content and how well they teach it.

After graduating, adult education students will play an important role in developing the ICT literacy potentialities of their communities and individual learners. Their ICT knowledge and competence in the use of multiple computer programs and networks will contribute to the formation of citizens and informed workers. This chapter now examines the ICT knowledge and practices of adult-education student-teachers in Malaysia in terms of their capacity to make a progressive contribution to the ICT era.

A Window on the Future

This section reports on the main forms of ICT interactions these student teachers have during their study program. One hundred and fifty-nine (159) final year student teachers were invited to participate; they came from three adult teacher education programs in northern Malaysia. The twenty-two (22) male and one hundred and thirty-seven (137) female participants reflects the typical male:female ratio for students enrolled in teacher education programs in Malaysia. There were one hundred and five (105) Bumiputera-Malays, forty-eight (48) Indian-Malays, and six (6) Chinese-Malays. The ages of participants ranged from nineteen to twenty-five years. All of them had passed the Year 12 school leaving examination with at least a credit in English.

Questionnaires and group interviews were used to gather data. Section A of the questionnaire solicited information on the personal background of each student, while section B comprised questions relating to their ICT practice. In addition to questionnaires, the student teachers were also asked to participate in focus group interviews to obtain insights into the nature and quality of their ICT interactions. The first part of the study sought responses on the status accorded to the English language in the teaching/learning environments of the student teachers. Although contested, English is claimed to be an important contributing factor towards meaningful participation in ICT activities. The mastery of English, one of the key prerequisites, or anti-market forces, determining people's capacity to participate in the global ICT economy.

Reading Preferences of Students of Adult Education. The student-teachers mostly read print newspapers in their daily lives, with 44 percent preferring to read English-language newspapers, 22 percent reading books in English, and only 15 percent reading journals and research papers in English. Almost 50 percent of the students indicated that they read their lecturers' notes and prescribed textbooks. This finding is consistent with previous research that found that only 20 percent of university students read in English (Pandian, 1999). Most Malaysians aged twenty-five and below read mainly for the purpose of passing examinations, a trend that suggests that these students may also be reading for the same purpose.

Oral/Aural Interaction of Adult Education Students. In relation to the student teachers' oral/aural interaction, more than 80 percent preferred not to speak English. Only 19.5 percent of the students indicated that they actively participated in discussions in English, while only 10 percent indicated that they attended seminars and workshops related to teaching of English. The students' reluctance to converse in the English language could be due to many factors, including, for instance, pressure from their peers. 80 percent of the students do not speak in English because they fear that their college-mates might label them as "proud," and 83 percent indicated that they are afraid to speak in English to their college-mates because they fear rejection. In addition to this concern, 74 percent of the students indicated that their college-mates mocked them when they spoke in English. This suggests that peer-group pressure is one of an unknown range of factors contributing to students' reluctance to speak English in public.

This suggests that the student teachers may have a negative disposition towards English. Their negative reaction towards those using English could be contributing to poor aural/oral proficiency in English among student teachers. The social atmosphere in these teacher education colleges is not conducive for the teaching and learning of English. The atmosphere of the teaching/learning environment provides students with the encouragement and spirit to share ideas and experiences necessary to enhance cognitive and affective learning (Musa, 1999).

The Use of Popular Audio and Video Culture. The interactions of student teachers with audio and video technologies suggest that 60 percent of them listened to English-language songs and music, though only 30 percent of them stated that they "switched on" to English language channels. Meanwhile, 72 percent of the student teachers indicated that they watched English-language programs on television. The pleasurable aspects and ease of access to television and radio facilities may account for the high percentage of the student teachers consuming popular audio and video culture. These pleasurable activities remain to be exploited to enhance the learning of English among the student teachers. Film is an effective meaning-making device in the hands of skilled adult educators who take this curriculum resource beyond its function as an entertainment medium (Kist, 2000). Likewise, young adults analyze, assess, and use television as a form of communication. The ways young adults understand television, its programs, and system and the fact that it may be mobilized to improve their English-language proficiency suggests strong reasons for radio, television, and film as media in adult teaching/learning.

ICT Interaction. Most of the student teachers (48.9 percent) used about 6–10 hours per week for computer-related activities, with 27.7 percent investing less than five hours per week on the computers. 51 percent of the student-teachers stated that they were competent in ICT skills, while 49 percent felt that their ICT skills were moderate to less competent. This suggests that almost half of these student teachers did not have a good understanding or confidence in their abilities to use ICT creatively in teaching/learning settings. Different modes of meaning-making and knowledge production have emerged as a result of developments in multimedia technologies. As a result, the demand for student teachers to acquire sufficient knowledge to effectively use the myriad of multimedia possibilities has increased.

This understanding of ICT becomes more problematic when the student teachers were asked to describe the most important purpose of ICT activities. Only 39.1 percent of the student teachers used the computer for academic and knowledge development purposes. Gathering news (25.6

percent) was another significant purpose underpinning their computer activities. 18.6 percent of the student teachers indicated that e-mail and chat relays were considered as the most important activity linked to computers, while 16.7 percent considered leisure and entertainment most important.

Issues for Students of Adult Education in Interacting with ICT

Group interviews were conducted to provide qualitative insights into the student teachers' knowledge and practices with ICT. This section reports on the key issues that emerged around several themes.

ICT and English

The student teachers acknowledged that English was an important language, one that had secured a powerful and a privileged role in the competitive world economy. They also recognized that a good command of the English language was necessary to establish the efficient use of information and communication technologies as well as a high-performance workplace. Many of the student teachers noted that they did not use the computers for English-language learning purposes; mostly such learning was confined to formal classroom settings. Nevertheless, they emphasized that browsing through the Internet and writing to friends through e-mail and chat relays enhanced their English-language learning and expanded their use of it. Capitalizing on these uses of English in computer classes presents itself as an important learning opportunity.

The Pleasure and Perils of Seeking Information. Many student teachers sought information on the Internet which presented different perspectives on current affairs and political issues in Malaysia. The student teachers pointed out that they encountered difficulties in interpreting news items, as they found that their truth claims differed markedly across these competing sources. These student teachers had difficulty assessing these news items as their education had not provided them with any of the knowledge and skills needed to question these conflicting reports.

The negative implications of the Internet were also discussed by the student teachers who referred to pornography and electronic games with violent themes. The student teachers noted that pornographic sites were popular but added that surfing these sites engaged them only in a "playful manner." Some student teachers noted that people could be "addicted" to certain websites if they lacked social awareness or respect for people. Others pointed out that surfing the Internet was an interesting, fun, and enticing pastime at this point in their lives, especially given that there are many taboos surrounding pornography and sensitivities concerning electronic games with violent themes. Just what adult education programs might do to address this issue is unclear.

Evaluating websites is an important activity, as it enables users to consider the reliability of information sources, the accuracy of content, the clarity of the material presented, and the purposes served by the sites. Many of the student teachers have not learnt the skills to evaluate the websites that they encounter. They have not learnt to identify the authors and owners who developed the sites, nor how to question the advertisements present at these sites. Further the student teachers have not learnt about the construction of community texts for use in social action and other forms of citizenship. When asked if any one of them was an active member of any civil or non-government agencies, none of the student teachers stated so.

An Under-utilised Thinking Tool. The student teachers acknowledged that there were many websites that were useful for educational purposes, particularly in sharing ideas from other parts of the world. However, due to time constraints and a lack of computer facilities, since most did not own their own computer, many of them could not develop their learning activities in a systematic way. Most of the student teachers observed that computers were largely used for word-processing purposes in accomplishing their assignments. They seldom used this technology for references, information, seeking or web-searching purposes associated with knowledge accumulation, creation, and distribution. The student teachers also indicated they were often overwhelmed with information and faced difficulties in searching for information that related specifically to their assignments. However, they did note that the traditional learning resources, namely, reference books and group discussions, were still found to be most useful in accomplishing their assignments.

E-mail and Internet Chat Relays. Many of the e-mail and chat relay conversations among these student teachers were linked to their personal lives rather than the public sphere or their educational program. The informal ICT education involved were acts of friendship building, leisure, and pleasure. While the ability to get and send e-mail to people from different parts of the region and the world was exciting, most reported that it was not capitalized upon as part of their formal education program. On e-mail, the student teachers discussed daily difficulties related to relationships among friends, family and loved ones. They also forwarded interesting and amusing stories, jokes and puzzles as leisure pursuits. Only a few of the student teachers used e-mail to seek clarifications, ideas and information seeking for their course assignments. Some had used e-mail and chat relays for civic purposes.

The Limitations of English: Proficiency and Preference. There are a number of challenges in preparing adult educators for "new times," The negative disposition among these student teachers towards the English language was evident in poor proficiency and a preference not to use English. The social atmosphere present in the formal and informal learning settings did not encourage the use of English-based activities. There was also resistance to an English-language reading culture, with student teachers seeing the most English could offer was the study of their lecture notes and prescribed textbooks for examination purposes. Not surprisingly, most of the student teachers engaged with very few ICT activities in English. Given the considerable efforts invested by powerful interests in making the English language dominate global interactions, this is a matter which demands attention. The Malaysian Ministry of Education is currently pursuing policy changes that give a renewed national/global status to the English language in teaching/learning at all levels of education.

Technical and Creative Imagination? The group interviews indicate that the courses on ICT emphasized technical competence where student teachers developed skills in word processing, graphic creation, and accessing websites. The student teachers themselves engaged predominantly with word processing, Internet chat relays, and e-mail, but did not necessarily use these tools to the best effect. The conception of ICT interaction is one that is fraught with problems, especially where it encourages deference and conformity and where it is narrowed to skills acquisition that occurs devoid of critical inquiry and creativity. The student teachers recognized the need for innovation to stimulate critical reflection on different ways of engaging in multi-modal texts, thereby enhancing their scope to author and design multi-modal texts. The shift from presenting ICT education as a technical activity towards more creative and imaginative activities is a major challenge for all involved in adult education programs.

Developing Critical Literacy. ICT interaction within these education programs for preparing adult educators was not situated within a critical literacy framework. Student teachers were not educated to reflect and construct knowledge but, rather, the emphasis was on learning to consume information. They want to know-how to use ICT to transmit information and to become productive authors, generating knowledge and building online community relationships. The aspirations in this regard resonate with the view of a knowledge society as one where all its members are enabled to undertake reference work and develop the critical thinking and creative facilities that promote informed and active citizenship (Leu, 2000).

Conclusion

The advent of the information age and the rapid development in information technology as a means of communication as well as knowledge creation has made it imperative for teachers to be knowledgeable and active participants in the ICT arena. In this context, a crucial function of adult education is to nurture student teachers who can develop professional identities that facilitate the construction of community texts for use in citizen social action. Adult educators have the power to shape and produce the next generation of teacher-citizens who possess excellent ICT knowledge and practices. If the findings of this study can serve as a guide, then it is likely that many student teachers in Malaysia may lack the ICT skills that are needed for their roles as adult educators in these new globalizing times.

The barriers to English-language learning have to be addressed, given its dominance as a global language and its role as the command language of the globalizing economy. The mastery of this language would seem to be an imperative for active participation in the global political economy. English is to be the language of the supposedly "new" knowledge economy, but its dominance of the new technologies of human interaction, reflection and knowledge production is being challenged (Singh, Kell, and Pandian, 2002). Given the increasing significance accorded to contestation over English, the reluctance of student teachers in Malaysia to engage in learning the English language is a critical issue. Books, computers, and other print media have a complementary role to play in enhancing English-language learning. With Malaysia gearing itself towards becoming a "knowledge society," it is important that student-teachers become avid readers and knowledge producers in this language.

The curriculum for learning ICT needs to go beyond word processing techniques, the ability to construct graphics, and accessing of websites.

This skills-based learning places emphasis on technical competence and information consumption rather than critical enquiry and knowledge creation. It is the capacity for critical questioning and creative problem solving that needs to be developed in student teachers capable of contributing productively to a knowledge society. They can then have a better understanding of the mediation and manipulation of information, reflect on what they have learned, and then generate and disseminate knowledge about their daily life events.

There is a need to rethink the whole process of learning to use ICT. Having student teachers accomplish tasks without comprehending what they are doing only reinforces the domestication of education. Defining adult education as the transmission of information to adult learners generates passive people without the capacity to critique and improve their life situation or that of others. The knowledge society requires creative individuals with the capability to critique, think, and study about learning and the ability to connect these learning activities to the different ecological and social problems that concern today's global society (Valente, 1997). The transformation of adult education programs is important as the move towards a knowledge society demands that adult educators problematize our teaching ideas and practices. These changes in learning practices have to be supported with properly resourced policy measures at the level of national government, as well as interested parties at the local levels. Funding improved access for adult educators to computers is a necessary step on the road to creating a knowledge society.

References

Chan, K., and L. Cheah. "Multimedia in English Language Teaching (Melt): Issues, Changing Realities and Challenges for Literacy Now and in the Next Millennium." In *Global Literacy—Vision, Revision and Vistas in Education*, edited by A. Pandian. Serdang, Malaysia: Universiti Putra Malaysia Press, 1999.

Hall, S. "The Meaning of New Times." In *Stuart Hall: Critical Dialogue in Cultural Studies*. edited by D. Morley and K. Chen. London: Routledge, 1996.

Kist, W. "Beginning to Create the New Literacy Classroom: What Does the New Literacy Look Like?" *Journal of Adolescent & Adult Literacy* 48, no. 8 (2000): 710–17.

Ministry of Education Malaysia. *Conceptual Blueprint on Smart Schools*. 1997.

Musa Md. R. et al, "Creative Writing in Malaysian Schools: A Case Study of Literacy Development Using Action Research." In *Global Literacy—Vision, Revision and Vistas in Education*. edited by A. Pandian. Serdang, Malaysia: Universiti Putra Malaysia Press, 1999.

Norizan, A. R. "Computerised Reading for ESL Learners." In *Global Literacy—Vision, Revision and Vistas in Education.* edited by A. Pandian. Serdang: Universiti Putra Malaysia, 1999.

Pandian, A. "Advancing Literacy in the New Times: Happenings in Contemporary Malaysia." In *Literacy Matters: Issues for New Times.* edited by M. Kalantzis and A. Pandian. Seaholme, Victoria: Common Ground Publishing, 2001.

———. *"K-English Teachers, K-Society and K-Economy."* Paper presented at the Malaysian International Conference on English Language Teaching (MICELT), Malacca, 15–17 May 2000.

———. "Whither Reading in Malaysia: Confronting Reading Reluctancy among Pre-University Students." In *Global Literacy—Vision, Revision and Vistas in Education.* edited by A. Pandian. Serdang, Malaysia: Universiti Putra Malaysia Press, 1999.

Singh, M., P. Kell, and A. Pandian. *Appropriating English: Innovation in the Global Business of English Language Teaching.* New York: Peter Lang Publishers, 2002.

Valente, J. A. "The Role of Computers in Education: Achievement and Comprehension." *Prospects.* XXVII, no. 3 (1997): 403–13.

Chapter 13

On-line Supplementation of Adult Education: A Change in Pedagogy and a Pedagogy of Change

Andrew Scown

> The new cognition...rests on awareness of the limitations of positivist methods and on skepticism about grand narratives, data collection, and data analysis techniques, without falling into the epistemological nihilism implied by ultra-relativism. Such cognition seriously takes into account the uniqueness of the object of study, the historicity of the life-world, and the heterogeneity of social subjects and their evolving identities.
> (Marginson and Mollis, 2001: 602)

The "new cognition" poses a significant challenge for adult educators and learners alike. This chapter provides an account on work towards a "new cognition" of pedagogical practice in on-line adult education that encourages diversity rather than sameness. A pedagogy based on negotiating difference in power relations and promoting heterogeneity in adult education, designed for an on-line adult education course in Educational Leadership and Management will be illustrated. This pedagogy, known as the Evidence-Critique-Impact (ECI) model, is employed as a mode of teaching and learning in an international on-line adult education program.

Adult Education in a Globalized Environment

Globalization constitutes the basis for much reflection and action in adult education. These influences are observable in universities where once the prevailing notion of the scholar who enjoyed academic freedom and autonomy has given way to new governing narratives in association with neo-conservative globalization, namely, performativity, cost efficiency, economies of scale, the assurance of quality, accountability, return on investment, and frameworks of excellence. Neo-conservative globalism's meta-narratives are transforming the cultural practices of adult education, calling into question the identity of the adult learner through the politicization of pedagogy and the construction of a global marketplace for adult education enabled by information and communication technologies. Through manipulation, judgment, and overt policing, both within the academy and by national governments and funding bodies, the homogenizing press towards conformity and compliance is exerting increasing control over adult education.

These developments are grounded in contestable claims. It is assumed that students only want credentials, and that low market demand for education products is a sign of poor teaching. These low-demand courses are thought not to be providing positional advantage to students and accordingly should be replaced with courses that are in demand and return financial advantages. These assumptions lead to disillusionment and disempowerment of adult educators. Perhaps more importantly, these assumptions undervalue the role of adult learners in co-designing a curriculum that suits their needs. It disregards well-established theories of adult learning, and ignores the capability and desire(s) of adult learners to be involved in designing educational processes that respect and reflect learners' life-world(s) and evolving identities. A curriculum grounded in pedagogical practices that responds to the different life-worlds of adult learners can promote diversity and find strength in the appreciation of relations of difference around gender, class, sexuality, and ethnicity. This is preferable to regimes that create a compliance with the notions of sameness that characterize many on-line education offerings.

Approaches to adult education that revolve around homogenized curricula and rely on pedagogies offering linear flows of information assume a stereotypical learner. This chapter draws on a case study to argue that this does not facilitate adult education and so needs to be challenged. Adult educators cannot underestimate the truth of the maxim "Linearity Kills." This challenge for adult educators (and institutions that host the education of adults) is to identify these homogenizing forces and to create practices that move towards fluid, multi-dimensional pedagogies that recognize and promote diversity.

Homogenizing Adult Education

Increasingly, on-line adult education programs are subject to homogenization. This was observed in the case study site in the curriculum design and implementation, the linear and inflexible use of technologies of human interaction, community formation, and knowledge production, and the decision making that privileges neo-conservative accountability over sound theories of adult education. These homogenizing trends in adult education not only constrain teaching and learning but also reinforce threats to the sustainability of diversity. Sameness trumps education for diversity and precludes its valuing and promotion. On-line teaching is emerging as a repetitive activity of didactic and linear transmission controlled by instructional technologists and their corporate managers who speak the language of systems capabilities, cost effectiveness, and time efficiency. Any prudent understanding of pedagogy is marginalized for adult education and the place of adult learners in the education process. This sameness in method, content, and evaluation detracts from productive adult learning.

Curriculum Design and Implementation

On-line curriculum quickly assumed the characteristics of a standardized approach predetermined by instructional designers rather than adult educators with disciplinary and pedagogical expertise. This disallowed on-line teaching and learning being grounded in pedagogies characterized by negotiation and co-design. The opportunity to develop a curriculum where adult learners co-design relevant content and negotiate learning processes and objectives was not readily taken up in on-line courses. Instead, a standardized curriculum approach characterized by sameness in both content and teaching processes became the dominant style of on-line education. The result of this homogenized curriculum that the voice of adult learners often goes unheard.

Learners become subject to working their way through prescribed "click and drag" exercises and navigating multiple choice or cloze (fill in the missing word) test activities that limit learning. Within this process, the success of teaching and learning was judged by quantitative measures that demonstrate mastery of pre-determined capabilities that are norm-referenced for ease of marking and ranking. Typically, opportunities for adult learners to request purposeful assessment strategies that are negotiated on relevant criteria (to both learner and educator) are ignored.

University support processes preserved and promoted homogenized the curriculum. "Quality standards" were used to produce curricula that conform to standardized designs for all on-line curriculum products rather than allowing for each offering to be unique. Adult educators argued that curriculum designed for on-line learning should acknowledge and embody the tenets of productive pedagogy, allowing for negotiations with adult learners in order to promote deep, situational learning. Negotiating the curriculum would, they argued, increase respect for the life-world of students, thereby making on-line offerings distinctive. This approach would allow students to differentiate between competitor programs as they make their selection of appropriate learning experiences in a marketplace of extensive (and expensive) offerings.

On-line products that do not recognize and productively engage diversity pose a significant challenge to adult education. They package attributes, capabilities, and competencies that are peripheral to real-life applications into sequences that the students must complete in order to satisfy course requirements. Adult educators argue that curriculum that is responsive to student needs requires more than providing on-line resources and the prescription of rigid "click-and-drag" exercises. Possibilities for students to negotiate alternative graduate capabilities or to elect to by pass stipulated capabilities in preference for others that were more relevant or appropriate to their situation(s) were held to be more appropriately characteristic of on-line learning programs. The preference was for on-line learning that is responsive to students' learning needs and styles. This necessarily makes it difficult to judge effective teaching and learning using criteria that privilege predetermined standards of achievement selected for ease of measurement.

However, e-textbooks and threaded discussions were often constructed as the normative model for on-line adult education. This was challenged by adult educators keen to develop alternative models. The preference was for a focus on life-world evidence, engaging learners in the reflective analysis and critique of different perspectives to inform and challenge knowledge, and application leading to personal and community transformation. This redesign of e-learning provided possibilities to ground on-line learning in pedagogy rather than to promote practices that reinforce myth-making about there being "one best approach to curriculum." To do so, these adult educators needed courage and support to challenge the inappropriate practices of on-line curriculum design, implementation, and learning that were fast becoming the norm in university settings.

Linear and Inflexible E-Learning Technologies

The advent and growth of e-learning technologies in adult education has proscribed teaching and learning that encourage dialogue and communication. Whilst the flexibility of synchronous and asynchronous chat provides opportunities for distant engagement, the communication afforded by these technologies is disembodied and prevents the engagement between on-line participants that builds the corporeality and relationality which is a vital dimension of pedagogy (van Manen, 1990). Discussion groups are limited by the capacity of technology (e.g., 500 characters per entry in synchronous chat groups), determined by the time zone in which participants reside, and reliant on the technological infrastructure of a particular country to support broadband technology.

The reliance on a single technology to construct, deliver, and evaluate teaching and learning can create inflexibility. No single approach to teaching/learning can cover every situation, convey every concept, or cater to every student. Technological system requirements that only permit bounded approaches to on-line teaching and learning are limiting. A core component of adult learning is experimentation, and a key capability for adult learners is the ability to judge what approaches work best in different scenarios. "Learning for transference" is far more effective than compliance with any technical specification. The practice of mandating a bounded approach to on-line teaching and learning through strategies that govern what can and cannot be done disenfranchise the key players in adult education, namely, the students and teachers. The "teach to the test" syndrome is an example of the manipulation of curriculum orientation that was emerging in this on-line environment.

Organizational support for flexible delivery is based on the assumption that adult learners want on-line computer-mediated teaching. It is assumed that by this adults gain more control over the time and place of their learning, and that e-learning technologies are a satisfactory replacement for face-to-face delivery. The claims are that every person has the skills and resources to access this technology, and that adults learn best individually—by themselves. The view is held that they want to focus their learning on workplace issues, and that adult educators need only write content that can be facilitated for on-line discussion groups by the participants themselves. All of these assumptions have been found erroneous.

These assumptions are grounded in economic rather than educational concerns. While frequently clothed in educational rhetoric, e-learning is primarily driven by questions of profit-making through achieving economies of scale. Much effort has been invested in debunking the practice of gathering students and teachers together for lectures, seminars, tutorials, and study groups, and in boosting claims about the alleged cost efficiencies of cyber-linking many-to-many on-line participants in a/synchronous chat groups. In this case study, many adult learners who were limited to programs that were only available on-line found that they were not comfortable with this mode of learning and opted out (or did not participate), preferring instead face-to-face offerings. The adult educators involved argued that decisions made regarding on-line provision should take into account the principles of curriculum design, whilst implementation strategies need to be resourced adequately to ensure that multiple pathways (and multiple technologies) allow for multiple approaches to teaching and learning.

Privileging Neo-conservative Controls over Worthwhile Education

The provision and management of adult education is aligned with broader changes to the public good. These include the enforcement of national(ized) curriculum standards, restricted resource allocation, and increased surveillance (accountability). The impact of these on adult education providers was once unimaginable in higher education circles. In universities, the move is to judge the merit of programs of research and teaching using so-called business rules. Teaching and Research Assessment Indicators and resource allocation are then aligned between individual institutions and their performance on these indicators. The criteria on which these "Ivy-League" performance tables are calculated assume a student population that is characterized by sameness, and promote a homogenized curriculum that appeals to this like body of students. The instruments employed for data collection tend to rely solely on sanitized and positivist approaches that assume the benchmark of sameness as the indicator of success. When the results of these evaluation exercises are employed in processes of decision making, then the poor performers (both adult educators and courses) are faced with threats of program closure and potential redundancy.

Such processes demonstrate a lack of understanding of the need for diversity in educational processes. They also underestimate that need for individualized pedagogies for every student in a class, dismiss the genuine desire of students to learn for the virtue of learning, and amass the responses from all students from undergraduate certificates through to PhD into like categories for ease of comparison. However, the processes and outcomes of adult education cannot be captured in simple Likert scale questions that are constructed in difficult and confusing language and that ask questions and demand responses that typically are irrelevant to making decisions about the needs and interests of subsequent cohorts. Whether these evaluation exercises are to lead to betterment in teaching and learning is questionable given their current format. All parties need the opportunity to interpret, to challenge the results of these assessment exercises with supporting data, and to construct alternative strategies for both teaching/learning and course evaluation.

The foregoing issues reflect the debates in adult education around the new technologies of teaching and learning. It is against this backdrop that adult educators are trying to develop theoretically informed and empirically grounded practices within the on-line environment that meet the needs of adult learners. The following section describes a pedagogical framework that has been developed amidst this situation in the attempt to overcome these homogenizing influences and to promote difference in on-line teaching and learning.

Evidence-Critique-Impact

Adult educators adapt practices from different pedagogical theories and synthesize these into workable models for the situation at hand. Whatever the genesis of the approach, there seem to be certain characteristics of successful on-line adult education. These include a constructive response to the challenges of what it means to be and to learn in today's world. To this should be added a critical awareness of theories and practices of adult learning, an empathy with adult learners whatever their situation or prior experience, and an understanding of the contemporary challenges in which adult learners are placed. The Evidence-Critique-Impact (ECI) pedagogical model is one attempt to respond to these challenges within a framework of on-line learning for an adult education program. It was developed collaboratively by a team of academics and educational technologists through a process of curriculum design and course renewal.

The rationale for the ECI model arose in response to an opportunity to develop and deliver a program in Educational Leadership and Management in partnership with a private education provider in Southeast Asia. A key factor in the success of this program was the degree of freedom and vision of innovation held by the course team. This enabled the customization of the program of workplace education for corporate clients, the individualization of learning tasks and agreements, and the negotiation of assessment strategies for each student in accordance with academic regulations. The program embraced the notion of diversity rather than assuming that a "one-size-fits-all" approach would work for adult learners.

Because students need the opportunity to respond to diverse geographical, political, administrative, and economic systems, the program had to embrace diverse cultural and linguistic settings. Thus, it was essential to develop a pedagogy of on-line teaching/learning that allowed for each student to find a place within the program. This encouraged each student to respond with her or his different learning styles and prior learning experiences. By combining their formal learning with the competing demands of their professional workplace, the students were able to enhance the benefits they gained from their on-line education programs. Whilst the initial program was developed and provided in the English language, plans are in place to offer the entire program in other languages and to have local adult educators work with students in their local language. However, this facility needs to be considered alongside the quality assurance requirements of the host University that degrees offered and awarded are delivered in the English language with any translation providing supplementary material.

The ECI model draws on theoretical ideas in curriculum design developed by the co-designers in adult education from the perspectives of hermeneutic phenomenology (Scown, 1998), multiliteracies and the design of social futures (Cope and Kalantzis, 2000), and the use of information and communication technologies in education (Tsembas, 2001). Since the development of this model, it has been employed in delivering on-line courses for students in Australia, Vietnam, Indonesia, Malaysia, Singapore, the United States, and China. The feedback from these students demonstrates support for adult education that achieves difference.

The following section provides an account of the theoretical framing for this model and outlines the pedagogical approach of the ECI model. It concludes with reflections on attempts to work innovatively within/against the limitations of the dominating currents in on-line adult education.

The Life-worlds of Adult Learners

To journey with adult learners provides opportunities to engage with their life-world(s). Such opportunities need to be invitational, as adult educators cannot impose our presence into the life-world of another without first being welcomed into their dwelling place. Yet students often declared that they were uncomfortable with the process of on-line adult learning because of the intrusive and imposing nature of the facilitator, the learning process, or the technologies of instruction. This imposition was particularly noticeable when the usual communicative relationships were limited by technology, especially where an on-line "facilitator" invoked interrogative questions in the attempt to establish a communicative relationship so essential to genuine learning. The parties to learning remain virtual and disembodied. On-line learning runs the risk of being an experience of alienation where it promotes sameness for ease of managing educational costs.

The scenarios listed above limit the usual procedures of communication experienced in the embodied teacher-learner relationship. To move beyond the "firewalls" that block pedagogical communication, the designers of the ECI model sought to create a conceptual basis and a pedagogical model that recognizes difference and diversity amongst their students. This promoted a teaching and learning model that enabled pedagogical relationships of openness and inclusion. This model uses the lived experience of adult learners as a platform for learning. This meant working with the current phenomena of globalization in processes of critiquing these phenomena from multi-disciplinary and multi-literacy perspectives. The adult learners were supported in their efforts to transform knowledge and knowing in ways that impact on individuals, the community, and the world. The ECI model takes as its starting point the life-world of each student participating in the program. It encourages difference as it draws forth reflections on each student's life-world, rather than trying to simulate a life experience and have people process this as if it were an experience held in common.

The concept of "life-worlds" (Husserl, 1970) taken up in work on hermeneutics and phenomenology, invites students to become consciously aware of their lived experiences. The focus is the world, as the student' experience it in their everyday life, rather than how they imagine it could be or how others idealize what it should be. To imagine that we inhabit one life-world would be naïve; our existence is lived out in "multiple and overlapping communities" (Kalantzis, 1997). There are "multiple and different life-worlds that belong to different human existences and realities" (van Manen, 1990: 101). To work with another person and to enter the life-world of that person is to recognize, value and encourage the diversity that already exists among us. Life-worlds are as different for each individual as is the identity of the person who inhabits that world: "gender, ethnicity, generation and sexual orientation are just a few of the markers of these differences" (Cope and Kalantzis, 2000: 15).

It is through negotiating their life-world/s and the life-world/s of others that students negotiate their identity and constitute the realities of life, living, and learning. Yet, very often students are not conscious of their lifeworld. They live, work, plays and recreate—the experiences of daily living—and yet they are unconscious of that which constitutes their being. Similarly, adult educators, managers, and leaders can unconsciously assume and encourage sameness and uniformity as they try to teach student workers ways to conform to the standards of the organization, the culture of the workplace, the voice of the nation. A key question the designers of the ECI model grappled with was: "How as adult educators can we work with the reality of life-worlds of adult learners?"

In exploring this question (more so than arriving at an answer), it became manifest that the immediate evidence of the life-world is the foundation upon which to scaffold students' work. It provides the evidence needed for learning: "This foundational basis cannot be anything other than the life-world and the immediate evidence of students' lived experiences, the term "evidence" referring to the immediate self-presentation of the objects involved" (Kockelmans, 1994: 336). This evidence provides a basis for learning and for the construction of knowledge; it allows students to recognize the capacity for learning and development that is intrinsic to their world. Rather than relying on exogenous curriculum specified by people outside the pedagogical relationship, it provides for evidence-based knowledge.

A Pedagogical Model for E-Learning

To work with the lived experience of adult learners and to engage in a process of learning that focuses on the life-world(s) of the participants demanded the clarification of agreed principles of adult teaching and learning on which to scaffold the pedagogy. Seven operating principles emerged to guide this work.

- First, a pedagogy of sensitivity and critical awareness to the existential realities of each students' life-world, lived through space, time, the body, and in relationship with others (van Manen, 1990);

- Second, an approach that allows for global communication and encourages a critique of theory and practice from different socio-political perspectives as a way of transforming practice based in new knowledge and new ways of knowing and being;
- Third, embedded content that encourages students to move beyond the surface to subsequent layers as they negotiate the meaning contained within the realities of their life-world, and in guiding theories and discourses;
- Fourth, recognition that having engaged successfully in authentic learning, adult learners and communities will be different. Passive knowledge needs to be continually worked and reworked through processes that empower adult learners and the learning community to be self-transforming. This transformation needs to be sensitive to plurality and difference;
- Fifth, adult learners are productive performers who relish the opportunity to create and to share their work. Interplay between adult learners is essential to providing the critique of knowing and knowledge that each student produces. Adult learners need opportunities to research, to create and to disseminate their work and to receive critique on this knowledge by other adult learners;
- Sixth, the concept of on-line authoring and editing provides many opportunities for adult learners to harness the capacity of information and communication technologies in creative and educational forums, and
- Seventh, the concept of read-only materials does little more than foster sameness through adult education, what is needed for an e-learning pedagogy is an on-line platform that promotes difference and that is different from other pedagogies that are best suited to face-to-face learning.

The Evidence to Impact (ECI) model attempts to embrace these principles of adult education. The model contains three perspectives on knowledge: an Evidence angle, a Critique angle, and an Impact angle. These three perspectives are described as follows. Evidence: working with information and everyday experiences as found in the life-world of each adult learner. It includes observation, data collection, and reflection on personal experiences. Critique: working with concepts and theories that describe the underlying structures and processes of the real world. This involves each student in reflecting critically upon the social, economic, political, and cultural interests served by structures and processes, and invites the students to theorize as a way of contributing to informed debate on current bodies of knowledge. Impact: applying knowledge and new learning to the real world. It includes innovating and driving the change process to reflect the new learning/s that accompany the varying stages of the life journey of learning.

This model seeks to engage adult learners in the creation of knowledge and new modes of being in our world. It draws on personal experiences from the life-world of adult learners, promotes the clarification of values, recreates personal meanings, and designs new frameworks for making sense of the changing world in which they live.

This pedagogy involves an active process of critiquing the theories that constitute the content of the discipline(s). This is done by engaging the adult learners in testing these theories in their own life-world/s. To engage in this process of critique demands certain evidence to be brought forward so that adult learners can see the ways that theories shape their interpretations of lived experience.

Through this self-presentation of the experiences of their life-world(s), adult learners are encouraged to reflect on current knowledge, to critically analyze prevailing discourses and the reflections of others. This "Critique" challenges adult learners to consider the interpretations they place on their life experiences and leads them to generate new interpretations. It calls on them to consider the work of other scholars who have reflected on the same phenomena within their life-world/s and who have written, spoken, acted, painted, and danced their new interpretations into being. Adult learners are also challenged to consider how they can design new ways of thinking and doing to arrive at richer insights into life and living, and to impact on the world in light of this new understanding. It encourages other participants in the learning process to offer input and to negotiate communication that may lead to renewed insights.

"Impact" through learning is essential to the ECI process. To learn for the sake of learning is not as unacceptable as some would have students think. However, to learn and to be able to make a difference in the way adult learners experience their world and to influence how the world operates around them is essential for the sustainability of their world systems. To achieve impact through learning requires a practical application of their new knowledge, which serves to test, clarify, and further new knowledge and understanding.

On-line Supplementation of Teaching and Learning

In developing teaching/learning approaches for an on-line program founded on the ECI model, key aims were to encourage heterogeneity and to reward diversity rather than sameness. Essential to the model was the idea that adult students be presented with opportunities to approach course materials in whichever ways best suited their needs, interests, and preferred learning styles. An on-line multi-media multi-literacy approach allowing for interactive communication was a key element of the program.

A learning/knowledge matrix was developed to categorize the course material into three key themes. The material for each theme focuses on the different angles for engaging knowledge—Evidence-Impact-Critique. Table 13.1 provides an overview of the content for a program in "Leading and Managing Change."

These three angles on knowledge do not represent separate ways of knowing or types of learning, nor are they necessarily engaged in a linear sequence. Often, more than one kind of knowing and learning happens simultaneously, as adult learners shift between these learning opportunities. The approach of the ECI model promotes iterative movements between each of the components of the learning framework. The vertical dimension unfolds the material in a thematic progression from one concept to another. The horizontal dimension unfolds the material from the perspective of the three angles of knowledge: working with experience and context (Evidence), critically reflecting on theory and generalizing concepts (Critique), and acting on knowledge and applying new learning to remake the world (Impact). Students may move through the material in any sequence. Some students elect to move through Theme 1 thoroughly, studying it from all three ECI angles, before moving to Theme 2. Students with a strong preference for theorizing elect to immerse themselves in the Critique material in all three themes before acquainting themselves with the Evidence themes and then progressing to the Impact themes.

The program design allows an entry point and learning progression that suits each student. The only constant is that all themes are covered from each of three ECI angles.

Students are encouraged to nominate their own assessment submission and to negotiate with the adult educator the assessment criteria by which work will be assessed. Through the process of assessment, students are required to demonstrate knowledge of all themes (the vertical dimension). They are also required to demonstrate understanding and/or use of the knowledge from all three ECI angles (the horizontal dimension).

Their submissions are assessed on all aspects of the ECI process. Students are also invited to critique the work of other students through the on-line platform.

Table 13.1:
The ECI Matrix for Leading and Managing Change

	Evidence	Critique	Impact
Topic 1: Exploring the Phenomenon of Change	Change is a life experience which challenges us in many diverse ways.	To make meaning of how we react to change involves an understanding and critique of the theories of personal development.	To lead and manage change successfully calls forth a mastery of management change at the personal level.
Topic 2: Managing Change	Change is a dynamic process that involves many complex variables.	The successful change agent develops a theoretical framework upon which to critique and scaffold strategies for managing change.	By understanding the variables in the change process, models and strategies can be selected that are appropriate to each change scenario.
Topic 3: Leadership and Change	The capability of managing change is an essential component of leadership.	Teams that can develop and learn together have a stronger capacity to embrace change.	To lead and manage others in and through change demands that we have a sound understanding of this process.

Their critiques form part of each student's assessment tasks. Working with this model calls for each student to personalize how she or he approaches learning. Many students are challenged on a number of levels as they negotiate the meaning and process of being an adult learner.

Reflections on ECI in Practice

The ECI pedagogy has been employed as a model of on-line teaching/learning since the beginning of 2000. Research into this model has been conducted systematically since that time, as have course evaluations of the on-line platform. Student feedback includes such comments as:

> At last I am beginning to make the links. For many years I could not see why it was that change was happening—why we had to disrupt our comfortable ways. I can now see the evidence in my own life that change and transition is sometimes as necessary as continuity. I am able to critique the many theories about change and evaluate these against the realities of my own situation. I accept also that I can contribute to leading others responsibly through the change process. The ECI model has helped me tremendously with this understanding. Thank you for helping me become aware of this! (Handaya, student pseudonym)

Other feedback suggests that students value being recognized as individuals. The ECI model respects local situations rather than assuming all students inhabit the same workplace or country of residence, thereby allowing for a more intimate engagement with other on-line participants. A key factor in the success of the program identified by these adult learners is the flexibility for them to negotiate their own learning agenda, their assessment tasks and assessment criteria, and to act as appraisers of the work of other students through the processes of critique.

Constructive negative feedback from the students has focussed on the limitations of on-line learning caused by the technological difficulties of accessing communication channels, systems reliability, and lack of broadband. Other criticisms include the cost of accessing Internet providers, the difficulty of time-delayed asynchronous chat, and the feeling of loneliness and isolation should other students elect not to respond to one's discussion posting. The evaluation of teaching and learning in these courses rate high, and the overall satisfaction rating for students participating in the course rate high. On-line qualitative data collection tools have been used to allow students to publish their thoughts and feelings about the program. This feedback is positive and the ECI model is usually singled out as excellent in terms of facilitating student learning:

> I am benefiting from this course a great deal because of the space negotiated and created by me with your guidance. Learning is non-linear. It goes in circles. You return back to previous topics and there are new insights and new questions as you probe deeper. This has been an education about education. The ECI model has led me to new understandings about what it means to learn as an adult. (Chan, student pseudonym)

This chapter has grappled with issues of adult learning in an on-line platform. Situated within the current scenario in adult education that encourage models of sameness through homogenous approaches to teaching and learning this chapter has offered insights into a pedagogical framework that promotes heterogeneity. The main features of the pedagogical model that supports diversity are summarized as:

- Adult learners are active participants in constructing curriculum;
- Negotiated assessment draws on the learning needs of participants;
- Adult learners determine the specific outcomes that are relevant for their situation;
- By utilizing multi-literacy approaches adult learners become publishers and performers. Linear technologies give way to multi-modal communication. Adult learners draw upon many theories of teaching and learning and engage with other learners to determine method(s) appropriate to their learning styles;
- Adult learners are the decision makers in the teaching and learning process—quality is internal rather than external to the learning group; and
- Adult learners know what they want and need from education and are keen to participate in the design process.

Conclusion

After many years of working as an adult educator in a variety of formal and informal settings, understanding that "what we do" is in fact "who we are" is not something to be taken for granted but a cause for celebration. Authentic learning through adult education is a way of being that gradually becomes so much a part of life and living that it is something that we need to embrace as a gift. The rewards of adult education can be celebrated in the confidence that the intrinsic gains far outweigh the material. This "gift" is a journey with other adult learners to make sense of the unknown, to find new ways of learning and knowing, and to recognize and encourage diversity. It is a rare privilege. Working with the ECI model provides an opportunity for renewal among adult educators and allows for an engagement with other adult learners. Diversity and difference in adult education are encouraged, not subjugated. To break through the barriers of homogenization that governments and universities create in response to globalizing neo-conservative forces is an imperative for adult educators in the twenty-first century. The Evidence is clear, Critique is not difficult, and the Impact of a pedagogy that supports diversity is encouraging. Heterogeneity is high on the agenda of adult education. Adult educators who eschew sameness in the quest of difference can be encouraged by the realization that support for diversity allows for far more lasting impact than one that limits adult learning to a mandated template based on sameness.

References

Cope, B., and M. Kalantzis. "Designs for Social Futures." In *Multiliteracies—Literacy Learning and the Design of Social Future.* edited by B. Cope and M. Kalantzis, 203–34. London: Routledge, 2000.

Husserl, E. *The Crisis of European Sciences and Transcendental Phenomenology—An Introduction to Phenomenological Philosophy.* Evanston: Northwestern University Press, 1970.

Kalantzis, M. *The New Citizen and the New State: An Australian Case for Civic Pluralism.* Sydney, N.S.W.: Centre for Workplace Communication and Culture, 1997.

Kockelmans, J. *Edmund Husserl's Phenomenology.* Indiana: Purdue University Press, 1994.

Marginson, S., and M. Mollis. "The Door Opens and the Tiger Leaps"; Theories and Reflexivities of Comparative Education for a Global Millennium." *Comparative Education Review* 45, no. 4 (2001): 581–615.

Scown, A. "Assisting the "Development of Professionals" through the Use of Phenomenological Inquiry." *Reflect: The Journal of Reflection in Learning and Teaching* 4, no. 2 (1998): 39–45.

Tsembas, S. "Internet Resource Discovery." In *Internet Resource Discovery.* edited by B. Cope and D. Mason, 21–37. Altona, Vic: Common Ground Publishing Pty Ltd, 2001.

van Manen, M. *Researching Lived Experience: Human Science for an Action Sensitive Pedagogy.* London: The State University of New York (SUNY), 1990.

Chapter 14

Learning Reflexively: Technological Mediation and Indigenous Cultures

Leanne Reinke and Paul James

> The night of the sword and the bullet was followed by the morning of the chalk and the blackboard.
>
> (wa Thiong'o, 1986: 9)

In adult education, the dominating trend is to fetishize the use of new communication technologies. The adoption of these technologies both in everyday life and the classroom is constructed as a necessary step in "keeping-up" with global modernization. At its extreme, this view assumes a techno-utopian position that fetishizes instant access, easy connectivity, and vast archives of information. It suggests that technologies of mediation provide *the* way to revitalize social connections, enhance teaching practices, and sustain community in a fragmenting world. Such thinking, derives from a hyper-modernist world-view. That this view appears so reasonable is indicative of its cultural dominance, both in the popular domain and in adult education. For example, Liu's (1998) work exemplifies a stance that is primarily concerned with encouraging adult educators to develop new learnings in order to make full use of digital tools as advanced knowledge resources. His is an example of work which promotes the adoption of technology as an unquestionably progressive resource. Liu conducts correspondence with students by e-mail in order to bypass the inhibitions that he argues students typically face when in each other's presence.

As an extension of this position, the possibility for using technological mediation to overcome the supposed awkwardness of face-to-face interchange is all too often expressed as a new form of "the white man's burden": overcoming the awkwardness of intercultural interchange. This is part of the imperative to bring Indigenous peoples into the contemporary globalizing world through the new technologies of communication and education—the Internet, the World Wide Web, and the computer—as a means of storing and codifying knowledge. Images of this crossover of worlds abound. In one advertisement, a suit-wearing white European man sits in the dark, talking with three Indigenous men around a campfire. The night sky behind them is deep purple, and across the sky is written the words, "Talk anyone's language: Windows 2000." There was no discomfort with face-to-face or intercultural communication here.

Advertising provides a window into the contemporary world with its heavily researched and creatively engineered reflections on and expressions of our times. These reflections warp the reality of social relations, but nevertheless take us into the intensities of its promises and dreams. Perversely, it is advertising images that best illustrate the contradictions this chapter tries to analyze and understand. There is a Vodofone advertisement that depicts a satellite picture of the globe, with clouds swirling over Africa, shrouding a Europe that is flattened by the parallax of perspective. The inscription on that advertisement reads, "Vodofone spoken here." Like the Microsoft advertisement, it denotes the process of technological extension as transcending but accentuating place, person, and difference. However, it is the all-pervasive Microsoft images that present our desires most acutely: "Where do you want to go today?

If that is the dominant mono-cultural view—namely, that technology will comfortably transcend all the awkward boundaries of different languages, generations, and communities—at the other end of the spectrum there is a less common but equally problematic view. Here, technology in itself is treated as *the* cause of the fragmentation of community and the dissolving of pedagogical intensity. Students exposed to the bright light of mechanic interfaces are said to lose the capacity for sustained face-to-face pedagogical interchange, and, because of the new technologies, by the time they reach adulthood they can only concentrate for the length of an average television segment. There is no doubt that the use of technologies of communication such as the Internet can have socially fragmenting and socially abstracting effects, but it is reductive to suggest that this occurs through the technology itself. The usual way out of this Manichean clash of indefensible positions is with pseudo-liberal appeals to present a "third way"—namely, we should not use too much technology, although a moderate amount is fine. This position provides a pretense of balance while naïvely allowing the dominant mono-cultural view to go unchallenged. It is our argument that all three positions—the technologically utopian, the technologically determinist, and the technologically naïve—involve one-dimensional renditions of the problem.

First, they are all technologically determinist. The technology is treated as if it works all by itself, either for good or evil, or, halfway in between, for blandness. Second, all three positions are culturally reductive. They either do not confront the ontological differences between ways of being in the world, from the tribal-traditional Indigenous to the modern European, or alternatively, they turn "difference" into one of civilizational development. Here we are drawing upon a fourfold analytical distinction between different ontological formations of social life: tribalism, traditionalism, modernism, and postmodernism. It is important to recognize that in any actual society, particularly those in intercultural contact, these formations exist as layers of practice and subjectivity, rather than as one-dimensional planes enveloping the whole of social life. So, for example, in the Yolngu communities of Arnhem land, parents, schoolteachers, and community leaders self-consciously set out in the early 1980s to find an intersection between modern schooling and Indigenous-traditional forms of knowledge. In taking a culturally reductive path, there is a tendency to treat the difference between these ways of knowing the world as akin to the difference between the learning patterns of children and adults. Acquisition of technological skills is implicitly treated as part of the process of growing up and joining the modern world.

Third, these three positions tend to be culturally patronizing and Eurocentric. By contrast, we argue that the effects of technology depend upon the social framing of its use. Keeping to the fore a deep suspicion of technological utopianism, we want to suggest that by using the new communications technology with a reflexive and critical understanding of its potential effects, it may be possible to maintain the strength of face-to-face relations while developing qualified practices of technological mediation. This is particularly salient in the context of thinking about face-to-face communities where people still live, at least at one level of their being, in the kind of relation to place and person that can be called "tribal-traditional."

We argue that it is possible to adopt abstracting communications technologies in a way that is beneficial, without abstract mediation dominating social practice. This is occurring with some success in both Indigenous education and adult education generally, even if the pitfalls are many. Education outside of the formal education system is of particular importance in the Australian context, being the focus of reconciliation between Indigenous and non-Indigenous Australians and non-Indigenous communities to have a better understanding of Indigenous peoples. There have been a number of innovative projects in the research and development of computer-based education and language resources within Indigenous communities of Australia. These projects include distance education for remote students, CD-ROM language packages, and the collation of words and meanings of some Indigenous languages. These projects are varied in content, effectiveness, and appropriateness. For example, developing a dictionary for an oral language that is no longer spoken is bound to be either an act of well-meaning nostalgia or meaningless scientific abstraction. In contrast, using abstracting technologies in the context of practices framed at more concrete levels of integration is more appropriate to enhancing cultural sustainability through reinvention and renewal.

After discussing the introduction of computer-mediated technology in adult education programs related to Indigenous communities, this chapter analyzes some particular projects. The projects examined are a Bachelor of Education being provided by the Victoria University of Technology through face-to-face interaction in an Indigenous community in southern Australia, and the Remote Area Teacher Education Program operating in north Australia through James Cook University. These projects demonstrate the capacity to incorporate technologies and techniques of mediation into face-to-face communities without emptying out the meaning of embodied social interchange, in other words, without annulling the meaning of sitting and talking to each other. Before getting to some positive examples, the chapter begins with a critique of the tendency to treat practices of "literacy" as a "good thing" for people living within oral cultures.

Technological Wizardry Meets Indigenous Cultures

In the past, Western education has placed little value on the oral mode of communication, emphasizing instead the importance of reading, writing, and books. However, the turn to the electronic mode of communication has brought with it a series of new twists. The first is that some Indigneous people are now embracing electronic technologies as a means of communicating the meaning of Indigenous oral cultures to and beyond White Australia. New technology is seen as an innovative way to teach

White Australia about Indigenous cultures, and also as a way to reinforce the culture of the Indigenous communities for themselves: creating a double focus for adult education. There are a number of CD-ROM packages and projects that document Indigenous communities' histories and cultures. Such interactive technology and digital imagery is presented as enhancing understanding and promoting reconciliation between cultures. Here, however, in the absence of a framing culture of oral exchange, or at least face-to-face explanation, the form of the address—that is, as unreflexively presented electronically mediated text and images—counteracts the content of the address.

One of these technological tools of reconciliation released in Australia is illustrative of this phenomenon. It is a CD-ROM multimedia package entitled *Lore of the Land* (1999). This extensive venture has been undertaken by the Institute of the Sisters of Mercy and the Mercy Foundation, in association with Indigenous activists, singers and elders. *Lore of the Land* is a CD-ROM package that has been marketed as a meeting of worlds: "Where the newest communication tool meets the oldest civilization." This multi-media tool is an interactive package with a connection to an Internet website. It purports to encourage understanding and reconciliation between cultures around spirit and place. The vision of the "evocative new interactive documentary" heralds digital forms of communication as shaping the future and enabling the crossing of new frontiers of knowledge. This package does not, however, offer anything new in terms of ideas to offset the one-dimensional technological mode of delivery. Rather, it provides the possibility of hearing the oral histories and the songs of the Indigenous peoples out of context.

A multi-media computer package is an opportunity for recorded stories to be heard in their oral, rather than written,, form. Nevertheless, it is still necessary to be sensitive to and reflect upon the way in which the stories are told, in what context and the impact of editing and scripts. In this production, there are relatively few Indigenous stories to make the most of the technological capacity to communicate oral recordings. Those that are presented are short, predictable, and not contextualized by any teachings about the Indigenous ways of life or visuals from the speakers' communities or urban situations. There is an overuse of still photography, accompanied by background Indigenous music presented without information about where or what is being displayed.

An interactive game primarily tests one's patience, as the player is instructed to move around images, supposedly representing a cave, to collect "artifacts" such as spears, boomerangs, and woven baskets. These images of material culture appear without any explanation of their cultural meanings. Indigenous people speak all too briefly about their connection to the land in terms that reinforce, rather than extend or challenge, the prevailing understandings of White Australians. It is paralleled with a middle-class suburban Anglo-ethnic family playing in their backyard, and a group of young Anglo-ethnic surfers speaking of their affiliation with the ocean. These examples make a mockery of the spiritual meaning of the land and denigrate the foundational meaning of place for Indigenous Australians. The claim that a 40,000-year-old culture meets the newest communicative tool illustrates the failure of this socio-technological undertaking to give a meaningful representation of Indigenous cultures.

The use of technology, as in the above example, does not engage with the ontological form of Indigenous culture but merely carries fragments without being contextualized in a multi-media format. While it may involve sophisticated techniques of representation, it does so only to suggest that Indigenous cultures can be whisked away on a magic carpet to a land where difference does not make a difference. The assumption behind using the electronic form is that it is the latest in a line of progress in communicative developments. This assumption has profound implications for those communities who have retained their oral traditions. While it is possible for the oral, written, and electronic media to coexist in a productive tension, the assumption that new technologies can represent Indigenous ways of life by "lifting" bits of graphic or aural activity effectively overshadows this possibility with an unacknowledged technological hubris.

Sustaining Oral Cultures Electronically

A second twist has occurred with the emergence of electronic technologies of communication. Namely, that the electronic can draw directly back upon the oral without being mediated by writing as the dominant mode of communication. This "drawing back" links the oral and electronic modes through their apparently similar practices of interactivity, where, in their rapid adoption of electronic media, Indigenous people can move directly from orality to the electronic society. Michael Rose (1996: xx) has commented on the connection between the oral and the electronic modes of communication:

> it should not be terribly surprising that for Aboriginal people who adopt European media technology, radio and television would be something they would generally

consider first. Radio and television production are much closer to the oral nature of traditional Aboriginal communication than printed-word newspapers, magazines or books. There is also the problem of language and literacy: a small television service or radio station can be set up and people in a particular community can, given certain basic equipment and training, produce and listen to broadcasts in their own languages without necessarily being able to read or write in English or any other language.

Accordingly, electronic communication technology is said to be more attractive to Indigenous communities than reading and writing. For this reason, it could be that the many technological communicative programs that have been developed are more culturally appropriate for Indigenous peoples. More commonly, however, technological packages designed for adult education are presented as bridging "the old with the new," more for marketing purposes than as an attempt at cultural appropriateness.

While there is a bridge between the oral and the electronic, the issue of electronically stimulating Indigenous languages is not so simple. The Australian Institute of Aboriginal and Torres Strait Islander Studies (AIATSIS) has an extensive program committed to sustaining diverse Indigenous languages. The Indigenous Languages and Interactive Technology project aims to encourage the sustainability of Indigenous languages. It claims to do this in three ways. First, through maintaining a large collection of computer-based information about Australia's Indigenous languages. Second, through the provision of advice to communities and educational bodies about the effective use of computers for the language work that they wish to undertake. Third, by publishing electronic materials through encouraging local communities to publish on the Internet. It is important to consider the focus of this program in relation to Indigenous language sustainability and its actual use within social contexts.

Some of the projects in this restoration program focus on the use of CD-ROMs for the storage of these languages in order to avoid their loss. The new technology allows for voices and texts to be accurate and contextualized. Handled well, this may indeed be the case, however, we suggest that a language stored on advanced digital equipment is different from a living language that is continually used within community-based integrative practices. Technological storage "fixes" the codification of a moment of speech and the abstraction of the body of the speaker. The association between spoken words and the written version is often taken for granted, so it is difficult to critically examine the recording of orality. The assumption that the recording of Indigenous languages in electronic form will "save" the languages is debatable. The recording of a language that is no longer spoken in a social setting means it cannot evolve and develop, and so bears little resemblance to a living language. A multi-media package on which spoken words can be heard offers little benefit unless the language is practiced in everyday social settings.

An example of a dictionary that has been produced for use electronically on the World Wide Web is that of the Kamilaroi/Gamilaraay language (Austin and Nathan, 2001). The website states that the Gamilaraay language from central-eastern Australia has a vocabulary of many thousands of words and quite a complicated grammar. This language stopped being used daily in the first half of the twentieth century due to the impact of British colonization. The World Wide Web version is a hypertext document that has many links to activate cross-referencing of words with similar meanings. The dictionary has a computer-generated finder list (reverse dictionary) and a thesaurus-style index. It has been designed to be attractive and easy to navigate. However, the impact such a program could have on the communities of this region in reinvigorating the use of their Indigenous language in their everyday lives is questionable. Nevertheless, this innovative language project has prevented the loss of records of this language's existence because it is now electronically stored.

The preference for the electronic over the written form, however, still holds relevance in some of these new developments. There are examples of the preference toward electronic forms within the education system in Indigenous communities within Australia. The Strelley Community displays the importance of the electronic form being introduced within the cultural framework of the community. Established in the west of Australia in 1976, the Strelley Community has maintained a strong Nyangumarta language and cultural maintenance program. Part of the program involves a series of "Culture Camp" field excursions that involve adults, particularly elders, in the learning process (Routh, 1997). This has been linked to the introduction of new technologies, such as CD-ROM and video, that have been used for projects in Nyangumarta. However, this culturally appropriate integration of the electronic form into pedagogy is not evident in many situations. There is too often a tendency to assume that the electronic technology itself will provide benefits through its capacity to store oral records. This benefit is thought to modernize communities that have retained face-to-face relations as their dominant mode of social integration.

Adult education policy makers are coming to recognize that progress in Indigenous education is not only achieved through the involvement of

Indigenous educators and the production of Indigenous curriculum, but also through the use of teaching practices which are appropriate for ensuring Indigenous cultural sustainability. Without understanding oral traditions in educative practices and Indigenous communities, the introduction of electronic technologies are unlikely to be beneficial. Many multimedia packages and enterprises offering technological wizardry will find their endeavors ineffectual if not grounded within the embodied, face-to-face practices of Indigenous communities that link people across the generations—young and old; child, adult and elder.

Integrating the Electronic

Debates about the adoption of technology in Indigenous adult education have generally been around the access and affordability questions. Yet it is not only these issues that need to be explored. The implications of disembodied communicative practices upon the constitution of social relations also need to be critically examined. The use of information technology has been promoted as a way for teaching to be carried out away from institutional settings and for allowing adults to learn at their own pace. This move away from face-to-face pedagogy has been advocated as part of the linear-progressive march of technology. There is a need to extend the debate over the implications on communicative practices that such an adoption of information technology may have. While the use of technology can be beneficial in bridging geographic isolation, this benefit often clouds some of the problems that it may engender, as does the automatic adoption of packages designed for White Australians for use with and by Indigenous adult learners. Henderson (1996) argues that the design of computer instructional packages needs to empower, extend, and enrich Indigenous students' culturally specific knowledge and ways of thinking. Unfortunately, this is not generally occurring.

Studies of teaching/learning contexts in Australian Indigenous communities place an important emphasis on informal adult education. This method of teaching incorporates the everyday practices of the social grouping into the learning environment. It is a process of adult learning that works well in situations constituted through face-to-face communicative practices. Stephen Harris (1980) has long argued that learning incorporates both informal and formal practices. Formal adult education maintains two distinguishing features: that language (written and/or oral) is the major means of transmitting knowledge; and that teaching and learning are carried on out-of-context, that is, outside of immediate everyday experience. In comparison, informal adult education is characterized by observation and by doing rather than by verbalization. Informal learning is situation-specific. Recognition of the differences in learning techniques is integral to any proposed developments in pedagogy. Given that these developments include the involvement of new technologies, it becomes important to consider the relations between different modes of communication. Lyn Henderson (1996: 102, 95) argues for the need to be aware of, and adapt teaching to accommodate, differences in learning practices, focusing on:

> the mental models, thinking processes, and teaching-learning strategies used by teachers and learners when interacting with electronic databases, interactive multimedia and the world wide web. ...For instance, questioning and justifying the validity of statements and analysis are endemic to academic discourse but are generally unacceptable in Australian Indigenous current-traditional ways of learning and teaching. Thus in one academic context, evaluation of Indigenous learners who are having difficulty with justification questions embedded in IMM courseware can identify the learners as deficient and, at best, remedial, and design feedback loops for context mastery. In a multiple cultural academic context, it is understood that Indigenous acceptance of the rationale for questioning and interrogating the knower (the White lecturer) and providing evidence based on objective research (rather than tradition and the authority of the elders) will need a cognitive apprenticeship approach.

This goes a step beyond the careful introduction of electronic communicative forms, such as occurred at the Strelley community. It not only means introducing the equipment to be used in a culturally appropriate manner, but also adapting the programs that are used to make them contribute to Indigenous cultural sustainability, which is a political and economic issue as much as anything else.

There are significant issues within the instructional design of computer technology that are essential to the debate over technology, adult education, and cultural specificity. Computer technology carries with it culturally specific meanings. Henderson (1996) points out that computer icons have little self-evident meaning for users: for example, all users have to *learn* that the question mark indicates "help," or the pointing hand means "go to," and the arrow means "continue." There are a number of reasons why instructional design shows evidence of being culturally one-dimensional and exclusionary. These include having an unconscious culturally homogenous approach, or wishing to avoid the possible controversy in the contradictory stances. Treating the user as an abstract "learner" with no situated identity can lead to mistaken assumptions. Multicultural educational software often adopts superficial tokenism, or such material is naïvely developed in the belief that it is inexpensive.

It is necessary, therefore, for any adult education programs implemented for Indigenous Australians to enhance Indigenous cultural sustainability if they are to be beneficial for the learners. This can be achieved through "bringing forward" cultural resources of their choosing. This entails going beyond "soft multiculturalism"—simply including various elements of other cultures. One of these dubious methods is to include myths and legends from around the world. Often, this instructional technique involves the students in devising their own myth and legend with authoring software. This tokenism indicates a serious lack of understanding of and respect for the spiritual significance of creation stories. Acknowledging these concerns, it is possible to illustrate educational programs operating within Australia's Indigenous communities that have reflexively adopted computer-mediated technology into their educational programs. These examples demonstrate the capacity of Indigenous people to adopt and adapt technology in ways that maintain the face-to-face practices fundamental to deepening and extending socially integrative communities.

Cultural Reflexivity in Educational Practice

Two programs are used here as examples of the self-conscious work of bringing Indigenous cultures forward through incorporating modern technologies within pedagogical practice. The Nyerna campus of Victoria University and Queensland's Remote Area Teacher Education Program illustrate the development of successful, innovative programs that emphasize the centrality of face-to-face interactions in an increasingly abstracted global arena of futuristic images and nostalgia.

The Nyerna program is offered through Victoria University of Technology, located in Echuca and Moama. These towns are situated in northern Victoria on the Murray River, the border with New South Wales. This tertiary course began in 1998 at the request of a delegation from the local Koorie community, which includes the Cummeragunja lands. The delegation traveled to Melbourne to approach the University with their request for a professional degree program in their local area. The aim of the program is to provide an alternative to regional students who feel alienated when forced to leave their family and country to study, and as a result often fail to complete their degrees. The center offers a three-year Bachelor of Arts in Sport, Recreation, and Youth Studies and a four-year Bachelor of Education program. There are also TAFE-accredited qualifications applicable to first- and second-year courses. To be culturally and locally appropriate, the program has been designed with flexible, integrated, informal, and enquiring approaches to teaching and learning.

The agreed principles for the Nyerna Studies program incorporate a participatory approach to learning and teaching. These include, first, a community responsiveness and partnership strategy between the students and the community based on mutual respect, interest, and authority. Second, the teaching and learning is based on an inquiry, learn-by-doing approach fostered through small-group workshops and seminars which enable students to build on real-life situations, encourage reflection, and analyze situations encountered in their community partnership programs. Third, there is a system of flexible pathways and outcomes where it is possible to exit the program at a number of points and achieve formal accreditation. Fourth, there is encouragement for students to determine their own questions, outcomes, and forms of assessment. Two additional principles were developed during the first two years of the program-in-practice. One was the recognition and incorporation of learning from the land in which the study center is located, and the other was the consideration of cultural sustainability in the program's support for open inquiry (Hooley, 2000).

There are different and varied ways of knowing whose interests and power should determine the form and content of teaching practices. The project has accepted the legitimacy of Indigenous ways of knowing. In this case, culturally aligned forms of community knowledge have been elevated to equal status with academic knowledge in the fields of education and youth studies (Hooley, 2000). The emphasis on community involvement is paramount to the Nyerna project. When a pedagogical project is undertaken with its way of knowing derived from the community in which it is based, it is operating at the most concrete level of integration. Face-to-face interaction frames the educational practices undertaken by the group. Within this social framing the students are able to use more abstract modes of communication in their learning activities without diminishing embodied learning.

Our second positive example, the Remote Area Teacher Education Program (RATEP), is based at James Cook University in Queensland and began in 1990. It was established in collaboration with Education Queensland and the Tropical North Queensland Institute of TAFE. The program is designed to educate Indigenous teachers who are located in remote communities in Torres Strait, Cape York, and the Gulf of Carpentaria. In addition to being studied through interactive multimedia computer courseware supplemented by other electronic technology and texts, this off-campus degree also includes local research centers and residential schools for students.

Unlike a strictly distance education mode of delivery, the provision of such flexible modes of teaching and learning require significant levels of funding and infrastructure. The Federal Government funded local tutoring, the educational centers, and the necessary links to the institutional base. The course is accredited throughout its three years to allow students to exit with either a Certificate of Community Teaching, an Associate Diploma of Education, or a Diploma of Teaching. The significance of RATEP is that the course has been culturally contextualized for Indigenous university students. However, while it is possible to commend this course for its cultural sensitivity, the largely disembodied form of its teaching program needs to be acknowledged.

RATEP has addressed the pedagogic and theoretical questions of designing an appropriate instructional interface between the learner and the interactive multimedia materials (Henderson and Putt, 1993). This program was specifically designed for Indigenous students as the usual methods of distance teaching where found to be inappropriate. The retention and graduation rate for special entry Aboriginal and Torres Strait Islander on-campus students studying the same Diploma of Teaching with the same lecturers was 30–40 percent. Long periods away from their communities were unacceptable for the teachers, as was carrying out the course by Internet-based programs or by written distance-education packages. Each teacher is now provided with a laptop computer, which has the required projects to be undertaken already loaded onto them. The actual design of the interactive material has also been designed and modified to suit the requirements of Indigenous learners. Henderson's research (1996) has found that non-Indigenous students are not disadvantaged by using these same culturally contextualized materials, but rather, that many find numerous personal and cognitive advantages.

The multiple cultural models which have been used for the design of RATEP aim to combine the academic, dominating, and Indigenous cultures in a coherent interplay (Henderson, 1996). The program is designed in a cyclic model to accommodate the specific learning characteristics of its students. They are directed to move between various texts to complete a task, the workbooks, textbooks, videos, and computer-based activities. This cycle of observation, demonstration, and practice with immediate feedback correlates with the methodologies of adult learning and teaching (Henderson and Putt, 1993). It is not only possible for this cycle to be repeated, but for it to occur privately, as there is a reticence among Indigenous adults to take risks publicly.

While RATEP is still substantially a distance education program enabled and dependent upon computer technology, it at least recognizes the need to contribute to Indigenous cultural sustainability in its instructional design. One of the challenges the program now faces, however, is that of the language it uses in its delivery. As RATEP operates across several remote localities, it consequently operates across several Indigenous language groups. Now it has to reconsider its dependency upon English as its carrier. Such a challenge to RATEP is indicative of the broader challenges facing adult educators at the interface of technology, adult education, and the sustainability of Indigenous cultural and linguistic diversity.

Conclusion

This chapter has addressed the popularization of electronic communicative technologies within adult education in Australia's Indigenous communities. We have argued that for effective Indigenous pedagogical practice it is necessary to address the specificity of cultural practices, not just as content but also as social form. The instructional programs in electronic forms must acknowledge the culturally specific practices in their design. The preferred mode of face-to-face communication must also be addressed in adult learning/teaching practices and be integrated with the disembodied electronic mode in appropriate ways. This has significant bearing upon Indigenous language sustainability and the language options that must be available for adult Indigenous learners. It also has significant bearing upon the identification and incorporation of Indigenous knowledges within new technologies.

There are a number of programs operating in Australia that have taken measures to acknowledge and incorporate practices that appropriately flag the need for adult educators to contribute to Indigenous cultural and linguistic sustainability. The examples that have been explored within this chapter suggest the possibility, however fragile, of Indigenous communities sustaining the characteristics of integrative community: reciprocal and embodied engagement with persons and place. This, we argue, can only be achieved in a sustainable way through a reflexive framing of the abstract forms of communication within social practices constituted at the level of the face-to-face.

References

Austin, P., and D. Nathan. *Kamilaroi/Gamilaraay Web Dictionary* 2001 cited 2 March 2001. Available from http://coombs.anu.edu.au/WWWVLPages/AborigPages/lang/gamdict/gamdict.htm.

Australian Institute of Aboriginal and Torres Strait Islander Studies. *Indigenous Languages and Interactive Technology at AIATSIS* 2001 cited 2 March 2001. Available from http://www.aiatsis.gov.au/res_rsc.htm#1git.

Darwin, N.T.: Professional Services Branch, Northern Territory Department of Education, 1980.

Harris, S. *Culture and Learning: Tradition and Education in Northeast Arnhem Land.*

Henderson, L., "Instructional Design of Interactive Multimedia: A Cultural Critique." *Educational Technology Research and Development* 44, no. 4 (1996): 85–104.

Henderson, L., and I. Putt. "The Remote Area Teacher Program (RATEP): Cultural Contextualisation of Distance Education through Interactive Multimedia." *Distance Education* 14, no. 2 (1993): 212–31.

Hooley, N. "Nyerna Studies: Learning as a Community Partnership." Paper presented at the Australian Indigenous Education Conference: Learning Better Together. Fremantle, WA, 4–7 April 2000.

Liu, K. "Electronic Communication, New Technology, and the Esl Student." In *Adult Esl: Politics, Pedagogy and Participation in Classroom and Community Programs*, edited by T. Smoke, 289–311. Mahwah, NJ: Lawrence Erlbaum Associates, 1998.

Lore of the Land: Reconciling Spirit & Place in Australia's Story. Alphington: Fraynework Multimedia, 1999.

Rose, M., ed. *For the Record: 160 Years of Aboriginal Print Journalism.* St Leonards, N.S.W.: Allen & Unwin, 1996.

Routh, R. "The Strelley Community School Nyangumarta Language and Cultural Maintenance Program." *Australian Journal of Indigenous Education* 25, no. 2 (1997): 27–32.

wa Thiong'o, N. *Decolonising the Mind: The Politics of Language in African Literature.* London: James Curry, 1986.

Chapter 15

Peoples' Power against the Empire: Re-framing Work-Related Teaching/Learning

Mike Brown

Introduction

For two decades, pressure has been brought to bear on Australian workplaces to reform their operations to ensure international competitiveness. These pressures have dramatically impacted on both management and workers. Take the case of the contract negotiations at the Toyota plant in Melbourne, where specially trained Japanese negotiators were flown in to conduct these talks. As part of their tactics, these negotiators walked their union counterparts through the factory in order to point out to them that all the machinery in this car plant was merely bolted down. This was their way of telling the union negotiators that all of this vast car manufacturing plant could be moved offshore if Australian workers were too expensive.

As elsewhere in the global economy, this threat underpins industrial relations in many Australian manufacturing companies. Sometimes this threat is real and at other times it is imagined. Judging by the decline in employment within Australian manufacturing it has been all too real for many. In this way, workers across the country are left with a threat of choosing between retaining their jobs or making a claim against their employer for increased wages and improved working conditions which could see their work moved offshore.

Living in a globalizing world has potential advantages and real disadvantages for us all. We need to know what these are so as to be informed about possible actions. Likewise, we need to discuss why we are heading in the directions that we are. Similarly, we need to enter into dialogue about future directions and explore alternatives. As a society, we need to consider issues and perspectives that are both local and international (Cornfield and Hodson, 2002). These efforts need to be ongoing.

There is a political project emerging here that has a substantial role for adult educators and adult learning to play. Part of the task is to galvanize the various networks and resources of adult education with those of community activists. This involves putting people first and asking questions about how we want to live, both now and into the future. This important debate is beset with competing arguments and agendas which need to be discussed so decisions can be made and actions taken. The question, then, is not whether we should undertake this project, but where do we start?

This chapter identifies some ideas that may assist in this transdisciplinary project of developing a curriculum framework for work-related learning. The argument is structured in three sections. The first section briefly outlines the context by presenting some general features of the interrelated processes of globalization/localization. The second section offers a series of disparate ideas, from a strategic naming of work-related learning to participatory economics as resources to aid this project (Butler, 2001). The final section in the chapter brings these ideas together as the basis of a tentative curriculum framework for work-related teaching/learning. This section concludes with four vignettes which stand as examples of the kind of case studies and stories which the curriculum can present to adult learners for further consideration.

Globalization/Localization

The project of creating a defensible framework for work-related teaching/learning can usefully be situated within the context of globalization and localization. While globalization is economic, cultural, social, and political, only the first two of these are discussed in this chapter. Economic globalization can be variously named as neo-conservative globalism, economic fundamentalism, the Washington consensus, integrated world capitalism (IWC), or as "empire." It is about the global integration of trade and financial markets, freeing these from the control of nation-states. Under global trade, the regulations of nation-states lose some of their significance as a cross-border trade becomes driven by the regulating power of market forces. Products are controlled for quality according to a specified standard, and the issue for business becomes sourcing the cheapest acceptable product and delivering it to markets where it will obtain maximum return. It is in this way that Australian consumers are offered oranges that are grown in Brazil and wealthy Arabs can drive Australian-made cars. Interestingly, global trade is a one-sided affair that is not extended to a freeing up of the labor market. For example, working people are not always free to cross borders, and for those who do get access to work in another country, this is no guarantee of further success (Mojab, 2001).

Some have referred to cultural globalization as "McDonaldization" and "Disneyfication." For instance, Ife (2002: 143) notes, "people in different parts of the world are increasingly wearing similar clothes, eating similar food, watching the same movies, listening to the same music and playing the same games." This is having devastating effects upon local communities and the sustainability of ecological, cultural, and linguistic diversity.

On the other hand, localization has arisen out of resistance and frustration to the effects of globalization from above. This has been led by community-based initiatives that seek to address the real needs of local people. Examples of localization include the establishment of community banks, local currencies, and cooperatives. Localization can also involve cultural initiatives, such as reclaiming local customs, languages and celebrating local histories. Likewise, in some instances and local political processes have been established as a reaction to feelings of dis-empowerment brought about by a perceived loss of relevance of national political parties. This can take regressive forms of resistance or progressive forms of projecting globalization from below.

The interdependent practices of globalization and localization have ramifications for adult educators. As we enter the twenty-first century, adult educators are considering whether these views on global/local relations are accurate, who is winning and who is losing in this process, whether this is desirable, and what might be done.

The dominating approach to adult learning for work at the moment is vocational education and training (VET). However, the curriculum for the kind of project that is being outlined here cannot be based on pre-defined competencies or outcomes. The VET system is one of the structures that the nation-state uses to service the needs of global/local capital. It is a sector that is focussed on processes and procedures that privilege and service the needs of employers. There is little space to question the desirability of this subservient relationship. The risk is that worker-learners graduating with VET qualifications may end up with an "education" that is not worth having. Only limited gains are likely to result from working within existing VET programs. What is needed is a reconceptualization of learning for, through, and about work. A democratic, negotiated project would involve those most effected by the decisions in making the decisions.

The following section explores a series of ideas leading to the re-imagining of work-related teaching/learning. This requires an understanding of the social, technical, and economic relations of work, complementary holism, and participatory economics. In the final section, these are brought together to provide a preliminary curriculum framework for work-related teaching/learning.

The Social, Technical, and Economic Relations of Work

As work-related learning includes the social relations of "doing work," then it is necessary to find ways to assist workers-learners in analyzing, understanding and critiquing workplace power relations. A starting point for this is the work of Amott and Matthaei (1996) on race/ethnicity, gender and class, historical moment, and location. After researching the multicultural economic history of women workers, they concluded that women throughout the USA have not experienced a common oppression as women, but that their experiences are mediated on the basis of race, class, and ethnicity. Recognizing this suggests engaging worker/learners in developing an analytical framework that focuses on ways in which race-ethnicity, class and gender relations of power combine to structure women's working lives. To this can be added the analysis of the transformation of these relations over time with the development of a global/local capitalist economy and continuing struggles against oppression.

Harriet Bradley (1999) has been researching workplaces in Britain for the last fifteen years. To understand workplace dynamics and power relationships, she argues that it is necessary to make sense of the overlapping dynamics of class, ethnicity, gender, and age. In exploring patterns of relations between men and women, she traces continuities as well as changes, and places these change within the context of global/local capitalist developments. Her work demonstrates how these processes combine to produce hierarchies of gender and class power within workplaces. Importantly, her framework evolves from, and is grounded in, research within workplaces whose dynamics are historically and contextually situated. Bradley's work provides a model for students to use in the analyzing and understanding gender and class relations, along with a resource-based account of power. This allows for the exploration of material and cultural elements while also offering a means to link structure and action, as well as the global and local. As workplace power relations are an important aspect of work, attempts to understand and learn about them are an integral part of work-related teaching/learning. However, adult educators cannot stop there. Strategic alliances can be developed between the academic world and the lived experiences of activists working within community projects.

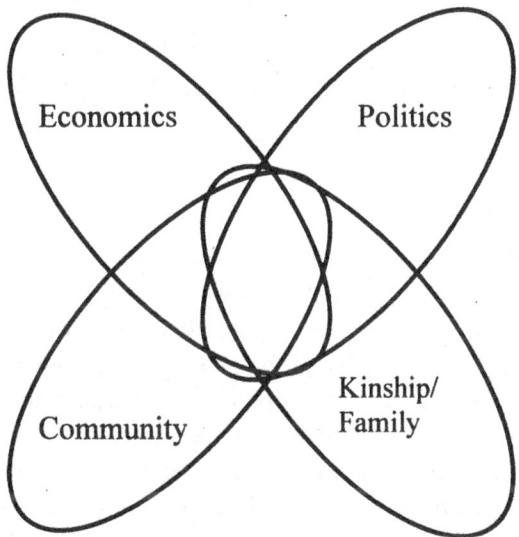

Figure 15.1: Complementary holism: The overlapping spheres of economics, politics, community, and kinship

Complementary Holism

"Complementary holism" is a concept that refers to ways of assisting people to analyze global/local society. It enables them to understand where we are at the moment; develop alternative aims and visions for that society; and develop strategies for moving from where we are to where we want to be (Albert, Cagan, Chomsky, Hahnel, King, Sargent, and Sklar, 1986). In other words, "complementary holism" attempts to capture a holistic view of global/local society, represented by four spheres, namely, community, kinship, economics and politics (see figure 15.1). Complementary holism invites the exploration of ideas, work and modes of organization within each sphere, as well as investigating the relationships across and between them.

Within the curriculum framework being advocated here, the concepts and themes drawn from each of these spheres need to be considered in relation to how these might impact on and influence the field of work-related teaching/learning. Major focuses within the "community" sphere are ethnicity, culture and inter-communalism. For the "kinship" sphere, major concepts to be explored are the influence of feminism, patriarchy, and sexuality on a range of family relations. The "political" sphere involves exploration of self-management and participatory forms of democracy. Interestingly, Bradley's (1999) analysis of ethnicity, gender, class and power within workplaces aligns with these four spheres of complementary holism.

Participatory Economics

Albert and Hahnel (1991) have begun to develop the "economic" sphere of complementary holism as a model of how the other spheres might be further developed, as much as it stands as an alternative form of political economy to that of neo-conservative globalism. For over a decade, Albert (1997; 2000) has been facilitating developments in "participatory economics" by critiquing neoclassical economics. One aspect of this criticism is the way that neo-classical economics labels the negative outcomes its policies and practices have on people and the environment as mere "externalities." This critique has fostered an oppositional approach to developing "a people-centered economics."

Complementary holism is part of a process for developing a vision that develops a value-rational approach to economics. Albert and Hahnel (1991), explain that the values and goals which they aim to enact are equity, solidarity, diversity, and participatory self-management, plus efficiency and classlessness, see also Albert, 1997. They explain that an economy is a set of institutions that facilitates and organizes people in the production and consumption of goods, services, and information. Chomsky (1988), a member of this project, though not always in total agreement, argues that

> the task for a modern society is to achieve what is now technically realisable, namely, a society which is really based on free voluntary participation of people

who produce and create, live their lives freely within institutions they control, and with limited hierarchical structures, possibly none at all.

Within this conception of participatory economics, work is carried out under the democratic arrangements of workplace councils using a principle of one person for one vote. Albert and Hahnel (1991) explain that there is no fixed hierarchy and that each worker has a list of comparable job tasks and responsibilities, a fair share of both desirable and not so desirable things to do, comparable responsibilities and opportunities, and is equally prepared to participate in decision making.

In regards to consumption, the consumers receive roughly equal shares of the social product, must make a reasonable attempt at predicting their consumption in advance, are entitled to one person one vote, collective goods are chosen by consumer councils, and participants enact equity and self-management practices.

Participatory planning under this approach to economics is a means by which worker and consumer councils negotiate and revise their proposals for what they will produce and consume. The proposal is that all parties relay their plans to one another via "facilitation boards." The system rests on a comprehensive exchange of information which workers and consumers use to revise their proposals in order to yield a match between consumption requests and production proposals (Albert and Hahnel, 1991: 12–13; Albert, 2000).

The other three spheres of complementary holism, namely, community, kinship, and politics, wait to be developed. This would follow similar principles to that of participatory economics, by foregrounding democratic values with a general aim of achieving a people-centered society. This task informs contemporary efforts to elaborate and articulate an appropriate vision for work-related teaching/learning.

Towards a Curriculum Framework for Work-Related Teaching/Learning

One possible direction is to think less of the curriculum as a matter of reproducing the world of the industrial era, but as offering a design for living in the future world of the emergering post-industrial era. A post-industrial curriculum aims to engage students (and teachers) in knowledge production, rather than reproducing the practices of "knowledge management" that arose under the industrial era and are now most evident in the domiant franschise model of business. Through such knowledge prpducing curriculum the students become socio-cultural subjects bearing a vision of their future agency in the world. It is these considerations about possible and preferred futures that provide the resources for critically reflecting on the industrial curriculum of the present, and thereby enable appropirate changes and continuities across and between these eras.

Given that the curriculum is a plan for learning, then pedagogy is necessarily important. Pedagogy gives the curriculum its orientation to the future—the future of students and their relations with family, community, politics, and the economy. Efforts by adult educators in developing a people-centered pedagogy for work-related teaching/learning are especially significant.

Work-related learning is a broad notion that could encompass all the learning that occurs in relation to work, not just learning *for* work, but also learning *through* and *about* work, both paid and unpaid. This includes the formal, informal, non-formal, and incidental learning associated with work performed in private and public sector industries, businesses, or service agencies as well as the work done in the home, local community, and on behalf of global/local civil society. A curriculum for work-related teaching/learning framed in these terms represents an expression of the principles of complimentary holism (see Figure 15.2).

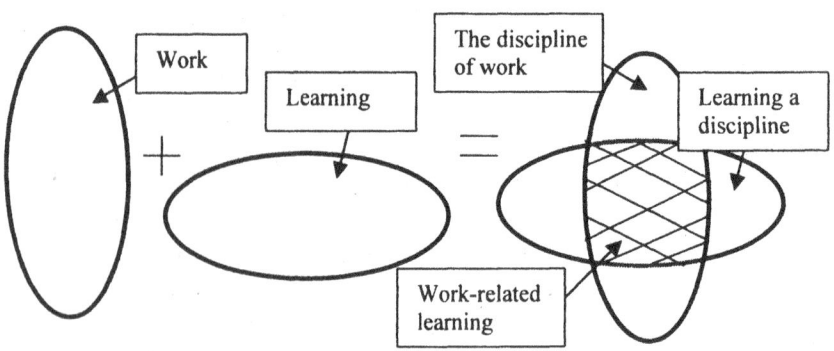

**Figure 15.2: Work-related teaching/learning:
The interdisciplinary intersection of work and adult learning**

In identifying and considering alternatives to integrated global/local capitalism, the study of both work and learning are taken as being broad and intersecting disciplines. Such an approach involves consideration of "work" within workplaces which is done for wages; unpaid work within the home and in the family situation; and also such notions as voluntary work within the community. Similarly, adult learning is understood as encompassing formal, informal, non-formal, and incidental learning (Foley, 2000).

The point here is that there are many important aspects of work which can be made the focus of systematic work-related learning that goes beyond performing technical skills. Work-related teaching/learning encompasses as legitimate curriculum content what worker-learners consider important issues as well as the debates about work and workplaces, from which working people are often excluded. Work-related learning provides a space for analyzing and critiquing existing forms of work, as it is does for considering and developing alternative possibilities.

Work-related teaching/learning offers an educational space for investigating possibilities for more democratic forms of work. Work-related teaching/learning also provides a place for collective consideration and collaboration in efforts to create, deepen, and extend democracy to a political economy now dominated by the ideology of neo-conservative globalism. Coming from two ancient Greek words, demos and kratia, "democratic" translates into "people power." Therefore, a democratically inspired project of developing a curriculum framework for work-related teaching/learning puts working people and their power at the center of knowledge production. It is the application of people power to the active and explicit study of the lived experiences and relations of work (Ehrenreich, 2001).

A Critical Pedagogy of Work-Related Teaching/Learning

Kincheloe's (1995; 1999) outline of a pedagogy of work addresses the political, economic, and social realities that shape education for employment and the conditions that produce the students who are affected by it. This pedagogy escapes technicist constructions by offering a conceptualization of work education as involving the creation of a vision, or design for the future, grounded in reconceptualized democratic ideals.

Such an approach challenges the comfortable taken-for-granted assumptions of corporate managerialism that have now infested virtually all work practices including those of adult educators (Simon, Dippo and Schenke (1991). This pedagogy engages worker-learners in evaluating work, its organization, and the key ideas driving these for their contradictions and the opportunities they present. Aligned with this is the influence of the discourse of neo-classical economics and the economy as the assumed logic and dominating discourse of how the life-world is organized. A critical pedagogy of work could provide a basis from which to critique claims about the efficiency of global/local market and to develop alternative theories and practices for adult education.

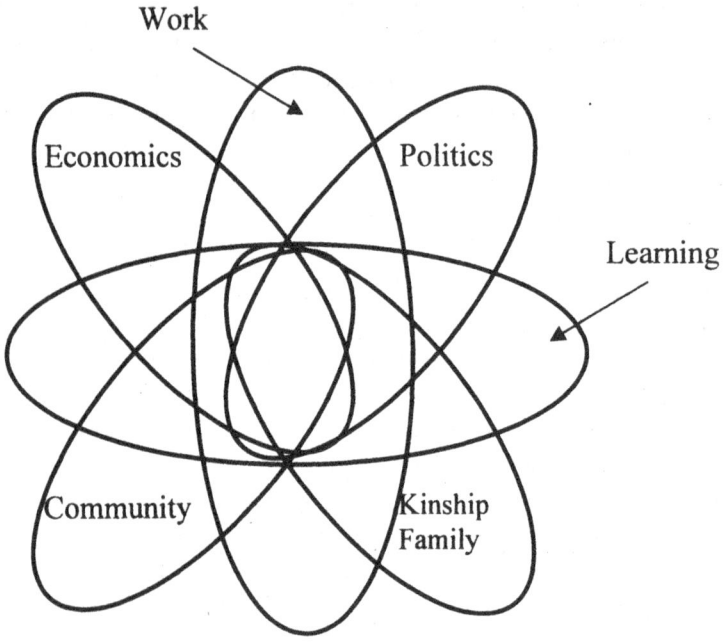

**Figure 15.3: A curriculum framework
for complementary holism and work-related learning**

Adult educators understand theories on self-esteem, community building, and identity formation are bound up with work. Respect for workers and the dignity of work may be promoted by working collaboratively with students to create more democratic forms of knowledge production. Notions of diversity and solidarity are important to assisting worker-learners to understand the cultural politics of their work and how this relates to the broader socio-political, cultural, and economic dimensions of globalization. Workers can begin to reframe and rewrite the meaning of their work as part of larger, global/local struggles against social and economic injustice. Such approaches develop worker/thinkers. The forms of work and the nature of workplaces can be a collaborative effort to be thought through by those most involved, namely, the workers. Such a project could be facilitated through adult education programs.

This chapter represents a preliminary articulation of such a curriculum framework for work-related learning (see figure 15.3). The aim of this research project is to devise approaches to curriculum that legitimize and facilitate various means by which worker/learners can learn to analyze, understand, and critique existing power struggles with the aim of formulating alternative visions for "people-centered" approaches to globalization. This is occurring in tandem with efforts to enable teaching/learning of practices for making judgments about these alternatives and to devising strategies for bringing these transformations into reality.

One useful strategy for facilitating work-related learning programs is for adult educators to have their students collect, generate, and analyze a range of case studies, vignettes, and stories. Four vignettes are presented below as examples of the possibilities for change that emerge from these considerations. Each vignette provides an example of work and learning that corresponds to each sphere associated with complementary holism.

Four Vignettes

Working within the Community

The Wyndham Adventure Playground. Wyndham lies on the western outskirts of Melbourne, Australia's second largest city. It is a multicultural, working-class community of 77,000 people with limited recreation facilities and sponsorship. In March 1996, a community-based committee was established to plan and build an adventure playground. By April of that year, the council had approved the selection of a site. The organizing committee created a further eleven sub-committees focusing on planning, promotion, funding and sponsorship, building, and materials, along with subcommittees for the provision of catering, childcare, and first aid during the building phase.

Leading up to a "design day," students from twenty-four local primary schools were encouraged to draw or build models of their ideal playground. The design day was held in May and a representative of the USA-based company, "Leathers and Associates" gathered ideas from 120 students. In June the committee received the first draft of a schematic design.

Two consultants from "Leathers and Associates" and a Melbourne builder oversaw the construction phase. On Monday, February 17, 1997, the site was pegged out, and holes for some 180 structural poles were drilled. Tuesday, February 18 marked the beginning of the work of some 2000 volunteers on the site. The volunteers were organized into three shifts. The first worked from 7:30 a.m. to noon, the second from 12:30 p.m until 5:00 p.m. and the third from 5:30 p.m. until nightfall at about 8:45 p.m. On Sunday, February 23 after eleven months of planning, and at a cost of $200,000, (though having a replacement value of $800,000), the adventure playground was completed.

It is suggested that careful consideration and review of projects such as this would assist students in identifying and validating the collective work of communities. Based on the learnings from this type of work, this could make it possible for other worthwhile projects considered important by the people in the community to be initiated using collaborative processes.

Work and Kinship: Childcare and Family-friendly Workplaces

The ABC Childcare Center Limited is a not-for-profit workplace that has twelve employees. It is a small organization that has shown understanding of the specific needs of its staff, establishing practices that enhance staff retention. The center has a very low turnover rate, even though some employees travel long distances. Similarly, it has recorded very high levels of satisfaction amongst its clients.

This center has institutionalized a number of important family-friendly measures. Staff can use the facilities for their own children and rostered days off are accumulated for use at the employees' discretion. Staff also have access to telephone and fax for their personal use. The center uses flexible working hours in a creative manner that is of benefit to the staff and clients alike. The juggling of work and family arrangements are issues that face everyone. The provision of family-related care for either children or aging relatives is a major challenge. The tensions associated with care giving are likely to be resolved in fair and equitable ways when a representatived cross-section of the stakeholders work together in creative and collaborative ways.

Work, Unions, and Political Organization: La Coordinadora

La Coordinadora is a union of Spanish longshoremen. Throughout the 1980s, this union attempted to work in a different way from most other unions. It practiced democracy based on a unique combination of three principles.

First, there was no group of unemployed waterside workers in Spain, as the union had control over hiring and every docker participated. The union established a system of hiring that shared out all the available work equally. Second, during the 1980s, La Coordinadora was Spain's only industrial union. At one stage, they had 80 percent support throughout their industry sector. The union operated as a loose network, with the branch in each port acting autonomously.

General assemblies made important decisions, while elected delegates had no power other than to carry out their mandate. Any docker could attend meetings, with the ultimate power resting with the assembly. Accepting election as a delegate meant volunteering to do a great deal of unpaid work for the union. These principles resulted in one of the most democratic labor organizations anywhere in the world. It is interesting to review the ideas, work, and decision-making arrangements such as these when considering what possibilities they may hold for contemporary work-related learning. In particular, there is the need to consider how paid work might be shared more evenly over a wider population of working people.

Work and Economics: Grasslands Grocery and Information Café

An organic grocery shop and information café, Grasslands is located in suburban Footscray (Australia) and is run as a cooperative by four friends. This group of informed and active citizens work on a paid and unpaid basis as human rights and legal advisers. Around 1996, they developed an innovative and ethical means of raising funds for social and political projects. In their own words, "they were sick and tired of seeing community groups sell their independence, principles and vitality for the promise of government funding."

The café opened in April 1999 selling organically grown fruit, vegetables, and nuts, as well as environmentally friendly soaps and cleaning products. Of every dollar that is spent in the shop, fifty-seven cents goes towards the wholesale cost of the product, twenty-six cents goes towards the cost of delivering the product to the customer, and seventeen cents is invested in projects and donations. After eighteen months of operation, this non-profit organic grocery business has donated more than $30,000.

Possibilities

Much of the learning associated with these vignettes remains hidden and unexplored. Foley (2001) has suggested that adult educators need to develop their understanding of the learning that such projects, events, and actions facilitate. He argues that this learning needs to be "read into" and made explicit with regard to the informal and incidental experiences these vignettes provide. From these cases, much can be learnt about the local/global and the historical/present. Their purpose is to initiate thoughtful consideration by adult learners of their understandings of work, learning, and work-related teaching/learning. From the four vignettes presented above, adult educators are left to consider questions such as: How can worker-learners be more involved in community-based work? How can worker-learners be more involved in considerations about childcare and family-friendly workplaces? How can worker-learners be more involved in learning about how work and workplaces are to be organized? How can worker-learners engage with ideas about innovative ethical work? In a free, just, and democratic local/global society, these questions need to be explicitly considered and addressed by those directly involved. Work-related teaching/learning can encourage, foster, and facilitate the self-activity of worker-learners. Chomsky (1988) explains:

> I would like to believe that people have an instinct for freedom that they really want to control their own affairs. They don't want to be pushed around, ordered, oppressed, etc., and they want a chance to do things that make sense, like constructive work in a way that they control, or maybe control together with others. I don't know any way to prove this. Its really a hope about what human beings are like—a hope that if social structures change sufficiently, those aspects of human nature will be realised.

This raises what is arguably a fundamental curriculum question for adult educators: "What can, and should be taught to whom, when, where and how?" This question provides a holistic entrée to curriculum development for work-related teaching/learning, that leads to the generation of a range of questions concerning participatory economics: How can working people be involved in learning about, from, and through the contemporary debates that inform their work? How can workers be involved in learning about the dynamics of the power/knowledge relations involved in work? What can working people learn through participating in the formation of visions of work, community, kinship relations, and political economy? How can work, learning, and society be democratized in this era of neo-conservative globalism? The development of a holistic framework for work-related teaching/learning is worthy of careful consideration by learners, working people, informed and active citizens, and adult educators.

References

Albert, M. *Parecon: Life after capitalism*. London: Verso, 2003.

———. *The Trajectory of Change: Activist Strategies for Social Transformation*. Cambridge: South End Press, 2002.

———. *Moving Forward: Program for a Participatory Economy*. San Fransisco: AK Press, 2000.

———. *Thinking Forward: Learning to Conceptualise Economic Vision*. Winnipeg: Arbeiter Ring Press, 1997.

Albert, M., L. Cagan, N. Chomsky, R. Hahnel, M. King, L. Sargent, and H. Sklar. *Liberating Theory*. Boston: South End Press, 1986.

Albert, M., and R. Hahnel. *Looking Forward: Participatory Economics for the Twenty First Century*. Boston: South End Press, 1991.

Amott, T., and J. Matthaei. *Race, Class and Work: A Multicultural Economic History of Women in the United States*. Boston: South End Press, 1996.

Bradley, H. *Gender and Power in the Workplace: Analysing the Impact of Economic Change*. Basingstoke: MacMillan Press, 1999.

Bradshaw, D. *Transforming Lives, Transforming Communities: A Conceptual Framework for Further Education*. 2nd ed. Melbourne, Victoria: ACFE Board, 1999.

Brechter, J., T. Costello, and B. Smith. *Globalization from Below: The Power of Solidarity*. Cambridge: South End Press, 2000.

Butler, E. "The Power of Discourse : Work-Related Learning in the "Learning Age." In *Power in Practice: Adult Education and the Struggle for Knowledge and Power in Society*. edited by R. Cervero and A. Wilson. San Fransisco: Jossey Bass, 2001.

Chomsky, N. *Profit over People: Neoliberalism and Global Order*. New York: Seven Stories Press, 1999.

———. *Language and Politics*. Montreal: Black Rose Books, 1988.

Cornfield, D., and R. Hodson. *Worlds of Work: Building an International Sociology of Work*. New York: Kluwer Academic, 2002.

Darrah, C. *Learning and Work: An Exploration in Industrial Ethnography*. New York: Garland Publishing, 1996.

Ehrenreich, B. *Nickel and Dimed: On (Not) Getting by in America*. New York: Metropolitan Books, 2001.

Foley, G. *Learning in Social Action: A Contribution to Understanding Informal Education*. London: Zed Books, 1999.

———. *Strategic Learning: Understanding and Facilitating Organizational Change*. Sydney, N.S.W.: Centre for Popular Education (UTS), 2001.

———. *Understanding Adult Education and Training*. 2nd ed. Sydney, N.S.W.: Allen and Unwin, 2000.

Hahnel R. *The ABC's of political economy: a modern approach*. London: Pluto Press. 2002.

Holloway, J. *Change the World without Taking Power: The Meaning of Revolution Today*. London: Pluto Press, 2002.

Ife, J. *Community Development: Community Based Alternatives in an Age of Globalization*. French's Forest, N.S.W.: Pearson Education, 2002.

Kincheloe, J. *How Do We Tell the Workers? The Socio-Economic Foundations of Work and Vocational Education.* Boulder: Westview Press, 1999.

———. *Toil and Trouble: Good Work, Smart Workers and the Integration of Academic and Vocational Education.* New York: Peter Lang, 1995.

Kress, G. *Writing the Future: English and the Making of a Culture of Innovation.* Sheffield, England: National Association for the Teaching of English (NATE), 1995.

Lummis, C. *Radical Democracy.* Ithaca: Cornell University Press, 1996.

Mojab, S. "The Power of Economic Globalization: Deskilling Immigrant Women through Training." In *Power in Practice: Adult Education and the Struggle for Knowledge and Power in Society.* edited by R. Cervero and A. Wilson. San Fransisco: Jossey Bass, 2001.

Simon, R., D. Dippo, and A. Schenke. *Learning Work: A Critical Pedagogy of Work Education.* New York: Bergin and Garvey, 1991.

Stilwell, F. *Changing Track: A New Political Economic Direction for Australia.* Sydney: Pluto Press, 2000.

Chapter 16

Learning in Complexity: Work and Knowledge in Enterprise Cultures

Tara Fenwick

Introduction

Changes in work are occurring at great speed. Definitions of "workplace" and questions about appropriate roles for workplace educators are confounded by organizations and jobs so flexible that they sometimes do not outlive educational programs. Some claim that the boundary-less "career" is revolutionizing employment as the rise of "entrepreneurialism" is redefining modes of engagement in the so-called new economy. Meanwhile, notions of worthwhile work-based learning hover between dizzying choices of theories and clamoring voices proclaiming just purposes. Current formulations of working knowledge tend to focus on experiential or practice-based learning, with careful attention to the role of workplace structures, cultures, and communities of practice as these influence an individual's knowledge construction.

Extensive critiques of these environments have lamented educational efforts to manage and subvert workers' learning to organizational goals of material profit and productivity. Sharp scholarly concern has particularly targeted neo-liberal educational responses that reproduce capitalist market relations, with their imbalances of power and wealth, and their exclusions and distortions of human welfare. Adult education that aims for nothing more than adapting individuals to the game plan of the new economy erodes social and environmental responsibility and spawns the individualism of style-absorbed consumers that perpetuates inequitable power relations, capitalist excesses, and labor-destroying turbo-technology. How are adult educators to proceed amidst fast-melting traditions, while assaulted by critiques of skills training for globalized markets?

In this chapter, I argue for an orientation to work and learning of both individuals and organizations that foregrounds pedagogical approaches to enable just, democratic, and life-giving work (Fenwick, 2001). This orientation involves a shift away from individualist constructivist theories of learning to a more ecological understanding of knowledge. Based upon complexity theory, an ecological learning theory holds that human beings, environments, and cognition emerge together as intertwined systems. By contrast, constructivist learning theory suggests that knowledge is a substantive "thing" to be acquired or ingested by learners as isolated cognitive agents. Individuals are then viewed as independent knowledge-constructors, or meaning makers. However, ecological learning theory describes knowledge as situated within biological and discursive systems of cognition that flow continually, are mutually participative, and cannot be reduced to particular individuals' construction of meanings.

Here I explore an ecological approach to learning in and for work. The context is a research project focussed on adults who all left organizational jobs to enter the ranks of the self-employed, becoming entrepreneurs in the so-called new economy. In their sites of learning and work, prevailing power relations dividing workers, managers, and owners were blurred, for their identities and activities crossed these roles regularly. In particular, three dimensions of ecological teaching/learning theory are argued to hold heuristic value for understanding and enabling knowledge and identity development in contested sites of work. First, that knowledge unfolds in systems, whereby cognition co-emerges with environment, individuals, and activity. Second, that understanding is embedded in the conduct and relationships among systems and subsystems, rather than the minds of individual actors. Third, that learning is a continuous invention and exploration linked to disequilibrium experienced in systems. These three dimensions suggest approaches for adult educators that are outlined in the last part of the chapter. However, in the first part, the notion of an ecological learning theory is introduced, drawing from the study of the newly self-employed. The learning experiences reported by these adults as they negotiated the fluid world of enterprise not only provide useful examples of ecological learning theory but also suggest a new future for work which presents unique opportunities and challenges for adult educators.

Ecological Learning Theory: Work Knowing as Co-Emergence

Work-based learning is a socio-cultural process of changing participation in the culturally designed settings of everyday life, variously termed situated "cognition" and "communities of practice." However, many situated perspectives still treat the environment as merely supplemental to the individual consciousness. At best, they describe an individual subject who develops through participative interactions in a community of practice. The concept of the autonomous individual mind—learning to participate—remains fundamentally unchallenged.

Somewhat different from these situated perspectives is a concept of knowing called ecological learning theory. Grounded in evolutionary biology and complexity theory, ecological theory explains the co-emergence of knower and setting in complex adaptive systems (Maturana and Varela, 1987; Varela, Thompson, and Rosch, 1991). Everything from a weather system to an economic system to a human being is regarded as a complex system, rather than simply a complicated one with a mechanical, predictable system of parts, such as a car or a coffeemaker. A complex system is never stable or fixed, but always adapting in unpredictable ways. The key to a healthy system, that is, the ability to adapt creatively to changing conditions, is diversity among its parts.

A human body, for example, relies on highly specialized subsystems (biological, sensory, mental, and emotional) that not only each respond to different circumstances and different needs, but also have learned to cohabitate and communicate with one another. These systems in turn are made up of parts, like organs, which are complete systems in themselves. But a person is also a part of other systems: family systems and social systems, which in turn are nested in national systems, which are part of larger forces like global market systems, all of which are part of Earth's environment. A system is self-modifying, sensitive, and responding to changes within it and around it through constant dialogue with its environment. Its many components are always alive, always interacting creatively with parts around them. Because these interactions form patterns without external organization, these complex systems are described as self-organizing. The outcome of all these dynamic interactions of a system's parts is unpredictable. So much is occurring simultaneously that the system is quite literally impossible to understand by analyzing its parts, or reducing it to causes and effects.

All complex adaptive systems "learn," where learning is defined as transformation that expands a learner's potential range of actions. Research on HIV-AIDs systems, for example, demonstrate that the immune system remembers, forgets, recognizes, hypothesizes, makes errors, adapts, and thus learns (Davis, Sumara, and Luce-Kapler, 2001). Forest eco-systems, weather systems, human communities, and market systems all learn. Part of this learning is the continuous creation of alternate actions and responses to changing situations, undertaken by the system's parts. More sudden transformation can occur in response to a major shock to the system, throwing it into disequilibrium. Computer-generated images of systems undergoing disequilibrium show that they go through a phase of swinging between extremes before self-organizing gradually into a new pattern, or identity, that can continue co-habiting with and adapting to the other systems in its environment.

So the first premise of ecological learning theory is an ontological one: the complex adaptive systems represented by person and context are inseparable. The second is epistemological: that change, or "knowing," occurs from emerging systems affected by the intentional tinkering of one with the other. When two systems coincide, the "perturbations" of one system excites responses in the structural dynamics of the other. The resultant disequilibrium and "coupling" creates a new transcendent unity of action and identities that could not have been achieved independently by either participant. This is "mutual specification" (Varela, Thompson, and Rosch, 1991), the fundamental dynamic of systems constantly engaging in joint action and interaction. Knowing exists in the interstices of a complex ecology or organismic relationality (Davis, Sumara, and Luce-Kapler, 2001). Change occurs through disturbances amplified through feedback loops within and among complex adaptive systems.

Thus, human understandings, both voluntary and unconscious, are embedded in their conduct within these webs. What some call tacit knowledge is viewed by ecological learning theory as existing not within individuals in ways that drive actions, but unfolding in circumstances that evoke these actions. Much of this joint action exceeds and leaks out of individual attempts to attend to and control unconscious action through critical reflection. The problem lies not in underdeveloped critical abilities that should be educated, but in a false conceptualization of the adult learning figure as separable from the contextual ground. The focus is not on the "learning event" and its components (which other perspectives might describe in fragmented terms: person, experience, tools, community, and activity), but on the relationships binding them together in complex adaptive systems.

New Work Contexts: Shift to Enterprise Culture

Conceptions of co-emergence and ecological learning illuminate the development of working knowledge of adults among economic structures increasingly emphasizing flexibility, fluid knowledge, and enterprise. The contemporary context of adult learners requires a brief explication. Edwards (1998) argues that in current regimes of "reflexive modernization" and flexible specialization, workers must construct their own biographies, choosing between different lifestyles, subcultures, social ties and identities. Workers are encouraged to regard the increased casualization and temporization of work as an opportunity, and to accept as their duty the obligation to continually recreate themselves as a shape-shifting portfolio of capacities that meet unpredictable corporate demands.

As workplaces are restructured, adult education has focused on forming worker identities that elicit individualism, market responsiveness, flexibility, and innovation. Organizations, both public and private, desire self-reflexive entrepreneurial workers who thrive on uncertainty, are measured by innovation, and accept responsibility for the risks attending their actions and choices. Thus, organizations seek to recruit or create "autonomous, self-regulating, productive individuals...[with] energy, initiative, self-reliance and personal responsibility" (du Gay, 1996: 60). Entrepreneurial employment is postured as a means to personal fulfillment and self-development.

Accordingly, amidst the discourses of flexibility and individualism, the identity of the "enterprising self" has gained ascendancy, particularly in analyses of worker identity re-formation. "Enterprise" refers not only to the priority allocated to commercial interests above civic, social, and ecological interests, but also to "enterprising" characteristics such as initiative, risk-taking, self-reliance, and self-responsibility. du Gay (1996) argues that an "ethos of enterprise" now pervades all spheres of our consumerist risk society, such that the dominating project of adult workers is constructing and self-regulating their own human capital (their work capacities, biographies and success) in an "enterprise of the self." In other words, the "character of the entrepreneur can no longer be represented as just one amongst a plurality of ethical personalities but must be seen as assuming an ontological priority" (du Gay, 1996: 181). The adult learner's circumstances are irrelevant, as the enterprise discourse represents all as possessing the desire, capacity, obligation, and opportunity to engage in reflexively constructing and reconstructing their own human capital.

One result of this entrepreneurial reductionism has been increasing cultural preoccupation with self-created enterprise, or "me, inc." as a way of life. Individuals are leaving organizations to pursue a variety of more fluid and self-directed forms of employment, ranging from small enterprises to "portfolio" careers, a term indicating a package of work arrangements and clients in various contexts. Perhaps this is a consequence of messages about the changing culture and political economy of work increasingly emphasizing individual responsibility for creating work, developing knowledge and skills, managing one's career, and maximizing individual opportunities for successful micro-enterprises in global/local capitalism. Of course, the reality is far more oppressive, gendered, and marked by race, class, and age stratification than prevailing enthusiasms indicate.

Women appear to be a significant part of this rising enterprise culture. Women's business start-ups have risen dramatically in the past decade, doubling the rate of men's (Industry Canada, 1998). These women entrepreneurs indicate that their reasons for leaving jobs to choose enterprise involve a complex mix of personal and organizational factors (Moore and Buttner, 1997). The 109 women entrepreneurs across Canada interviewed for this study left jobs in organizations, and had been self-employed for at least four years at the time the research was conducted. Participants narrated their challenges and strategies in this process, the knowledge they valued most, and their understanding of how it developed. About two-thirds said they had left unhappily, citing reasons of inequitable gendered power relations evident in "glass ceiling" issues, serious ethical conflicts around corrupt practices, and lack of recognition and creative opportunity. Many said they had decided to start their own business as an opportunity to "do it my way": live out a creative dream, create their own work environments, contribute meaningfully to their communities, and gain more personal flexibility and control over their work and lives. Part of their struggle against the conventional entrepreneurial virtues of competitive growth and profiteering was learning what alternate visions they were seeking, and learning to adapt and transform within enterprise systems.

Of the 109 women entrepreneurs interviewed, a large majority (62 percent) had started businesses in the service sector (8 percent in health care, 14.5 percent in education, 8.1 percent in organizational consulting, and 28 percent in business services such as accounting). 16 percent were in retail,

8 percent in manufacturing, four percent in high tech industries, 4 percent in food and entertainment, 3 percent in construction, and 2 percent in transportation industrial sectors. In terms of their highest level of formal education, 54 percent of these women had obtained post-secondary degrees (31 percent with bachelor's, 17 percent with master's, and 6 percent with doctoral degrees), 37 percent had earned a post-secondary certificate/diploma, 6 percent had completed high school, and 3 percent had not completed high school. Only 12 percent had any formal business training such as a course, workshop, or degree in business. Of the 109, forty-three employed 2–5 staff, ten employed 6-10, fifteen employed 11–20, six employed 21–50, and five employed more than fifty. Seven worked alone but hired additional contractors for each project as needed, and twenty-three were the sole employee. The participants included three Black Canadian women, five Asian-Canadians, six Middle Eastern Canadians and East Indian Canadians, two Aboriginal Canadians, nine European-Canadian immigrant, and eighty-four Anglo-Canadian-born women. Fifty-seven were married with children, twenty-nine, single mothers with children, nine, married with no children and fourteen were single with no children.

Knowing on the Fly

Entrepreneurs' stories embody what Edwards (1998: 382) envisions as "active, creative, reflexive, risk-taking workers with certain degrees of autonomy in how they define and achieve their work goals." Most of them work in environments unbounded by institutionalized roles, norms, and disciplinary knowledge. They choose the relational networks in which they will participate, the physical settings, and the overall activities comprising their everyday tasks. Like other workers in an age of flexibility and enterprise, they mobilize resources, seek opportunities, and act quickly. They engage continually in innovative problem solving, where invention is a way of being. This is especially so in the case of small businesses, where owners must cross many boundaries of knowing, from management and financing to product design and marketing, from daily operations to long term visioning. In many respects, these people have the power to define what counts as "knowing" in their choices of work activity. But, in any case, the production and assessment of knowledge is of uppermost concern for these new entrepreneurs.

The ecological conceptualization of cognition offers three key ideas that are useful for explaining certain processes of knowledge production described by these enterprising individuals. First, that knowledge unfolds in systems, whereby cognition co-emerges with environment, other people, and activity. Second, that understanding is embedded in the conduct and relationships among systems and subsystems, rather than the minds of individual actors. Third, that learning necessarily involves continuous invention and exploration, linked to disequilibrium experienced in systems and amplified with feedback loops. These three concepts are discussed together with illustrations from experiences narrated by enterprising individuals.

Ecological theory assumes that human beings are connected in communities of other actors, objects, and forces, all of which together create complex systems. Each complex system is nested—simultaneously a unity and a collective of unities, and part of a larger unity. Complex systems modify themselves, adapting to unexpected circumstances and even transforming their activities and relationships with other systems. For example, the women explained that the process by which an enterprise emerges defies rational planning models that dominate conventional understandings of business development. An idea for an enterprise was often embedded in social action—through an unanticipated opportunity or a contracted activity that expands or suddenly morphs into an enterprise.

After inception, the enterprise unfolds in unpredictable ways. According to entrepreneurs narrating this process, knowledge of business procedure, politics, and social relations, as well as more broad-based knowledge about the enterprise's purpose and the adult learner's identity, all emerge and shift together in response to points of disequilibrium encountered along the way. Many entrepreneurs reported that the enormity of what had to be learned hit them soon after they made the commitment to a business start-up; fewer than 10 percent of the women interviewed had any formal business training. A never-ending series of dilemmas arose which were associated with the internal systems of the enterprise itself, as well as those associated with other external systems. For example, unpredictable changes in customer trends require the ability to continuously improvise: "You can put ten products out there but never know which one will go."

Beyond clients, the enterprise was nested within and dependent upon a series of relationships—systems of financial accountability to lenders and staff, internal production processes, external distribution networks ranging from marketing to material processes of product flow, and networks of suppliers—all of which fluctuate. For many women, activity in their family and social networks were also integrated with their enterprise. In all of these networks, a dynamic balance was created of self-interest and reciprocity. The owner of a home renovation service explained, "If my staff are happy, if my family is happy...if I'm managing to do most everything that I've got on my plate, and if everybody is reasonably happy, including myself, I feel that the balancing act is working."

Entrepreneurs described accessing a variety of resources to learn what was needed to manage these dilemmas and relationships. First, disequilibrium became an accepted condition. One consultant to other women entrepreneurs explained, "You have to let go of control...there's always something else around the corner." Second, most sought to align themselves with supportive social networks, including mentors, staff, and other enterprises, to help "ride through" the disequilibrium. An urban event-planning consultant explained:

> I have surrounded myself with people who are where I want to be and that think the same way that I do. I have a whole resource of people around me that I can share whatever it is that I'm going through, and they work through it with me. And I do the same for them.

Entrepreneurs described their work knowing process as "knowing on the fly," "navigating the mess," "do or die learning," and "discovering our way." Learning was all-at-once, becoming "a Jill of all trades" while flying through judgments about which trade and where in the heat of daily pressure to act. A significant step involved learning how to focus: separating messy dilemmas into tasks, then discerning and choosing what needed to be learned. As one explained, "We invent it and then figure out what it is." Continuous invention included learning to discern what was emerging, naming it, and then representing it to others. Emotions of exhilaration and fear often accompanied this sense of inventing one's way into business. The figuring-out process was described variously as "learning by stumbling and stumbling," "flying by the seat of your pants," and "tinkering." Learning to act amidst uncertainty and complexity without a sense of mastery became for many a way of working, a way of being. Standards were invented according to what worked best for a particular context and purpose.

This theme is well-explicated by ecological theory, which casts learning as continuous invention and exploration produced through relations among consciousness, identity, action and interaction, objects, and the structural dynamics of complex systems. There is no absolute competency defining proficient conduct, because conduct flows and grows ceaselessly.

Maturana and Varela (1987: 39) suggest that subsystems in a series of increasingly complex systems together invent changing understandings of what is "adequate conduct" in this particular time and situation, or "consensual domain." New possibilities for competent performance are constantly emerging among the interactions of complex systems, and thus learning occurs in the possibility for navigating unpredictable shared actions. Knowledge cannot be contained in any one element or dimension of a system, for knowledge is forever spilling into other systems. As one example, these entrepreneurs frequently referred to the positive work environment that had developed as their enterprise grew as a marker of their "success." One woman who ran a contracting company in a rural area employing seventy trades-people explained:

> We worked hard to create an atmosphere for people to work that was humane, rewarding and challenging. They had successes as well as me. We were kind and caring. We recognized that they were individuals with dignity.

While emphasizing the importance of learning to the emergence of their enterprise, individual entrepreneurs often had difficulty articulating the actual "lessons they had learned," that is the "knowledge" they accumulated through their business/learning activities. Changing markets, economic conditions and networks continually altered their web of relationships, requiring continual innovative experimentation. Unanticipated opportunities—and inspirations—frequently presented themselves. A person operating a management consulting firm described knowledge as something that evolved during the doing of a project:

> When we've achieved that, we're finished with that. I'm going to try the next thing—whatever it may be. I love spontaneity. Let's not plan this for a year. Why don't we just figure it out and do it tomorrow morning?

Thus work and knowledge are entwined in the process of creation that involves but does not necessarily serve labor, production, and acquisition. They are not linear or pre-planned, but unfold spontaneously and continuously on many levels. Knowing is fluid, not substantive "human capital" that can be transferred from one situation to the next. Entrepreneurial knowing co-evolves in a complex relation of identity and daily choices that create and re-create the enterprise, which interacts with the evolving systems within and around it in spontaneous and adaptable ways. Davis, Sumara, and Luce-Kepler (2001) describe this phenomenon in ecological terms as the continuous enlargement of spaces of possibility. In other words, people participate together in what becomes an increasingly complex system. New, unanticipated possibilities for thought and action often appear in the process of inventing the activity, making prior decisions non-viable in the unfolding system dynamics. For this reason, explained some entrepreneurs, they did not like the rigidity or presumptions of business management plans. A woman who started a "human resources" consulting firm stated:

> I have no intentions because I always believe there is something else around the corner. I don't want to commit myself to something and disappoint somebody. Where else it will take me I don't have a clue yet. Everyday in this business I meet more people and make more connections that take me on new adventures. I never know what's going to happen.

New Adventures for Adult Educators

The experiences of these adults' learning and working among rapid changes of enterprise culture might be construed as a harbinger of the future face of work and learning. Institutionalized education and programmatic pedagogical interventions could constrict "knowing on the fly" which is essential to survival and balance within multiple complex systems. However ecological learning theory invites some critical challenges. Although a comprehensive critique is beyond the scope of this chapter, four points are worth stating here.

Complexity theory poses troublesome questions about the agency and identity of adult learners. A perspective of adult learning as being tossed by the dynamics of continuous systemic adaptation may ignore these issues. How, for example, are the moral purposes of adult learners related to complex system dynamics? Second, this theory suggests seamless-ness between cognition and interaction in a community. There may be aspects of an adult learner's cognition that are not available through dialogue or present in action. The relationship of knowers to theoretical knowledge existing apart from a particular community of action needs articulation. Third, from the perspective presented here, ethical issues of socio-economic justice which are fundamental to adult education become problematic. How can an adult education project driven by a commitment to changing social injustice be formulated so that it adequately accounts for the complex ongoing systemic perturbations, without being illusory? Finally, the influences of inequitable power relations on patterns of co-emergence exerted by culturally determined meaning categories such as gender, race, sexuality, class, and religion may not be discernible from an ecological perspective. Consequently, the support for dominating interests in complex systems by particular knowledges and cultural practices may be obscured. These arguments, posed from a critical perspective, are incongruent with basic principles of complexity theory which eschew frames of dominance-oppression. Ecological learning theory argues instead that disequilibrium and patterns created by difference are continuous (Davis, Sumara, and Luce-Kepler, 2001). However we still need to ask, Is all learning and knowledge to be valued the same? Is the "agency" of adult educators and their students redundant in the politics of complex adaptive systems?

These issues help to trouble the faddish and uncritical acceptance of complexity discourses in pedagogical discussions and also prompt us to find ways to reconcile ecological teaching/learning with critical, cultural orientations to adult education. How might spaces of possibility be opened for "learning on the fly," without forsaking the importance of adult education in redressing social and economic injustice? Rather than attempting to instigate change through control, pedagogy can seek to open spaces for the learning system to experiment with change itself. Adult educators can also help all participants to see their own involvement in co-creating the system, and seek ethical ways to record the expanding space and its possibilities. In more specific terms, adult educators promoting ecological modes of teaching may undertake work as noisemakers, interpreters, and mapmakers, as well as enabling attunement, facilitating disequilibrium, and building courage in complex learning systems.

As noisemakers, adult educators may plan starting points or disturbances to introduce into a system of learners, then observe carefully. They watch subtle particularities being created through myriad interactions in the system, amplify or make space for these, and remove barriers. Educators can also be alert to disturbances and paradoxes that occur in an organization, showing their significance. For example, strategies for creating organizational "noise" might include highlighting the contradictions and silences in corporate policies, perhaps by elaborating a variety of meanings for the key concepts that give energy to corporate rhetoric. Adult educators can encourage learners to try going "the wrong direction," by appropriating corporate rhetoric to make these keywords say things in unexpected ways and then to see where they might lead.

As interpreters, adult educators can assist people to name what is unfolding around them and inside them, to continually rename these changing nuances, and to unlock the tenacious grasp of old categories, or restrictive or destructive language that strangles emerging possibilities. Karpiak (2000) argues that the adult educator's responsibility is to help a collective connect its parts to the whole system—individual learners to the learning community and its creations, the community to the larger systems with which it interrelates, and learners to the inner parts of themselves.

As mapmakers, adult educators can help trace and create meaningful interactions of the actors and objects across the expanding spaces. They may help adult learners to make a communal sense of the patterns emerging among these complex systems, for example, showing others how to watch for changing power relations between different people, seeing knowledge fluctuate as new understandings emerge in small corners. Adult educators not only track and show system's changes, but also draw attention to the system's own disturbances that create potential for organizational learning. Karpiak (2000) describes this role as attuning adult learners to disequilibrium. Adult educators may help amplify generative disturbances by drawing attention to the new possibilities these create, and help divert patterns that may start creating undesirable conditions, unsafe spaces, or power inequities. Throughout their activities, adult educators must reflect carefully on their own entanglement and interests in the emerging systems of thought, action, and power.

As facilitators, adult educators can help adult learners through the disequilibrium they may experience in one or more systems. Adult educators can also enhance feedback loops in a system of adult learners as they experiment with different patterns arising from these disturbances. Educators can show, for example, how the processes unfolding in multiple experiments at the fringes of an organization reflect patterns going on in interrelated systems. Feedback loops assist the system to self-organize by detecting, selecting, and creatively adapting itself to new patterns emerging within itself. However, what appears to be messiness in this process often induces an impulse to create controls, to assert boundaries, and to create rigid structures that actually suppress and choke the flow of creativity. Educators can help others to forestall the urge to predict and contain, remain more flexible and adaptable, and work through disequilibrium creatively.

Because adult learning is co-emergent, there is little certainty, and there is limited use in planning a grand direction for learning through a work-based project. So, adult educators can encourage learners to be inventive, to try small experiments simultaneously, to reflect on what happens, to adopt a "good enough" vision rather than cling to rigid arbitrary standards, and to focus on those experiments that seem to be working best for the time. As the enterprising women represented in this chapter illustrate, the courage to decide, act, and invent when one lacks skill and confidence is an important stance for adult learners to acquire in conditions of multiple changes among complex systems. Adult educators not only can assist adult learners to become "unstuck" when paralyzed by uncertainty, but can model "going-on" strategies. Contingency is the only predictable condition, so adult educators must expect it, enjoy it, prepare for its many possibilities, and attune themselves to learner activity in imaginative ways.

Conclusion

In this chapter, examples of women's experiences of knowledge production in and through entrepreneurship illustrate ways that knowledge, identity, and environment are co-emergent. Adult learning is embedded in conduct and relationships, and involves continuous invention and exploration linked to disequilibrium within and among systems. Ecological learning theory holds potential for illuminating the relationships among subsystems, dimensions of learning collectivities, and the ways that knowledge is produced and transformed in contemporary enterprise culture.

Finally, the stories about these enterprising women offer hope in themselves, amidst the pessimistic discourse of "inevitable" globalized capitalism fuelled by the lifelong learning of managed subjectivities. As participants in a globalized enterprise culture, these women seem to resist certain neo-liberal marketplace imperatives. According to their own narratives, they are crafting new models of work, entrepreneurship, and success. Further, they are creating spaces for learning that are not limited by dominating notions of worthwhile work knowledge and processes for its production. Their enterprises enact vivid environments and subjectivities through networks of knowing and relationship. In an age of lumbering corporate obsession to capture and codify "intellectual capital," these "small" environments of enterprising action move swiftly and freely. In their fast-paced flexible work arrangements, knowing co-emerges "on the fly" with a project, community, and attendant identities. Reified knowledge and "learning outcomes" are all too rigid, if not irrelevant, in the unpredictable, fluid, and ambiguous contexts facing adult educators, worker/learners, and entrepreneurial enterprises.

References

Davis, B., D. Sumara, and R. Luce-Kepler. *Engaging Minds: Learning and Teaching in a Complex World.* Mahwah, NJ: L. Erlbaum Associates, 2001.

du Gay. *Consumption and Identity at Work.* London: Sage, 1996.

Edwards, R. "Flexibility, Reflexivity and Reflection in the Contemporary Workplace." *International Journal of Lifelong Education* 17, no. 6 (1998): 377–88.

Fenwick, T. "Work Knowing "On the Fly": Enterprise Cultures and Co-Emergent Epistemology." *Studies in Continuing Education* 23, no. 2 (2001): 243–26.

Industry Canada. *Shattering the Glass Box: Women Entrepreneurs and the Knowledge-Based Economy. Micro-Economic Policy Analysis Branch* On-line government report, 1999 updated, cited 20 January 2001. Available from http:// strategis. ic. gc. ca/sc _ecnmy/mera/egdoc/o4.htm.

Karpiak, I. "Evolutionary Theory and the New Sciences." *Studies in Continuing Education* 22, no. 1 (2000): 29–44.

Maturana, H., and F. Varela. *The Tree of Knowledge: The Biological Roots of Human Understanding.* Boston: Shambhala Press, 1987.

Moore, D., and E. Buttner. *Women Entrepreneurs: Moving Beyond the Glass Ceiling.* Thousand Oaks, CA: Sage, 1997.

Plexus Institute. *Edgeware Applications* June 2001 updated 2001, cited 5th July 2001. Available from http:// www.plexusinstitutew.com/edgeware/archive/think/main_app-h.html.

Varela, F., E. Thompson, and E. Rosch. *The Embodied Mind: Cognitive Science and Human Experience.* Cambridge, MA: MIT Press, 1991.

Conclusion

Pedagogies of Global/Local Hope: Disobedience in the Face of Globalism

Michael Singh and Sue Shore

Neo-conservative Globalism's Framing of Adult Education

Adult Education @ 21st Century recognizes and develops the distinction between globalization and globalism. "Globalization" has been represented, variously, as cooperation across nation-states and continents, a powerful form of neocolonialism and the internationalization of capitalism.

On the one hand, globalization gathers, redefines, and creams off local human and environmental cultures for uses elsewhere. By this means, the reservoir of biological and multicultural resources from anywhere around the world are drawn into selected transnational spaces, tailored to the particularities of these different localities. On the other hand, efforts to work "globally" require the development of local connections. In this way, capitalist globalization needs local diversity as a resource for product innovation and niche marketing. It needs to be acknowledged that these processes of de-location and relocation do not mean the salvation or renaissance of each locality.

As a complex combination of historical practices, this "globalization from above" is marked by the increasing ascendancy of Euro-American power and interests throughout time and space. The dominating representation and material reality is that of neo-conservative Anglophone "globalism." This subject position alienates many, causing resentment to manifest itself in fundamentalist nationalisms and regressive parochialism. Neo-conservative globalism is the ideological project that seeks to secure Anglophone globalism by encouraging people throughout the world to willfully accept these interests as their own, and to ignore their own alienation and disaffection and their causes. When this ideological interest cannot be achieved otherwise, the awe and power of military force is often invoked.

Within *Adult Education @ 21st Century,* a global perspective is addressed with reference to countries as diverse as Germany and Malaysia. References here are to neo-conservative globalism being used to moderate the scope of change possible through adult education. Familiar though problematic claims for possibility and social change are being cycled through official publications renaming the field and toning down the limits of change. International "development" is reframed as "structural adjustment" programs, and the imposition of "quality" assurance regimes, drive the corporatization of university and post-compulsory training programs. In contrast, others are working to change the unjust appropriation of the world's resources by Anglophone nations across the three most recent eras of globalization.

The discourses on "globalization from below" represented in *Adult Education @ 21st Century* resonate with familiar empowering and liberatory discourses that have peppered the history of the field. These discourses suggest that global/local public goods such as democracy, citizenship, peace and security, human rights, the preservation of nature in and for itself, and economic and social justice can be renegotiated, and that adult education can contribute to this work. We see this as an appropriate response to the incessant socio-economic conservatism at the forefront of adult education these days.

The researchers in this collection have argued for those of us with capital or significant policy-making power to acknowledge the investments we have in colluding with the colonizing power of bureaucratic regimes to maintain "the way things are done around here."

Through their own efforts, the authors demonstrate the small, but nonetheless significant opportunities taken to disrupt racialized, gendered, and classed divisions of labor and those relations of power that are rooted in the privileging of speculative capitalism above all else. That is what we mean by pedagogies of global/local hope: the belief that by thinking and acting globally, across the boundaries of time and space, we need to—and can—work collaboratively at making local adult education better. By thinking and acting globally, adult educators can work to limit the dangers and endangerment of the world.

A Transnational Historical Moment

How are the legacies of the past shaping what is happening now? For decades, adult education has been marginalized within the public sphere of many nations around the world. For a long time, its knowledge base, accreditation system, and aims were ruled outside nation-centered policy-making forums and funding mechanisms concerned to prepare students for work and citizenship. Apart from extension programs, universities were largely absent from the debates about adult learning until the 1980s, despite the fact that they were inherently sites of "adult teaching and learning." In many countries, especially those bearing the legacy of the British imperial era of globalization, the establishment of Workers' Education Associations, workers' institutes, and adult education programs for the armed forces gave form and substance to the field's history. This has, however, resulted in limited critique of adult education practices that have worked counter to a project of social change for Indigenous communities, many women, and lesbians/homosexuals. Not surprisingly, given that its history has always involved a conflation of contested programs with contradictory aims, there are necessary tensions associated with the use of the term "adult education."

From the fifteenth century onwards, much of the world was globalized through incorporation into the western European empires as economically, politically, and technologically dependent colonies. *Adult Education @ 21st Century* acknowledges that contemporary neo-conservative globalism is embedded in, and makes advantages of, the history of these colonialist practices. Although these are being reconfigured in these "new times," their effects on Indigenous and local knowledges are unsurprisingly similar. Analysis of and engagement with the historical, material, and discursive practices of neo-conservative globalism is necessary to speaking back to its dominance.

Re-imagining the global/local framing of this work must of necessity foreground the advantages secured by the British Empire and the heated struggles of the cold war. The meaning of the local has changed and should therefore force a reassessment of local practices as part of the wider sphere of restructured and de-structured global/local relations. As the war against Iraq demonstrated, the world is being reconstituted as a single socio-political space and a single, unfettered market, with the Anglophone victors from the times of empire and cold war asserting their power and interests globally. The neo-conservative Anglophone alliance, led by the confederation of political interests from the south of the USA, would now seem to constitute a global hyper-power.

The tensions between the legacy of past approaches to adult education and the mounting challenges to them create conditions for shaping innovations that identify and create spaces which are the hybridized product of these social, historical, and economic interactions. Nevertheless, innovation and hybridized products were also the ground on which empires were founded, making innovative adult education dangerous work if it aims to avoid the pitfalls of the past.

Non-compliance in the Face of Corporate Managerial Boundaries

Innovation activists such as Mike Brown and Liv Mjelde are giving expression to (re)newed possibilities in, through, and for adult education via transnational mesh-works. Many of their practices and their accompanying theory-building for professional and continuing education, human resource studies, community education, and workplace learning are being directed towards global/local change. The aim is for transformation of anthropocentric, gendered, racist, classist institutions into sites of sustainable, socially just, and democratic practices. Harreveld has demonstrated what this means for tactically generating spaces for adult education that respond to and express the challenges posed by the neo-conservative, Anglophone empire.

These various innovations, with their provisions for teaching/learning in paid and unpaid workplaces, provide substantial opportunities for transnational employment and associated access to socio-economic and multicultural mobility. Nevertheless, all too often, adult literacy campaigns and industry-based training programs for women, Indigenous communities and bilingual workers make evident the borders against which innovation activists struggle to form a new generation of transnational workers, global/local citizens, and learners for life.

Amidst these uncertainties, existing patterns of inequality are replayed with considerable predictability. One of the concerns driving Roger Harris and Michele Simons is the kind of preparation required to work, teach, and learn in this unfolding environment. The voices represented in *Adult Education @ 21st Century* provide important examples of working in and against the hegemony of globalization from above. Likewise, the authors are conscious of the dangers of optimism, or the naïve belief that things will inevitably get better of their own accord, given the political, cultural and economic processes of restructuring and de-structuring taking place around the globe.

Adult education policies are never about the simple, local application of directives from central positions of bureaucratic power. Neo-conservative globalism selectively draws attention to its preferred changes while ignoring or downplaying the changes that are *not* taking place to ameliorate social justices manifested by increasing poverty and violence. Reinke and James make this evident in the reluctance by nation-states to recognize the place of Indigenous dispossession in adult education, work, and citizenship. Situating the focus of work and training in global cities gives a metropolitan focus that marginalizes regional and rural communities, where most of the world's population still lives.

Similarly, corporate education reinforces linguistic imperialism, repressing the specificity of linguistic diversity and inviting or coercing adult educators to do likewise. Leanne Reinke and Paul James argue that adult educators and students engaged in border crossing in the global public sphere are involved in intellectual production. They are uniquely situated with opportunities to engage in everyday acts of multicultural translation and negotiation. These border crossings are sites in which Reinke and James discover the multicultural creativity to formulate innovative adult educational practices, ideas, pleasures, and relationships. They raise ethical questions about what it now means for adult educators to assert their educational authority as critical knowledge-workers: a professional attribute increasingly suppressed by the politics of neo-conservative globalism and dismissed by the fictions of corporate managerialism. Central to the innovative work of these adult educators is dismantling the boundary between what Eurocentric, elitist exporters of adult education regard as "high" mono-cultural commodities and the "low" multicultural products of Indigenous Australia, Asia, or Africa. In the contemporary globalizing education economy, standardized White dialects of English have become one of the major forms of exports and anti-market mechanisms in the world's multi-lingual knowledge economies.

We referred earlier to the problematic nature of the generic term "adult education," with its tendency to capture every form of post-school education. Many countries around the globe make no distinction between the schooling of children and the opportunities available to adults. The latter are intricately connected to the quality and political capacity of schools to meet the cultural and political needs of diverse "ethnic" and gendered adult groups. Corporatist managerialists have been working hard to represent the meanings of adult education in forms that articulate with and give expression to neo-conservative globalism. Taken individually, the examples of theoretically-informed and tested practice offered in *Adult Education @ 21st Century* are in danger of affirming this trend, even as each struggles to portray the "project" of adult education otherwise. This problem arises not only because adult educators are located in the material lifeworld created by the dominating project of neo-conservative globalism, but because it too hunts down and appropriates whatever resources it may find useful to its project of "natural" dominion.

Nevertheless, adult educators struggle to find ways of reclaiming pedagogical, political engagements between and across learners, the political economy, and the knowledges they produce. In particular, corporate discourse on adult education has given rise to new code words that claim to empower adult educators across a diverse range of sites. However, Koo Yew Lie reminds us that adult teaching/learning is not a neutral enterprise; critical—creative—innovative corporate literacy is a requisite skill. The language of "learning to learn" and "lifelong learning" are, however, critical discourses in gaining acceptance for the idea of job insecurity, individual responsibility for the failure of speculative capitalism, and the redundancy of teachers in the educational process.

Furthermore, adult education institutions are not the only sites targeted by this project of global/local political and economic restructuring and destructuring. There is also a need to reflect on those initiatives that are financed through global systems of funding linked to structural (mal)adjustment policies. Peter Kell argues that these tend to obscure local adult education requirements as policies are mapped onto and against the training, curriculum, competence, and provider registration requirements that accord with the hegemonic expectations of globalized US-American neo-conservative interests. This mapping is aided and constituted by an endless array of self-serving, overpaid consultants with little stake in the lived particularities of adult education students or teachers. Pedagogic encounters aimed at learning *with and from* others are indeed a challenge in the presence of real and guarded nation-centered borders.

Such "learning" environments point to the stark need to recognize the politics of meaning-making in sites as different and differentially resourced as literacy campaigns in rural and manufacturing settings, the anti-globalization and anti-war protests throughout the world, in universities where adult teacher education programs are devised and delivered, and in all kinds of policy (re)making settings. Critical—creative—innovative meaning-making is the responsibility of adult learners, educators, and *their* educators.

Reclaiming Innovation

Not everyone agrees that the colonization of diverse ecological and multicultural spaces by neo-conservative globalism is desirable. For instance, Shore's work invites us to challenge the role of adult education in reproducing colonialist constructions of "the adult learner," asking us to critically reflect on the undesirability of such constructions and their effects on rethinking the subject of change. Anglophone adult education has for a long time been imbued with orientalist representations about Others and, more recently, entrepreneurial education providers (re)producing racist and sexist constructions anew. Is it desirable for issues of morality, of what it means to be human, to be dissolved in corporatized practices that categorize work-related teaching/learning as a politics-free zone? Humanity is now, this century, confronted with the dangerous possibility that the imposition of neo-conservative globalism from above is contributing to the homogenization of the world. This is occurring at the very moment when the sustainability of diversity is essential for remaking new global economies, citizenries, and learnings.

The peripheral location and status of adult education necessarily raises problems about the possibilities of adult educators bridging the organizational boundaries imposed by corporate managerialism and dissolving the boundaries created by dominating neo-conservative frameworks. This is complicated by the problem of distinguishing corporate managerialism's many borders from those of neo-conservativism. The community-building, knowledge-creating work of adult educators also confronts the interrelated power differentials of race, sexuality, ethnicity, class and gender, of all involved. The productive, innovative work of adult educators necessarily mediates and mitigates the contradictory and contested relations among these dominating socio-economic formations.

The problem of institutionalizing innovative policies and practices in adult education in response to and as an expression of these globalizing times is frustrated by the resistance created by corporate managerialism. Bobbie Harreveld argues that adult educators are faced with mediating the particular dangers of corporate managerialism embodied in the power of postmodernist entrepreneurs and surveillance auditors, and the perils of neo-conservative globalism embodied in a nation-state that continues its disinvestments in underwriting the socio-economic risks confronting its citizens and their society. Harreveld points to the dangers of bounding adult education within a dated, pre-networking business framework by challenging the ways in which new teaching and new learnings are categorized. Corporate managerialist containment, co-option, and contamination of innovations in adult education are framed within exclusionary boundaries. This delimits the possibilities for reconceptualizing worthwhile educational innovations by inscribing rarefied, abstract business "models" as the norm.

At other times, this is manifested in an inherent opposition between the humanities and the scientific and technological dimensions of adult education. Gayle Morris and David Beckett argue that the pleasure and interest that adult educators and their students take in teaching and learning are sources of dismay and problems for defenders of the contested politics of corporate productivity. The framing of adult education by corporatist myth-making falsely misrepresents the humanities as necessarily separate from and opposed to the techno-scientific dimensions of adult education. The conjoining of mono-cultural, political, and economic reductionism reinforces its resistance to innovations in adult education, innovations that cannot be contained within the singularity of its framework.

The tactical appropriation and elaboration of corporate managerialist vocabulary for progressive means affirms the performative dimensions of adult educators' multicultural work. Tara Fenwick's research is informed by a critical corporate literacy, whereby corporate projects are innovatively reread and rewritten as innovations in the lives of workers. As a site of a dialogical struggle, the identification of boundaries and their location by students and teachers alike is a critical matter of adult educational practice. Fenwick interrogates corporate managerialism from the perspective of the experiences of worker/learners, while at the same time enabling them to interrogate the work and working conditions of their learning.

Roger Harris and Michelle Simons have found that adult educators have to be skilled in translating corporate critiques, as well as locating the contradictions in neo-conservative globalism. This is necessary in order to produce innovations that are committed to democratizing and (re)articulating the changing relationships between citizens, the nation-state, and supranational and transnational organizations. This involves interrogating the constantly shifting corporate framework that struggles to fix the boundaries that curb possibilities for innovation in adult education.

Through the work of both-ways interrogation, using one to show the limitations of the other, Harris and Simons argue that adult educators are in a position to engage in the critical appropriation of the best possibilities present within the blindness of corporate managerialism. This enables them to re-deploy resources in the interests of adult education, using all that the ideas of "public" and "education" signify.

Corporate managerialist boundaries that separate adult educators and students from pleasure and desire in the quest for compelling cost reductions, return on investment, and profit sharing among board members are complexly imbricated. The importance of curriculum and pedagogy in stabilizing the identity of adult educators is, according to Barbara Toepfer, being greatly undermined by the political economy of neo-conservative globalism and its associated postmodernist project of fragmenting and disaggregating the work of teaching. Recognizing that our research and teaching is embedded in a context hostile to democracy and citizenship, Toepfer sees adult educators using tactical pedagogies to negotiate corporate claims to authority. Toepfer recognizes that the identities and moral labour of adult educators are being interpellated to service dominating corporate managerialist interests. Against this, she positions her research and teaching by grounding the interests of adult education in issues of class, gender, and ethnicity.

Andrew Scown challenges the dominating business "models" of adult education that serve to limit innovations by adult educators. Corporate managerialism's fixation on centralizing control through new techno-culture imagines itself giving effect to the production of teacher-less, re-useable "learning" objects. Scown argues that this is underpinned through the dislocation and regressive displacement by the corporate techno-cultural imaginings of a labor-less, profit-seeking adult education industry. Corporate investment in the hype of techno-culture is increasing the manipulation of and work intensification experienced by adult educators. This techno-culture is being deployed to effect the repressive and regressive fantasies of corporate managerialism. It is being used to reinforce privileged stereotypes of irreconcilable differences between the humanities and techno-scientific dimensions of adult education. However, they too are actively using the openings it provides for effecting innovations in adult education through reinventing key elements of worthwhile education on-line. Scown demonstrates that adult educators have the capacity to challenge corporate imaginings, especially when self- and corporate critiques are embodied in their work.

Work Points

What might possibly be done? What strategies successfully incorporate "sustainability" under these conditions? A recurring theme in adult education is the powerful positioning of the everyday as practice and theory. *Adult Education @ 21st Century* demonstrates that innovation in adult education requires recognition of and engagement with both the limitations of this field and our own complex and contradictory investments in neo-conservative globalism.

Adult educators are edgily positioned. Shahrzad Mojab argues that the efforts of adult educators are being radically opposed and co-opted by the dominating socio-economic formation. The latter possibility sees us being integrated into an agenda that resists innovations in adult education. Mojab argues for the importance of recognizing progressive interpretations, forms, and expressions of the dominating mono-cultural politics of corporate managerialism. These need to be filtered through understandings that recognize their complicity with the overarching project of managerialism. Herein lies a critical difference between innovation activists and the subject positions of enterprising educators popular in contemporary policy literature. The permeability of borders and the generic purity of postmodernist business models of entrepreneurial, corporate managerialists obscures the distinctions the models seek to produce between citizenship, education, and critical reflection. Mojab calls into question the limitations of corporate managerialist distinctions between privatized intellectual property and public knowledge, and its division between worker education and work-related learning.

Shore engages with critiques of orientalist approaches by White, Anglophone studies and teaching of Others, raising concerns about the role of neo-conservative globalism in the suppression of multicultural diversity through agentic Whiteness. Conversely, thinking of the distinctive attributes of contemporary globalization in terms of hybridity and unlimited expansionism, then a key (political) agent in innovation is the mobile and culturally diverse multitudes of the world. For instance, the productive flows of international students give shape and substance to new forms of educational life and community. Tactically, the focus is on (re)appropriating the immanent possibilities present in the contradictions and crises of neo-conservative globalism. The aim is to construct sources of hope and productive change by refusing to comply with the limits of opportunity discourses and push the limits of the dominating political agenda and the resentment politics it incites. Thus, while curriculum refurbishment is driven by neo-conservative economic imperatives, as multicultural political work it is subject to strategies such as, reinterpretation, counter-construction, mimicry, and interpretive elaboration.

To produce an innovatory curriculum for teaching about the ideological, historical, and localizing practices of globalization, adult educators consciously mediate and mitigate the legacies of "globalizations past" that inform their own identities as much as the curriculum. The view that "globalization" is a unique phenomenon of the post–cold war era is misleading. Contemporary intensification of inequitable flows of power has added to the tensions associated with periods of globalization created by Western European imperialism and the superpower cold war. This latest phase adds to, coexists, and interacts with these rather than leaving them in the past. Adult educators engaging in activist policy and pedagogical innovation recognize the continuing influence of these earlier eras of globalization on our work today. The residual and lingering effects of past eras of globalization create the need to engage with and respond to these histories in the remaking of the disobedient curriculum.

Elaborating Partial Knowledges

Adult Education @ 21st Century provides examples of different starting points for practice and theory relative to conventional pedagogies. Each of these adult educators suggests that pedagogical engagement has a purpose that is very clearly about producing partial knowledges. What their students do with this partial knowledge depends on the collaborations involved and the aims to be achieved.

If adult education practice and theory is premised on partial knowledge, then meaning-making offers much in the way of situating this knowledge in wider practices of "globalization from above" or neo-conservative globalism. Whilst the politics of critique may differ, the task for adult educators situated in corporate programs not wedded to socio-economic justice is to keep an "eye on the big picture." This involves recognizing and making explicit the connections to people's daily lives, their work as informed and active citizens, and their links to progressive social movements. This kind of "practice/theory" builds hope through encouraging partial understanding, recognizing the need to strategically situate this understanding more broadly, acknowledging that there are choices to be made about where one begins, what social action one advocates (or rejects), and how to proceed with a project of learning and "social change."

Reflexivity

This strategy of elaborating partial knowledges is premised on the practice of reflexivity which unsettles the all-powerful discourses of knowing that are so influential in the making of corporate managerialists approaches to adult education. The elaboration of partial knowing can supplement forms of theory building and knowledge production that render visible the cul-de-sacs and blind spots created by efforts to reduce the complex, contradictory and contested life-worlds of adult educators and students and erase their historical connections. This supplementary knowledge has the power to disrupt the corporate managerialist practices that circumscribe transnational work and life-worlds as simply the perspectives, needs, and concerns of individuals. Hence, the scrutiny of neo-conservative globalism in *Adult Education @ 21st Century* gives insight into the constrained range of responses to these pressures. This examination of the everyday theory and practice of adult education as a function in and of relations of ruling is premised on quite different understandings of self/Other relations than those informing the neo-conservativism of the dominating cultural norms.

Crossing Borders

Peter Kell argues that adult educators are skillful in negotiating between the old capitalist economy and techno-corporatist imaginings of a neo-conservative economy of mindless labor. Imaginings of past orientations to knowledge meet the present superficialities of dot-point public relations information. The devaluing of the identity of adult educators is being effected through the enhanced status of reusable learning objects for corporate entrepreneurialism. Kell sees adult educators pushing in multiple directions, representing multiple ways of being critical, active intellectuals traversing corporate managerialism's forbidden borders. Caught betwixt and between the politics of neo-conservative globalism, Kell recognizes their efforts to make the transition to new forms of adult teaching, learning. For Kell, the work of adult educators points to ways of crossing the thresholds which corporate managerialism portrays as distinctly separate borders, blurring face-to-face teaching and on-line learning, merging teachers and students in action learning, and generating work-creating projects.

Adult Education @ 21st Century provides details of how adult educators "cross borders" by mediating and mitigating the coercive power of corporate managerialism. Pushing through the barriers affects their creative and

Pedagogies of Global/Local Hope

intellectual work. In their productive and enabling undertakings, Shore recognizes that adult educators are engaged in something which is potentially damaging, if not self-destructive and potentially counterproductive to a process of "social change." Rather than working under totally liberating conditions Shore recognizes the risks that adult educators have to manage in confronting corporate managerialism, entrepreneurial education and neo-conservative globalism. These pose dangers for the displacement of adult education as much as adult educators.

Nevertheless, Morris and Beckett argue that adult educators persist in publicly naming their interests by invoking their distrust of and critiquing the erosion of democracy, the reduction of citizenship to consumerism, and socio-economic injustices. These adult educators do even in the face of corporate faddism and postmodernist chic. Morris and Beckett point to the many similarities that exist between past and present histories of efforts to create teacher-less reusable learning objects and to convert adult educators into surveillance auditors and corporate enterpreneurs. Their work presents evidence of attempts to create socio-economic spaces for the reinvention of adult education without the benefit of affirmation and material rewards once secured through governments committed to underwriting the public's socio-economic security.

Even so, Morris and Beckett nurture a troubled consciousness, not knowing whether their border crossings transgress and repudiate the dominating political economy that their research actions and educational commitments warrant, or whether they are in reality complicit with its replication.

Efforts to exclude adult educators from the multicultural traditions of adult education express their marginalization from and by the dominating imaginings of corporate managerialists. Koo Yew Lie argues that adult educators face the predicament of crossing borders marked by language, community, and nations. Their efforts to construct meaningful new teachings and learnings are beset by the resilience of borders within the entrepreneurial corporations within which they labor. These are the borders they wish to dissolve.

Supplementary Frameworks

In making tactical border crossings, adult educators risk the occupational hazards of no longer belonging to the adult education profession, as well as corporate co-option in its efforts to privatize and globalize local, public intellectual property. Pandian and Baboo alert us to the difference between productive pedagogies for profit making and productive pedagogies for sustaining all forms of life. Their project resonates with Nair-Venugopal, who explores the willingness of adult educators to engage with the existing political economy of adult education. She finds adult educators willingly manipulating the mask of corporate managerialism as but one means in the struggle for worthwhile adult education. The boundaries of corporate managerialism attempt to demarcate a line between adult educators and self-regulating adult learners, by denying the place of teaching in life-long learning. Nair-Venugopal points to the mounting pressures adult educators face from a larger global constituency challenging the imposition of neo-conservative globalism from above.

The relationship between adult educators and corporate mono-cultural politics is one of contradictions and contestation, grounded in critiques of the commodification of public education, public knowledge, and public identity formation. Michael Singh and Lynne Li's argument helps us to see the ways adult education is being turned into a profit-oriented product for consumption by automatons; a political tool for encouraging passive conformity to industry, reinforcing authoritarian forms of corporate governance. The commodification of adult education continues to be a privileged object of corporate faddism. Singh and Li suggest that the ability of adult educators to contribute to the negation of the dominating socio-economic formation is minimized by corporate super-exploitation of the moral economy—the passion and commitment—adult educators have for their students, their disciplines, their profession, and the public good.

Nevertheless, Singh and Li contend that corporate faddism has not successfully colonized the minds of adult educators, despite recurring takeover bids, retrenchments and mergers. Rather, adult educators engage in complicated "negotiations" that contest the practices, relationships, and meanings being imposed on adult education. For Singh and Li, the education of adult researchers is a site for the construction of global/local citizens, workers, and learners, a key terrain in the conflicts over the impositions of and manipulations of neo-conservative globalism from above. Adult educators consistently work to redefine the boundaries of their work as delineated by corporate, financial, and political discipline, reframing the focus of teaching/learning and constructing broader frameworks within which students can pursue innovative modes of teaching, learning. Bobby Harreveld argues that adult educators shift, redraw, and sometimes actually manage to dissolve the lines that corporate managerialism uses to demarcate and discipline its preferred borders. This may be achieved by engaging and analyzing institutionalized corporate procedures. Harreveld focuses on both the material means and methods employed by corporate managerialism and on the examination of the ideas, feelings, beliefs, and representations embodied in and promulgated through the artifacts and practices of the entrepreneurial education corporation. This leads not to the erasure of the corporate borders as such, but, rather, to making visible the complex and heterogeneous borders used to create divisions that separate adult educators from students, the curriculum and pedagogy, their disciplinary communities, and communities of interest. Working mobile points of intersection, Harreveld argues that this makes it possible for adult educators to broaden the frameworks within and across which to pursue and elaborate innovations in adult education within global/local contexts.

Deploying New Literacies for Meaning-making

Using the notion of innovation activists as an organizing principle for the work of adult educators presumes a shift in the literate practices required of adult educators working in/against neo-conservative globalism. Pedagogies of global/local hope are not "add-on" techniques which guarantee pedagogical success. New literacies build on the premise that adult education practice and theory is deeply implicated in the European colonialist project. Neo-conservative globalism is an extension of these earlier imperial undertakings, rather than a radical departure from them.

New literacies for meaning-making are therefore not an addition to adult education, nor are they recently developed pedagogical technique. It is not a matter of critically reflecting on the syllabus and proceeding as if the desired changes will automatically follow. New literacies draw on a long tradition of connections, reflexive engagement, and situated action learning, combined with a global/local consciousness that appreciates the perils and pitfalls of embodied pedagogies, as well as their possibilities. New literacies are critical given the contemporary state's dis-investment in underwriting the social, cultural, and economic risks confronted by its citizens because the state has allied itself to serving neo-conservative interests. Mojab and Kell remind us that adult learning occurs amidst disparate global economies where industries move their business offshore when the going gets tough locally. The adult education industry is also active in making these shifts.

The ideological, historical, and localizing practices of globalization from above and below reveal disheartening contradictions. Harris and

Simons observe that adult educators experience neo-conservative globalism in unequal and uneven patterns. With the automation of jobs or their outsourcing, some have experienced it as unemployment, while for others it has meant the casualization of their work. Others face increasing insecurity in employment conditions at the same time as their work and its control and surveillance have been intensified. Transnational employment opportunities and cosmopolitan lifestyles for some stand in stark contrast to the expropriation of public security, the drawing of workers into debt, the intensification of labor, and the acceleration of environmental degradation. Much of the corporate-friendly de-structuring of citizens' common wealth continues as nation-states engage worldwide socio-political, cultural, and economic forces largely beyond the control of established state institutions.

In responding to these changes, adult learners are unlikely to benefit from pedagogies framed in terms of cultural imperialism, postmodernist neo-conservatism, or regressive parochialism, all of which we might argue are really so un-American, un-European, un-Asian, and un-African. On the contrary, adult educators who examine the possibilities presented by globalization from above and below may be able to help their students learn to make an advantage of the opportunities flowing from these risks. Rather than confirming students' sense of hopelessness and reinforcing passivity or resentment identities that exploit racist, patriarchal, and religious fundamentalisms, there is a need for pedagogies to make "global/local hope" a reality for adult learners.

Relocating the Local in the Global

To make pedagogies of global/local hope a reality, adult educators can work with their students to examine the possibilities presented by linguistic:repertoire and de-structuring to look for the opportunities in the global difficulties we face. Pedagogies of global/local hope may help in thinking beyond economic reductionism as well as Eurocentric, patriarchal, and anthropocentric interests. The challenges posed by unsustainable consumption can be studied in relation to creating the conditions for the sustainability of the world's ecological and post-patriarchal diversity. This is necessary not in the least because an image of a future filled with hope is needed to enable adult learners and educators to make meaning out of, and to give fullness, to their lives. This is being done in small but nonetheless significant ways by initiatives that emphasize the sustainability and biological and cultural diversity generated in global and local communities. Such initiatives are among the resources that adult educators can gather for the project of engendering global/local hope.

The maintenance and rejuvenation of the local now requires increasing deliberation and action on a global basis. Any given locale cannot be justified, shaped, or renewed in seclusion from the rest of the world. An appropriate slogan for energizing innovation in adult education might be "thinking and acting globally to make the local viable." Within this perspective, the local is understood as an expression of and response to the global, while the global is mediated and mitigated by the local. The sustainability of the local now needs to be institutionalized globally through transnational organizations of civil society and supra-national state agencies. Innovatory approaches to adult education construct the local and global as mutually constituted and as equally problematic in the opportunities and challenges they present. Thus, adult educators cannot carry on as before. It is now necessary to relocate local expressions of adult education within this changed global context. The viability of adult education might be made possible and actual through relocating and renewing local innovations in relation to changing global connections.

Contributors

Shanthi Balraj Baboo is attached to the Film and Television programme at The School of Communication, University Science Malaysia. She is also involved with activities related to awareness raising and information dissemination on renewable energy and is presently conducting a study on the reporting of environment and energy issues in the Malaysian newspapers. Her previous work examined the representation of children in the media and media literacy in Malaysia.

David Beckett is a senior lecturer in the Department of Education Policy and Management, the University of Melbourne. This work, both empirical and conceptual, centers on adult education, as it is apparent in professional development, policy analysis, and in workplace and lifelong learning.

Mike Brown is a Senior Lecturer at RMIT University. His main research interests are in adult education, work and work-related learning with a focus on curriculum and innovation.

Tara Fenwick is an Assistant Professor in the Department of Educational Policy Studies, University of Alberta, Edmonton, Alberta, Canada T6G 2G5. Her research focusses on socio-cultural and post-structural understandings of working knowledge, examining identity, power, knowledge and language in terms of equity and democracy in knowledge production. Her published books include *Learning Through Experience, A Handbook for Adult Education and Lifelong Learning*, Krieger Publishing Company (forthcoming). Email address: tara.fenwick@ualberta.ca.

Bobby Harreveld is a lecturer in professional and vocational education in the Faculty of Education and Creative Arts, Building 355, 240 Quay Street, Central Queensland University, Rockhampton, Queensland.

Roger Harris is Director of the Centre for Research in Education, Equity and Work (CREEW) and Associate Professor in adult and vocational education at the University of South Australia, Holbrooks Road, Underdale, SA 5032, Australia. His recent research includes a range of nationally-funded projects on workplace trainers, VET staff development, VET professionals' work, apprenticeships and traineeships, Training Packages and workplace learning. He is Vice-President of the Australian VET Research Association (AVETRA) and Editor of the *Australian Journal of Adult Learning*.

Paul James is an editor of Arena Journal and Professor of Globalism and Cultural Diversity at RMIT, Melbourne. He is Director of the Globalism Institute and author or editor of seven books including, Nation Formation (1996), Work of the Future: Global Perspectives (1997), and Tour of Duty: Winning Hearts and Minds in East Timor (with photographs by Matthew Sleeth, 2002).

Peter Kell is associate professor of Adult Education at the University of Wollongong. Associate Professor Kell is an executive member of the Australian Vocational Education Research Training Association and a Co-Director of the Universiti Sains Malaysia-Wollongong University International Literacy Research Unit. He is a joint author with Professor Michael Singh and Associate Professor Ambigapathy Pandian of *Appropriating English: Innovation in the Global Business of Teaching English*, published by Peter Lang. His research interests include the internationalization of education and training, workplace and adult literacy, and transnational developments in education markets. Peter Kell has also published on nationalism, race, and sport, authoring *Good Sport: Australian Sport and the Myth of the Fair Go*, with Pluto Press, in 2000.

Koo Yew Lie is a lecturer at the School of Language and Linguistics, Faculty of Social Sciences and Humanities, National University of Malaysia. She undertook a doctoral research project on the intercultural literacies of multicultural readers at the Institute of Education University of London on a Commonwealth Academic Staff Award. She is currently involved in research involving the plural literacies of multicultural meaning makers in changing spaces. Her areas of interests include intercultural discourse-communication and literacies, English as an additional language, and the politics of English in multicultural spaces.

Lynne Nengying Li (PhD) is a senior research associate in the Department of Language and International Studies, RMIT University, City Campus, 441 Swanston Street, Melbourne 3000, Australia. Her interest is in ESL teaching, bilingual education, and linguistic globalization. She is presently involved in a research study of the roles of international education in reshaping enterprise university in the multi-lingual knowledge economy context.

Liv Mjelde is professor at Akershus University College, Institute of Vocational Pedagogy in Oslo, Norway. She is a sociologist specializing in the Sociology of Education. She is an expert on studying the changing relations between vocational and general education from psychological (forms of knowledge), didactic (workshop and classroom learning), and sociological (division of mental and manual labor) perspectives. One of her research fields is the gender divisions as they can be observed directly in vocational education, in male and female fields, in relation to movements on the manual labor marked and in family ideology. Address: Akershus University College, Ringstabekkveien 105, 1356 Bekkestua, Norway, tel. +47 6711 7000, fax.+ 47 6711 7000. E-mail address: Liv.Mjelde@hiak.no

Shahrzad Mojab is an Associate Professor, teaching at the Department of Adult Education, Community Development, and Counselling Psychology, The Ontario Institute for Studies in Education of the University of Toronto. Among her areas of teaching and research are anti-racism education; critical and feminist pedagogy; social justice and equality; feminism and nationalism; women, state, globalization and citizenship; and women, violence and learning. She is the editor of *Women of A Non States Nation: The Kurds* and the co-editor of *Of Property and Propriety: The Role of Gender and Class in Imperialism and Nationalism.*

Gayle Morris is a learning and teaching specialist in the Faculty of Economics and Commerce at the University of Melbourne, having previously worked as a lecturer in industry, professional and adult education. Her research interests include the philosophy and practice of adult learning, professional learning of educators, adult literacy and diversity management. E-mail address: gemorris@unimelb.edu.au

Shanta Nair-Venugopal is an associate professor in the School of Language Studies and Linguistics in Universiti Kebangsaan Malaysia. Her books include *Language Choice and Communication in Malaysian Business* (2000) published by Universiti Kebangsaan Malayasia Press, and a jointly edited publication *Language and Globalization* (2000) by Pearson Education. Publications in which her papers appear include *The International Journal of the Sociology of Language, World Englishes, Paasa, Babel* and the *RELC Anthology Series Singapore.* Her research interests are in the sociolinguistics of choice, the New Englishes, and the discourse of intercultural communication and identities.

Ambigapathy Pandian is the head of Literacy Research in the School of Humanities at the Universiti of Sains Malaysia and co-director of the Universit Sains Malaysia and Wollongong Univerity International Literacy Unit. Dr Pandian has published widely on English and Literacy in Malaysia, authoring a book in Malaysia and editing a volume on global literacy. Ambigapathy Pandian is a serving member of the Penang Education Consultative Council and chair of the Tamil Schools Special Working Committee.

Leanne Reinke is a researcher with the Globalism Institute in the Faculty of Education, Language and Community Services at RMIT University, 411 Swanston Street, Melbourne, Victoria 3000, Australia. Leanne was awarded her PhD from the School of Political and Social Inquiry at Monash University in 2001 for a thesis that dealt with changing communication technologies within education and social protest. She is currently working on projects relating to community formation and transformation under globalisation.

Andrew Scown is currently employed by the Faculty of Education, Language, and Community Services of RMIT University where he is a senior lecturer and program manager for programs in Educational Leadership and Management. Andrew has worked in a variety of educational settings and is currently involved in the delivery and management of online programs in Singapore and Vietnam. Central to these program developments is the development and evaluation of pedagogies for online learning. E:mail address: andrew.scown@rmit.edu.au.

Sue Shore is a lecturer and researcher in the Centre for Studies in Literacy, Policy, and Learning Cultures at the University South Australia, Holbrooks Road, Underdale 5032, Australia. Her interests range across teacher education in adult and vocational training, adult literacy policy analysis, and mapping the effects of Whiteness in educational theory building. She has edited special editions of journals focussing on feminism and women in adult education and has just completed a six-year funded term of sponsored research in Australian adult literacy and numeracy in collaboration with a consortium of six Australian universities.

Michele Simons is a lecturer in post-compulsory education and training in the School of Education and senior researcher in the Centre for Research in Education, Equity and Work (CREEW) at the University of South Australia, Holbrooks Road, Underdale, SA 5032, Australia. She has a long standing interest in adult and vocational education as a practitioner and researcher. Over the past ten years, she has completed a number of research studies focusing on learning in the workplace, the work of VET teachers and trainers and managing change within VET sector institutions.

Michael Singh is professor of Education at the University of Western Sydney, where he is engaged in collaborative research into issues of social justice and socio-cultural diversity. His work in language and international studies led to the development of an internationally renowned research concentration in globalization and cultural diversity, The Globalism Institute. He also designed innovative bachelor's degrees in international studies, English-language studies, and teacher education. Professor Singh is the author of various research reports, including studies into innovations in the global business of English-language teaching; eco-cultural sustainability, the responsiveness of universities to Indigenous people's interests, the translation of studies of Asia into school curricula, and the use of performance indicators in education.

Barbara Toepfer is a vocational teacher and hotel economist. She was a team member of a German school advisory bureau on global education for four years and has specialized and published on global education for vocational education for almost twenty years. She is presently working at the Hessisches Landesinstitut für Pädagogik, a state institute for adult education for teachers, at the department "Berufliche Schulen," Erfurter Str. 22, 35274 Kirchhain, Germany. E-mail address: toepfer-woehl@t-online.de.

Index

A
adult education
  formal, 64, 146
  global/local, 22–23, 25–28, 30–34
  informal, 236
  literacy, 55, 65, 128, 158, 160, 162
  multi-disciplinary approaches to, 68
  pedagogy, 119
  policy makers, 235
  research on, 48
  vocational, 22–23, 25, 28, 30, 37–39, 42, 49–50, 145, 157, 159
adult learner
  identities, 129
adult learning
  embodiment of, 128
  principles, 112–115, 117–118, 120, 123
adult researchers, 169, 171, 173–175, 180, 184–185, 191–192, 289
advertising images, 228
agency, 6, 66, 84, 115, 117, 127–128, 132, 164, 250, 269
Agenda 21, 25, 32, 34
aid programs, 68
anti-capitalism, 22
  -globalization movement, 9
  -market mechanism, 61, 178
apprenticeships, 41, 46, 64, 145
audit tools, 174
Australia, 157, 293, 295
  adult education, 145, 148–150, 240
  adult literacy, 159
  education, 216, 231, 237
  English teaching, 55
  Indigenous issues, 233–234, 241, 279
  institutions, 142–143, 158
  research, 157, 173, 230, 253, 255
  VET system, 159, 165–166
autonomy, 60, 153, 177, 179, 210, 265

B
Bakun Dam Project, 59
Betzavta, 29
binarism, 16
biocultural sustainability, 66, 68
brokerage, 158, 160, 165–166

C
Cartesian
  dualism, 134
  epistemology, 133
class, 83, 123, 246–248, 264, 281
  and culture, 270
  differences, 38–41, 50, 74, 85, 87, 115, 210, 232, 253
  elite, 12–13, 81, 121
  language, 97, 103, 117, 215
  social, 40, 48, 80, 283
colonial administration, 93
  legacies, 66, 112
colonialism, 75, 106, 111, 113–115, 120, 122–123, 187
communication
  electronic, 233
  face-to-face, 241
  multi-lingual, 48, 106
  technologies of, 228, 232
communicative competence, 94, 159, 162
communities of practice, 160, 259, 261

competencies
  cross-curricular, 24, 26, 28, 33
complementary holism, 246, 248–249, 252–253
complexity theory, 260–261, 269
compliance
  and accountability, 148, 151–152, 162, 165, 183, 213, 278
  of workers, 61, 147, 160,
  regimes, 14, 142, 160, 164–166, 174–175, 210
  values, 57, 77, 157–163, 166, 210
computer icons, 237
constructivist theories, 260
control, 267
  colonial, 4, 12
  environmental, 10
  government, 12, 57, 58, 174–175, 245
  labor, 6, 107, 160, 174, 176, 181, 190, 255, 290
  pedagogical, 182, 185, 189, 210, 213, 270
  quality, 95–98
  social, 15, 87, 172, 179, 249, 256, 262, 264, 283
  social, 5
critical
  literacy, 206
  reflection, 112, 116, 118, 120–122, 205, 220, 262, 284
  thinking, 17, 61, 73, 81, 198–199, 206
critique
  literacy, 75, 230
  of theory, 219, 222–223, 269
  of pedagogy, 252, 277
  policy, 248
  process, 153, 207, 212, 220, 222, 224, 253, 286
  research, 128, 178
cultural
  hegemony, 92
  sustainability, 230, 235–238, 240
curriculum
  competency-based, 159, 163
  framework, 244, 246, 248, 251–253
  homogenized, 211, 214
decision-making, 161

Denmark, 39, 49
dialogic
  engagement, 82
  process, 165
difference, 209
  and diversity, 75, 84, 225
  educational, 113, 120, 216
  pedagogical, 215, 217, 219, 288
  poliltical, 40, 113–114
  power, 4, 122, 221, 270, 284
  social, 32, 74, 77, 111, 123, 133, 210, 219, 228–229, 232
digital imagery, 231
dilemmas, 29, 55, 60–62, 65, 121, 149, 153, 161–162, 164, 266–267
discourse theory, 127
distance teaching, 239
diversity
  biological, 65
  cultural, 86–87 253, 284, 295
  eco-cultural, 56, 170–173, 182–183, 188
  economic, 65, 143, 248, 261, 275, 281,
  educational, 46, 49, 77, 85, 127, 151, 210–212, 215–217, 221, 224–225, 291, 294
  language, 55–56, 95
  productive, 75
  social, 9, 74, 87, 129, 133, 136, 218

E
ECI
  model, 216–218, 221, 223–225
  pedagogy, 223, 225
  process, 221–222
eco-cultural sustainability, 169, 183, 185, 295
ecological
  sustainability, 55–56
  learning theory, 260–262, 269
economics
  participatory, 244, 246, 248, 249, 257
  people-centered, 248
education
  examination-driven, 75
  intercultural, 22, 26

Index

Malaysian, 75, 79–80
moral, 29
public, 13, 37, 39, 60–61, 173, 288
e-learning, 212–214, 219
embodied learning, 125, 132, 133, 239
employers, 30, 73
employers'
  preferences, 144
  expectations, 30, 141
English dialects, 61
enterprising self, 263
entrepreneurs, 180, 260, 264, 266, 268–269, 282
  women, 265, 267
environmental
  consciousness, 65
  knowledge, 60
Erasmus Program, 42, 46, 50, 54
ethical
  investment, 185, 187–188
  research, 187
  standards, 34
ethnic communities, 59
ethnolect, 97, 101, 104
Eurocentrism, 47
European
  Union, 7, 13, 15, 29, 38–39, 42–43, 45–46, 48
  Community, 43
Europeanization, 47, 49–50, 53
European-ness, 115
evaluating websites, 204
evaluation, 9, 30, 34, 38–39, 46–47, 51–52, 161, 211, 214–215, 224, 236
Evidence-Critique-Impact (ECI), 209, 215
examination, 24, 61, 75–76, 126, 134–135, 200–201, 205, 286, 289
exclusion, 11, 25, 44, 46, 113, 178

F
fragmentation, 60, 91, 163, 228
Freeport Gold Mine, 60

G
gatekeeper, 86

Germany, 6, 12, 21–25, 28–29, 32, 39, 47, 276, 295
global
  market systems, 261
  workers, 86
  power, 285
Global Compact, 31, 32, 34
globalism
  developmental, 60, 66
globalization, 5, 11, 24, 49, 53, 158, 209, 294
  co-operation, 275
  cultural, 245
  from above, 3, 11–13, 25–27, 39, 169, 183–184, 245, 275, 279, 285, 290
  from below, 25, 170, 245, 276
  localization, 244
  people-centered, 253
good practice, 33
governance, 173, 176–179, 184, 189–191, 288
government disinvestment, 61, 171

H
Hamburg Declaration, 17
hard trades, 40
hermeneutic phenomenology, 216
homogenization, 127, 211, 225, 281
human capital, 13, 61, 142, 157–158, 263, 269
Human Rights, 10, 22, 27, 31–32, 66, 255, 276

I
ICT and English, 203
identities
  hybridization of, 83
  re-formation, 263
illiterate adults, 8
ILO, 31
imagination, 75, 80, 113–114, 122
inclusive practice, 117
Indigenous
  communities, 59, 62, 230–237, 240–241, 277–278
  knowledge, 64, 182, 229

language sustainability, 233, 241
languages, 62–64, 230, 233–234
learners, 236, 240–241
pedagogical practice, 240
peoples, 59–60, 187, 228, 230–233
teachers, 239
Indonesia, 4, 57, 58, 60, 62, 66–67, 216
industrial relations, 142–143, 147, 150, 243
information society, 44
initial qualifications, 152
instructional
design, 236, 240
interface, 239
interactive technology, 231
intercultural competence, 25
interdisciplinary approach, 56
inter-ethnic
dialogue, 89
power relations, 76
international students, 152, 178, 184, 285
invisible norm, 116
Israel, 27–30, 34

J
journal reflection, 117
judgement, 136–137

K
kinship, 247–249, 257
knowing on the fly, 265, 267, 269
knowledge
academic, 85, 238
community, 238
creation, 76, 112, 114, 142, 199, 206, 207
economy, 87, 197, 206, 293
evidence-based, 218
multimedia, 202
partiality of, 121, 253, 286
production, 86, 120, 122, 206, 211, 250, 266
propositional, 13–134
research, 176, 251
social division of, 41, 51, 272
society, 84, 206–207
transformation, 217

transmission, 236

L
labor
divisions of, 52, 276
flexibility, 143
manual, 37, 40–42, 45, 48–49, 294
market, 21, 25, 27, 38–43, 45, 47–48, 58, 157, 170, 173, 245
mental, 49
patterns, 58
language
death, 64
proficiency, 61, 64, 107, 202
teaching, 61, 63, 68, 81, 173, 295
learning
as transformation, 262
authentic, 225
classroom, 38, 41–42, 294
evaluation, 30
flexibility, 223
for life, 24, 127
organizational, 47, 107, 183, 271
workshop, 38, 41
legitimation crisis, 59
Leonardo da Vinci Program, 38, 42, 44–45, 47–49, 51
impact, 46
liberal democracy, 15, 17
life-world, 78, 218–220, 252, 280
of learners, 84, 88, 212, 217
reconstruction, 66, 209–210
linguistic
capital, 101
diversity, 56, 64–65, 68, 83, 240, 245, 279
imperialism, 92, 279
repertoire, 100, 106
variation, 92, 101
literacies
dominating, 83, 88
resistance, 88
work-place, 87
literacy
academic, 81, 83
assertive, 79, 83
authoring-type, 76
everyday, 78, 81, 88

Index

literary practices, 78

M
mainstream, 112, 114
Malaysia, 69, 86, 89, 108, 276
  Bahasa, 62, 80, 82–83
  development, 59, 66
  economy, 58
  education, 74–76, 86, 105, 197–198, 293–294
  educational reform, 171, 198–199
  ICT, 197, 199–200, 216
  politics, 57, 62–64, 67, 203
  research, 55, 294
  student teachers, 206
  teacher education, 200
Malaysian English, 61–62, 82, 84–85, 91, 93–95, 97–98, 101, 103–106
markets
  global, 50
material culture, 232
meaning-making, 74, 77–78, 85–88, 132, 163, 202, 281, 285, 289
multicultural
  reciprocity, 188
  resources, 74, 85, 172, 275
multiculturalism, 73
  soft, 237
multiliteracies, 83, 216
multi-media, 221, 231–232, 234

N
national curriculum, 23
National Reporting System, 163–164
nation-building, 17, 56, 68, 76
neo-colonial dependency, 64
neo-conservative, 65–67, 157, 170–185, 189–191, 210, 275–290
  agenda, 6, 7, 50, 79, 115, 157, 211, 244, 257
  anti, 3, 9, 11, 16, 27
  globalism, 4, 9, 15–16, 38, 49, 55, 170–171, 182–183, 185, 190–191, 277, 280–281, 285, 287
  markets, 6, 9, 13–15, 56
  politics, 3, 13, 49–50, 61–62, 143, 225, 248, 251

new technologies, 21, 158, 179, 206, 215, 228, 232, 234, 236, 241
noisemakers, 270
normative code, 101
normativity, 91–94, 105
North American Free Trade Agreement, 4
Norway, 38–41, 45–46, 48–49, 53, 294

O
on-line
  adult education, 209, 211–212, 215, 217
  products, 212
  teaching, 211, 213, 215–216, 223
oppression, 10, 16, 111, 119–120, 246, 270
oral traditions, 232, 235
organismic relationality, 262
Organization for Economic Cooperation and Development, 39

P
Palestine, 27–30, 34
parsimony, 101, 105
participatory approach, 238
pedagogical
  division, 52
  model, 215, 217, 224
pedagogies of certainty, 122
pedagogy, 41, 116, 119, 184, 289
  adult education, 26, 28, 82, 122, 126, 177, 209–211, 213, 219, 250, 283
  English only, 100, 105, 173, 191
  face-to-face, 235, 237
  intercultural literacies, 88
  on-line, 216, 219, 235
  oppositional, 113, 165
  productive, 108, 190, 288, 212
  reflexive, 81, 118–119, 132, 182, 219, 236, 270
  vocational, 52, 251–252
performance, 126, 268
  anxiety, 61
  economic, 61, 150
  embodied, 127, 133, 137
  examination, 61, 65, 75

indicators, 163, 175–176, 179, 214, 295
workplace, 163, 203
performativity, 127, 174, 210
Philippines, 61, 67, 92
pleasure, 80, 204, 282–283
policy
   vocational training, 44, 45
   activism, 38, 59
post-
   colonial, 55–57, 62
   Fordist, 79
power, 75–79, 81–82, 117, 120, 158, 160–161, 165–166, 172–177, 245–246, 248, 255, 286
   competitive, 32, 182, 185, 253, 287
   economic, 67, 101, 180, 282
   Euro-American, 275
   global, 4, 12, 278
   in adult education, 85, 118, 206, 281
   labor, 13, 106, 112
   market, 15, 171, 259
   people, 251, 266
   political, 6, 15, 87, 114, 122, 133, 279
   relations, 84, 86, 94, 107, 111, 119, 120, 122, 153, 165, 182, 187, 209, 238, 257, 260, 264, 270–271, 276
practical consciousness, 134
privilege, 76, 80, 86, 95, 119–123, 132, 184, 187, 212, 225, 246
producing knowledge, 78
professional development, 116, 141, 149–154, 158, 163–164, 199, 293
professional identity, 142, 166, 175, 177, 206
Programme for International Student Assessment, 23

R
racialization, 88
racialized discourses, 112, 120
racist movements, 25
rational planning models, 266
rationality
   eco-social, 66
   technical, 66
reading preferences, 201

reformist, 11
refugees, 67
representations, 77–78, 113, 115, 122–123, 136, 191, 281, 289
research
   strategies, 170
   education, 169, 171–182, 184–186, 189–191
resources of hope, 88
restructuring
   global, 38, 50, 111, 291
   global economic, 49
revolutionary-Marxist, 12
Rio Principles on Environmental Development, 31
role
   balance, 148
   diversification, 147
   expansion, 146–147
   part-time, 144
   shifts, 146
   tensions, 149
   VET, 143

S
situated
   learning, 52, 152
   literacies, 73
social
   justice, 22, 66, 198, 276, 295
   mobility, 39
   movements, 9–10, 286
socially critical movements, 14–15, 18, 66
socio-cultural contexts, 75, 77
Socrates Program, 50
soft fields, 40
spiritual meaning, 232
streaming, 38
Structural Adjustment Programs, 11, 13
student centered, 162
submissive literacy, 79
Sweden, 3, 39, 49

T
target groups, 42, 48, 112
teacher-learner relationships, 163

Index

teaching
  ecological modes of, 270
Teaching and Research Assessment Indicators, 214
teamwork, 73, 79, 87, 150
technological utopianism, 229
terrorism, 4, 15–18, 67
tests, 24, 75, 175, 232
text production, 77
theory building, 111–116, 122–123, 286, 295
think-aloud protocols, 80
training
  competency-based, 127, 142, 160, 163
  packages, 127, 148–149, 161, 164
  reforms, 142, 145
transformation, 83, 85, 130, 143, 207, 212, 219, 246, 278
transformative potential, 84
translation, 85, 100, 187, 216, 279, 295
translocation, 59, 64

U

UN Human Development Reports, 7
understanding
  inferential, 135–136
  representational, 135
United Nations, 7, 21, 31–32

V

vernacular, 62, 78, 81–82, 84
vignettes, 244, 253, 256
voice, 73, 76–77, 83, 86, 88, 94, 117, 211, 218

W

ways of speaking, 79, 93, 100, 107
wedge politics, 67
White Australia, 231
workers
  moral identity of, 37
workforce
  differentiated, 150
  VET, 143, 154
workplace
  dynamics, 246
  restructuring, 263
  trainer, 145–146
work-related learning, 152, 176, 244, 246, 251–253, 255, 284
World Wide Fund for Nature, 171, 186

Studies in the Postmodern Theory of Education

General Editors
Joe L. Kincheloe & Shirley R. Steinberg

Counterpoints publishes the most compelling and imaginative books being written in education today. Grounded on the theoretical advances in criticalism, feminism, and postmodernism in the last two decades of the twentieth century, Counterpoints engages the meaning of these innovations in various forms of educational expression. Committed to the proposition that theoretical literature should be accessible to a variety of audiences, the series insists that its authors avoid esoteric and jargonistic languages that transform educational scholarship into an elite discourse for the initiated. Scholarly work matters only to the degree it affects consciousness and practice at multiple sites. Counterpoints' editorial policy is based on these principles and the ability of scholars to break new ground, to open new conversations, to go where educators have never gone before.

For additional information about this series or for the submission of manuscripts, please contact:

    Joe L. Kincheloe & Shirley R. Steinberg
    c/o Peter Lang Publishing, Inc.
    275 Seventh Avenue, 28th floor
    New York, New York 10001

To order other books in this series, please contact our Customer Service Department:

    (800) 770-LANG (within the U.S.)
    (212) 647-7706 (outside the U.S.)
    (212) 647-7707 FAX

Or browse online by series:
    www.peterlangusa.com